CULTURAL

DISENCHANTMENTS

La Città di CIVIDALE del FRIULI nello Stato Veneto.   Tom. XX

Frontispiece. Engraving of walled city of Cividale del Friuli
during Venetian period.

CULTURAL DISENCHANTMENTS

Worker Peasantries in
Northeast Italy

BY DOUGLAS R. HOLMES

PRINCETON UNIVERSITY
PRESS

Library of Congress Cataloging-in-Publication Data

Holmes, Douglas R., 1949–
Cultural disenchantments.
Bibliography: p.
Includes index.
1. Labor and laboring classes—Italy—Cividale del Friuli Region.
2. Cividale del Friuli Region (Italy)—Rural conditions.
3. Peasantry—Italy—Cividale del Friuli Region. I. Title.
HD8490.C582H65 1989   305.5′63   88-32492
ISBN 0–691–09448–9
ISBN 0–691–02849–4 (pbk.)

This book has been composed in Linotron Times Roman

Printed in the United States of America by
Princeton University Press,
Princeton, New Jersey

bc

To Barbara and Sarah

Contents

Illustrations

Tables

Acknowledgments

THIS project has moved in many different directions since its inception in the late 1970s. It has drawn me into professional and personal relationships that I value deeply and for which I have incurred many debts. In its formative stages, the work benefited from the participation of Pedro Carrasco, David Gilmore, Jane Schneider, and Robert Stevenson. My teacher Pedro Carrasco gave me a firm grounding in the theory and practice of anthropology, and introduced me to the challenge of blending anthropology and history. Most of all I appreciate his careful judgment, generous encouragement, and friendship. The peasant-worker matrix diagramed in chapter 7 was prepared with his assistance. David Gilmore and Jane Schneider provided me with two very rich perspectives on the potential of European anthropology. My encounter with them and their work instilled a preoccupation that has vexed me since the early 1980s. It also inspired the central, albeit unspoken, question of the text—what constitutes an anthropology of Europe? I hope they find my solution a provocative extension of their outlooks.

During 1983–1984, Ivan Karp spent an academic year in Houston during which we discussed many issues, brooded on weighty theoretical matters, and generally had a good time. His influence led me to abandon a rewrite of my dissertation and begin the study that follows. Ivan's wit and creative insights gave me the confidence to address the issues that form the core of this study. At about the same time, I began an exciting collaboration with Jean Quataert. Our work together provided an opportunity to extend my thinking into new historical and comparative areas. Much of chapter 3 is drawn from our raucous discussions and debates. The collaboration also permitted me to observe at close hand the craft of a superb social historian. Jean's scholarly rigor and intensity set standards that I hope to match in my own work. Above all, however, it is her warmth, energy, and good humor that I will always value.

Two readers for Princeton University Press—David Kertzer and an anonymous reader—reviewed the text thoroughly. Their critical comments helped strengthen arguments, clear up ambiguities, and correct outright errors in the data. More importantly, their suggestions provided a means to achieve an integration of the main theoretical and empirical issues of the text, a goal that had long eluded me. The review process, directed by my editor, Gail Ullman, was a challenging experience that significantly improved the quality of the text. Her patience and encouragement were invaluable.

Dusty Kennedy carefully read two early drafts of the manuscript. Her revisions and refinements helped give the prose clarity and vigor.

Jane Lincoln Taylor did an expert copyediting job, restraining stylistic excesses and establishing textual consistency. Fernanda Bignami Geiger offered detailed advice on the translation and interpretation of many of the Italian documents used in the text. The two maps of Friuli were drafted by Jeffrey Chatman and Cheryl Grabler.

Portions of the text were presented at the faculty–graduate student seminar in the Department of Anthropology at the University of Chicago in the spring of 1988. The insightful questions posed by participants influenced the final revisions of the manuscript. I would like to thank Manning Nash, Marshall Sahlins, and Raymond Smith for their hospitality during my brief visit.

The success of the fieldwork was due in large part to the remarkable qualities of Paolo Rondo Brovetto. Paolo has worked with me since the beginning of the study. His intelligence, his integrity, his natural charm, and his deep affection for his fellow Friulani permitted an exploration of areas that would otherwise have been beyond my reach. It has been a privilege to know and work with him. Elio Scaravetto and his wonderful family introduced me to Rubignacco and its inhabitants. They guided my early fieldwork and showed great patience with my endless questions. From long discussions in their kitchen, I first learned what it means to be Friulian; for that I will always be grateful. Violetta Feletig provided an important perspective on Rubignacco, through the life and history of her family. She also arranged interviews that were essential for the investigation of contemporary regional politics. Carlo Guildo Mor provided access to the archives of a rural estate in Bottenicco from which much of the documentary material in this book was drawn. He also generously lent me texts from his own library that introduced me to the superb regional scholarship he and his colleagues, notably Gian Carlo Menis, Giovanni Battista Pellegrini, and Amelio Tagliaferri, have developed for Friuli. Tables 3.2 and 3.3 are reproduced with the permission of Cambridge University Press. They appeared in volume 28 of *Comparative Studies in Society and History*.

I owe my greatest debt to the people of Cividale del Friuli and the surrounding areas who took the time to discuss with an awkward foreigner their daily routines, their intriguing beliefs and convictions and, in some cases, the most intimate aspects of their lives. My encounter with the Friulani enriched my life in ways I would never have foreseen, nor can ever adequately repay.

ACKNOWLEDGMENTS

Many friends and colleagues have patiently supported me during this project. They include: Barbara Butler, Terri Castaneda, Jerry Fryrear, Lauren Hansen, Mary Hodge, Nina Jody, Leonard Jordan, Jim Lester, David Malin, Kent Maynard, Marco Portales, Robert Reichlin, Anna Shapiro, Bahram Tavakolian, Teri Waite, and Priscilla Weeks. My dean, Wayne Miller, and two associate deans, Rita Culrose and Howard Eisner, provided steadfast administrative support and understanding. The Organized Research Program at the University of Houston, Clear Lake, funded the three summers of research in Italy on which this study is largely based. My students endured my eccentricities and have shown a gratifying degree of interest in my research. I hope this book satisfies some of their curiosity and further stimulates their interest in anthropology.

My family has tolerated the various demands of my profession. Barbara and Sarah Prouty made a home with me. They have brought great joy, even zaniness, to my life, and they have sustained me through this project. My mother and father also displayed unwavering support for the work during a very sad time for our family. My brother George gave generous encouragement, understanding, and advice. He also supplied me with a computer and helped clear my head on sailing outings in San Francisco Bay and on the Indian River.

CULTURAL
DISENCHANTMENTS

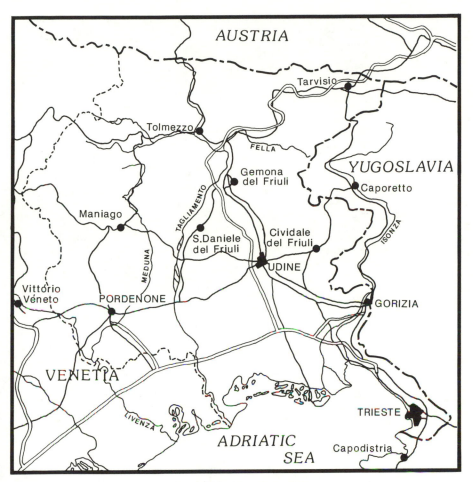

Map 1. Friuli–Venezia Giulia

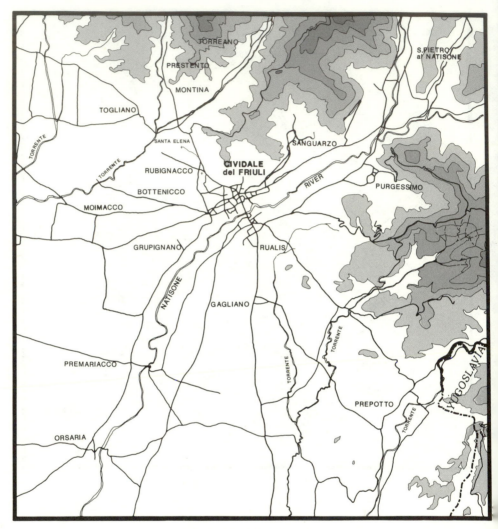

Map 2. Cividale del Friuli

Terrain of Inquiry

OVERVIEW

If one approaches Rubignacco from the southwest, off the highway that connects Cividale with Udine, the hamlet stands out against the foothills of the Julian Alps. The oak- and chestnut-covered hills suddenly rise above the plain. This backdrop changes from the rich verdant foliage of summer to the wet brown cover of autumn. Winter snows trace a telltale line across the pre-Alps. In late winter and early spring, the terrain is permeated with constant rain and mist. Patches of meadow and vineyard, as well as an occasional farmhouse, can be seen in the woodlands overlooking the hamlet. The parish church of San Marco dominates a cluster of buildings at the base of the foothills. Modest apartments and attached houses line two roads that converge in the middle of the hamlet. At the intersection of Via della Croce and Via Rubignacco, the pavement widens where an imposing steel cross marks the center of the parish. A narrow country lane winds from Via della Croce a few

Fig. 1. Steel cross marking the center of Rubignacco.

hundred yards past a decrepit kindergarten and along a ridge to the threshold of a small chapel, dedicated to Santa Elena. From the center of the hamlet to the south along Via della Croce, and to the west along Via Rubignacco, the density of settlement quickly thins, giving way to vineyards and cornfields that spread over the plain. Freestanding farmsteads dot the open countryside. The famous *benandanti*, or "good witches," of Friulian folklore would no doubt have noticed an arresting symmetry to the hamlet as they flew over the plain on the way to their nocturnal battles with spirits that threatened the countryfolk's harvest. As they hovered over Rubignacco, the benandanti could observe a matrix superimposed on the landscape by the Romans in the first century that continues to this day to align the roadways and settlement patterns in the hamlet.

A series of high-tension cables extending toward the snow-covered Alps traverse Rubignacco, as if to link the rustic to the modern. Some of these power lines terminate on the southern edge of the hamlet in a maze of transformers. The power lines and transformers abut a new industrial zone. Electric power conveyed from the mountains runs a compact steel mill and other new factories within the zone. Not far from the new industrial complex are two cement works. One, built early in the century, stands crumbling and abandoned; the other—more recently built—is in full operation, spewing sulfurous fumes from its huge furnace. Next to the abandoned cement mill is an austere structure that, during the first half of this century, was operated as a tannery. Through the broken windows of the cavernous main building, one can see the enormous vats where hides were dyed and processed. Two additional clusters of buildings stand on the other side of Rubignacco along Via Gemona. One group forms a silk mill and the other a brick factory. The silk mill is difficult to see from the roadside; its vacant structures, though attached to a splendid eighteenth-century villa, remain walled off on the fringe of the estate's formal gardens. An old canal faithfully channels water past the rear of the abandoned mill. By contrast, the brick factory is clearly visible from Via Gemona. Its high vaulted wood roofs give the factory a rustic appearance. An unsettling curve in the mill's towering chimney catches the eye. A major earthquake in Friuli during the spring of 1976 that bent the chimney also did serious damage throughout the region and killed almost a thousand Friulani. Even though the brick and silk mills are no longer in operation, sections of both were converted into small lumber mills that operated on and off into the early 1980s. Across Via Gemona is a technical high school that draws students from throughout the region for training in agricultural techniques and management. Further south—beyond the factories—lie the working class precincts that ring the urban center of Cividale del Friuli. Off in the east, two adjacent settlements, Bottenicco and Moimacco, spread over the plain. Each settlement surrounds the country villa and agricultural estate of a once-powerful noble family who for centuries controlled the land on the plain and the lives of the people who worked it.

The proximity of industry and agriculture drew me to Rubignacco. I was intrigued by the interplay between the segments of rural society tied to both the industrial wage economy and the family-based agrarian system. My early research, using conventional fieldwork methods, probed the nature of these agrarian-industrial interactions. In the fall of 1977, I established a routine of going door-to-door in Rubignacco, introducing myself to residents of the hamlet and beginning formal interviews that examined the economic involvements of household members. During the early phase of the research, however, I learned more from simply roaming the hamlet and having chance encounters. Following pathways along vineyards and across fields of maize and barley, down streets past factories and through working-class neighborhoods, I became familiar with the local social geography. At every opportunity I stopped to ask questions of field hands or engage passersby in conversation. These brief encounters yielded insight into the quality of the land, the making of wine (*vino*) and brandy (*grappa*), the ways silk was spun at the mill, the travels of migrants to sugarcane fields in Australia, the working conditions at the brick factory and cement mill, and the status of the harvest, the weather, the pig slaughter, and the like. I observed the comings and goings of the priest, and overheard conversations in kitchens, in bars, and in the street. From extended household interviews I gleaned family histories and data on the intricacies of workers' labor careers. Small pleasures highlighted my days: discovering faded religious frescoes painted on the interior walls of one farmstead; reading a boisterous sixteenth-century Latin dedication inscribed on the cornerstone of a peasant cottage. However, I also experienced frustrations with the languages, with reluctant informants, and with ambiguities in the data.

I concentrated on the commonplace and from the commonplace I began to piece together a comfortable view of the social regularities which ordered life in the parish (see Evans 1976). Only relatively late in the first stint of fieldwork did events begin to jar this narrow conception of the social order. A series of unconnected encounters and incidents suggested aspects of social reality in Rubignacco that were not fully captured in my early fieldnotes. The scarred hands of a retired silk worker, black fossils from a distant coal mine lining the shelf of a peasant farmhouse, the menacing provisions of a fascist agrarian contract, the medieval paraphernalia on display in a local museum—these did not fit with the picture I had constructed of the hamlet and its environs. During subsequent periods of fieldwork in the summers of 1983, 1985, and 1987, I began to pursue these irregularities with new sets of questions that moved the research from the relative tranquillity of the present toward an assessment of the unrest of the past. As I began to probe the layers of experience that had lain dormant for a generation or so in the memories of aging informants, dissonant undercurrents began to surface. Ancient animosities were rekindled and past anguish reawakened in the process. These latter episodes of fieldwork and archival research extended the boundaries of the work and set the tone for this presentation. These experiences, moreover, irrevocably altered my views on the nature of culture and social life in complex societies, as well as my assumptions regarding the potential and the limitations of anthropological research. I have tried to capture the social and cultural domains of Rubignacco and the surrounding rural districts in terms of the counterpoint between past and present. Although social life in Rubignacco has familiar contours, it is also cut by deep and unsettling contradictions.

At the core of this research are two sets of theoretical questions. The first set revolves around the identification of a type of social formation—peasant-worker society—that has largely gone unrecognized and unstudied. This aspect of the research is concerned with developing a theoretical framework for analyzing the social organization created at the interface of the urban industrial and the rural peasant spheres. The second set is rooted in Friulian cultural history. These questions bear on the transformation of the Friulian cultural domain from one infused with symbolic meaning to one dominated by social abstracts. This aspect of the study focuses on how the cultural realm was "disenchanted" and remade through the interaction between traditional representations of reality and the definitions and formulas emanating from church, state, and market institutions (*die Entzauberung der Welt*).[1]

Peasant-Worker Society

My analysis of the peasant-worker milieu emerged from a series of unexpected insights that developed during the fieldwork; the most important were derived from an examination of labor careers in Rubignacco. Social complexities revealed in labor histories of the Rubignacchesi forced a reevaluation of the basic assumptions of the research. The most flawed preconception was that the data would show, coexisting within Rubignacco, two distinct socioeconomic systems—one based on wage employment and tied to the industrial sphere, and the other based on domestic agricultural production and tied to the peasant sphere. I found, however, a single society that merges elements of these two social worlds in a rich and bewildering fashion and, more importantly, a society that has its own distinctive characteristics and dynamics. It became clear, furthermore, that this type of society was not new, nor was it unique to Rubignacco. On the contrary, it has a long and intriguing history that stretches back to the first stirrings of industry in the cottages and workshops of the European countryside (Holmes 1983; Holmes and Quataert 1986).

The material from Rubignacco reveals how peasant-worker social organization is composed of various "liminal" groups, each of which relates to the agrarian and wage spheres in its own characteristic fashion (Taussig 1980: 103; Turner 1967: 93–112). The members of each liminal group employ a mosaic of productive arrangements in their day-to-day lives and over the course of their labor careers. In rural households, individuals engage in agrarian and industrial wage work, mining, construction, and a range of scavenging activities, as the family moves through the domestic cycle. Despite the diversity of nonfarm employment, ties among family and kin to a common round of agrarian activities make the rural household the center of peasant-worker livelihood and society. Thus, worker peasantries are sustained by individuals who, in their efforts to secure a livelihood, create links between rural households and the wage nexus. Six major groups composed peasant-worker social organization in Rubignacco during the first half of this century. Each group was characterized by a slightly different constellation of productive involvements and hence a discrete set of relationships to landlords, employers, government offices, political parties, and even the church. As a result, each of these social groups displayed a different relative status and economic security, a different political predisposition, and a different potential for change and reconfiguration.

From a historical perspective, worker peasantries appear to evolve from the basic demands and constraints of rural livelihood which favor the integration of diverse productive involvements rather than the creation of narrow occupational identities. The pragmatic maneuvering among productive roles by rural populations gives this type of society its enduring contours as well as its propensity for change. Yet precisely these characteristics endow peasant-worker society with many of its ambiguities and, no doubt, contribute to its ill-defined status in the sociohistorical literature. The central paradox that rules worker peasantries is that, although this type of society, and the groups that embody it, historically have mediated many decisive rural transitions—most notably working class formation and repeasantization—the society itself

9

is *not* transitional. To understand worker peasantries fully thus requires transcending a mere delineation of peasant-worker social organization as a distinct phenomenon. Only by demonstrating how the dynamics of this type of society illuminate other related social phenomena can the broader historical role of peasant-worker society in shaping life in the countryside be assessed. One case will be important in the preliminary development of this argument: the emergence of a "working class" within a rural ghetto of Rubignacco, referred to by residents as Lazaret or the barracks (*le baracche*). The "social outcasts" of the ghetto were able to achieve a modest disengagement from the rural dependency relationships that enveloped the vast majority of the rural poor, and to forge distinctive social bonds based on a shared evaluation of their class circumstances. The case reveals how proletarianization can be incubated in a peasant-worker milieu.

Cultural Disenchantment

Elaborate agrarian contracts—defining with stunning precision various aspects of social and economic life in the rural districts of the region—are essential in any examination of Friuli's cultural history. These contracts first appeared in the eleventh century and continued to regulate agrarian relations well into the twentieth century. They have been conventionally viewed as leaseholding instruments which established the terms and provisions of agricultural production. Although this approach—which emphasizes the intricate socioeconomic elements of these agreements—is employed here, it serves only as the starting point for the examination. The broader premise of the appraisal is that these legal instruments mediated a fundamental cultural transformation—one that achieved a "disenchantment" of the traditional cultural domain.[2] That is to say, the contractual instruments introduced a formal rationality that reduced various aspects of social life to easily calculable systems subject to regulation by formal laws (Arato 1972: 35–36; Lukács 1971: 98; Mommsen 1987; Roth 1987; Schluchter 1987; Weber 1946: 215–16).

The theoretical foundations of this part of the study are heavily influenced by Max Weber, through the creative interpretation of Georg Lukács who linked Weber's analysis of Western rationality with key Marxist categories (Arato 1972: 30). Weber's use of the concept of "rationality" is very specific and thoroughly ironic. (Weber goes so far as to use Baudelaire's phrase *fleurs du mal* as a metaphor for scientific rationality.) Karl Löwith here captures both the irony and the specificity of Weber's stance:

The basic *motif* of [Weber's] "scientific" inquiry turns out to be the trend towards secularity. Weber summed up the particular problematic of this reality of our time in the concept of "rationality." . . . He attempts to make intelligible this general process of rationalisation of our whole existence precisely because the rationality which emerges from this process is something specifically irrational and incomprehensible. (Löwith 1982: 40–41)

The other concept that buttresses this analysis is "reification." This concept has a long Marxist pedigree and, as used here, comes closest to approximating Georg Lukács's formulation. Reification (*Verdinglichung*) refers to the induction of human characteristics, relations, and activity into abstract things.

Its basis is that a relation between people takes on the character of a thing and thus acquires a "phantom objectivity," an autonomy that seems so strictly rational and all-embracing as to conceal every trace of its fundamental nature. (Lukács 1971: 83)

Lukács, like Marx before him, saw this reifying process as the "essence of commodity structure." For Weber the role of commodity exchange was less crucial; rather, he explored the reified outcomes of formal rationality in the makeup of bureaucracy. Weber emphasized reified organization of bureaucracy as the most rational outgrowth of *discipline*, a phenomenon that sets the pattern in the factory, government bureau, military barracks, and virtually every other social institution (Tadic 1979: 291). The contractual instruments in Friuli readily lend themselves to a Weberian approach and thus support the Weberian position.[3] This part of the study will examine empirically how the principles of "rationality" transformed the "outer and inner life of society" on the eastern fringe of the Friulian plain (Lukács 1971: 84). This will involve an evaluation of the emergence of agrarian contracts from the feudal social milieu in Friuli, and their subsequent development as the pivotal legal-bureaucratic instruments in the countryside. The evolving terms and provisions of the contractual instruments ingrained a new cultural dogma, one that used essentially "economic" abstractions to establish social categories and productive formulas (Bourdieu 1979: 43–44).

Two complementary discussions bear directly on these same theoretical questions. The first concerns the unusual interaction between folk religion and the formal dogma of the Catholic church in Friuli from the sixteenth century to the present. Cividale, as a seat of the Roman Inquisition, was the site of hundreds of "witch trials" during which the bureaucratic logic of the church confronted and attempted to subdue the symbolic motifs and "ritual" practices of the Friulani. Carlo Ginzburg's (1983) superb study of the "cult" of the benandanti in Cividale and surrounding areas permits a historical evaluation of this clash of religious idioms in the carefully recorded dialogue of the participants. The peculiar interchange between Catholic dogma and Friulian folk beliefs that continued in rural hamlets well into the twentieth century will be examined from contemporary ethnographic data collected in the summer of 1985. The disturbing social consequences for the rural poor of what became a parasitic interaction between religious idioms will be evaluated in terms of popular beliefs and Catholic dogma regarding witchcraft.

The inquiry will be developed further in terms of the life histories of rural folk experiencing for the first time the challenges posed by factory work. The discussion is based on interviews with former employees—virtually all of whom are female—of Rubignacco's silk mill (*filanda*). Their ethnographic accounts depict the stark incongruities between the discipline of the factory and the norms and moral standards governing rural life. Accounting formulas for time, work, and wages, the relentless demands of machinery, and the often ruthless directives of overseers, thrust the workers into an alien environment dominated by a "rational" technology and business organization. The women who spent their work lives in this industrial setting faced arduous physical demands and vexing social dilemmas, surpassed only by the fears of destitution inherent in job loss. The rigors of factory employment intruded on the most intimate aspects of workers' lives and shaped their identities, marriages, and social position vis-à-vis coworkers, managers, and the outside community. The accounts emphasize these women's struggles to make sense of daily predicaments for which they had few—if any—cultural precedents.

Many times, this study was pulled in two different directions. Only gradually did I understand that the analysis of the cultural disenchantments in Rubignacco, its surrounding rural districts and urban precincts, folded back into the discussion of the worker peasantry. Indeed, the peasant-worker (*contadino-operaio*), more than any other figure in the countryside, straddles the enchanted and disenchanted realms.[4] From his rural household, where he speaks an obscure and ancient dialect, where he continues to harbor beliefs in witches and magical beasts, and where his family is bound together in an "uneconomic" agrarian routine, the peasant-worker ventures to distant outposts of the disenchanted world. In some cases with great shrewdness, in other cases with disarming naïveté, he negotiates the complexities of the wage economy.

Whether working in the local cement mill or in the oil fields of Vera-cruz, this mercurial figure maintains a deep and abiding tie to the en-chanted enclaves of his mysterious *patria*.

Comparative Significance

The peasant-worker phenomenon has been widely noted in the socio-historical and anthropological literature on Latin America, Asia, and Africa, as well as on rural Europe, but has escaped serious theoretical scrutiny.[5] The goal of my research is to develop a general—albeit pre-liminary—framework for the analysis of peasant-worker livelihood, so-cial relations, politics, religion, ethnicity, and identity. In chapters 3 through 7, a series of concepts is laid out to analyze, in as much detail as data permit, the nature of this type of society and culture in Friuli. These concepts serve as the foundation for a general theory capable of illuminating similar issues in an array of historical and cultural settings. The basic premise of this comparative approach is that a full spectrum of wage earning-involvements, and even industrial employment, can emerge and spread in the countryside without participants severing ties to agrarian holdings or divorcing themselves from indigenous culture. This situates the study at the center of sociohistorical debates regarding European industrialization and labor history. It also has a direct bearing on our understanding of rural development in the Third World.

Some specific issues in the work have a more focused comparative relevance, such as the discussions of agricultural development and con-tractual systems in chapters 2, 4 and 5; religion, ethnicity, and politics in chapters 4 and 5; Catholic dogma and folk beliefs in chapter 6; and bureaucratic organization and patronal relations in chapters 4 and 5; all of which have direct implications for European anthropology and social history. The depiction of women's experience in industry presented in chapter 7 and the general portrayal of the large agrarian operations, the *latifondi*, in chapters 4 and 5, have significance, both for the European context and beyond. The detailed examination of social relations, polit-ical outlook, and cultural sensibilities in the silk mill of Rubignacco is intended to contribute to the burgeoning literature on social life in early factory settings and women's experience in industry. Similarly, the or-ganization of the latifondi in Friuli has relevance for worldwide anal-yses of plantation systems. In the following pages, the tension between fieldwork experiences, and attempts to grapple with these experiences in a systematic manner, are explored.

13

The Research

Friuli is an area not well known to outsiders, foreign or Italian, nor has it been well traveled by anthropologists. No set of distinctive anthropological questions has yet been derived to address the beguiling character of the region. Though Friuli has not been overrun by anthropologists, it is an area for which there is a sophisticated body of regional history and folklore, and substantial works in social geography, economics, demographics, and politics. The obvious advantage of this literature is that it permits arguments, particularly those dependent on historical perspectives, to draw on complementary materials to enhance ethnographic analyses. This section—by no means a comprehensive introduction to this enigmatic region—sketches a series of opening questions and a selective ethnographic background to help the reader negotiate the discussions that follow.

The Setting: Rubignacco di Cividale

Rubignacco forms one of seven outlying rural settlements (*frazioni*) of the *comune* of Cividale del Friuli. The settlement spreads over approximately four square kilometers and has slightly fewer than five hundred residents. Until the late 1960s, Rubignacco formed a distinct administrative unit electing its own representative (*consigliere comunale*) to the communal government. At the time of the fieldwork, the frazione no longer constituted a separate political entity but had been combined with the frazione of Grupignano into a single administrative zone (*sezione*) of the comune. Since World War II, the Rubignacchesi have regularly voted for Christian Democratic candidates to represent them in the communal, regional, and national assemblies. Though it lacks a distinct political identity, the settlement retains its coherence as a geographic and religious unit (*parrocchia*). Most residents continue to view their parish as separate from the urban center of Cividale and to identify themselves as Rubignacchesi, even though many have difficulty specifying the precise boundaries of the hamlet.

From the Church of San Marco di Rubignacco it is approximately one and one-half kilometers to the center of Cividale. Cividale is a prosperous urban center (*centro*) with numerous well-stocked shops, restaurants, movie theaters, a department store, and dozens of bars that line the narrow streets and ring the open plazas. An unmistakable northern Italian lifestyle with a noticeable Venetian flavor is evident in local tastes in food, dress, housing, and automobiles. The Venetian influence runs from handsome urban villas and courtyards, to Verdi accompaniments blared over loudspeakers for children practicing on the communal soccer field. Venice's emblem, the lion of San Marco, decorates public and private structures throughout the comune.

Rows of myrtle and an occasional palmetto palm in gardens and courtyards reflect the temperate climate of the Friulian lowlands. Summers are hot and dry, with temperatures averaging just over twenty degrees Celsius in July. During the summer of 1983, a particularly dry season, farmers on the plain could be seen and heard launching small rockets to seed passing thunderheads in order to bring rain to the parched fields. The first rains of late August usually mark the end of summer and the beginning of the damp, cool fall-to-spring period. The weather systems that move off the Adriatic or across the Alps in the spring and fall tend to stall over Cividale, dropping the majority of the 1,800 millimeters of annual precipitation in spring and fall. Winter temperatures drop to a low in December and January, averaging a bit above freezing (Prost 1973: 27–28).

As they have since the Middle Ages, vendors fill two of the main plazas in the center of the comune, forming a large open-air market each Saturday. More than 150 vendors arrive early in the morning in small trucks with panels that unfold to display special goods and wares. These items include fruit, flowers, vegetables, cheese, linen, clothing, shoes, toys, and hardware. Evidence of the Slavic segment of the Friulian population can be seen and heard thoughout the market. Slovene-speaking farmers from the remote mountain settlements of the Natisone Valley descend on the comune to sell their produce and purchase inexpensive wares. Yugoslav license plates are frequently seen on the cars that line the side streets of the comune. Mingling in the market are farmers, workers, schoolteachers, civil servants, prominent landowners, professionals, an occasional priest, wives, children, flirting teenagers, and elderly pensioners. On these Saturday mornings one can without much trouble discern the Christian Democrat, Communist, and Socialist politicians working the crowds, spreading their aggressive charm and good humor. Early Saturday is also the best time to hear, among the various people moving through the market, the variety of dialects spoken in eastern Friuli. Again, Slovene and Friulian are prominent among the sturdily built, ruddy-complexioned farmers. Some urban residents are heard greeting each other in Friulian and shifting to standard Italian or occasionally to a Venetian dialect. The carefully groomed middle-class residents rely solely on Italian for their exchanges.

Most of the public architecture in Cividale, which includes schools, government offices, an archaeological museum, the cathedral, convents, and numerous churches and small chapels, is within the remnants

15

Fig. 2. A view of the urban center of Cividale del Friuli from the "devil's bridge."
The facade and tower of the fifteenth-century *Duomo* is in the center.

of the medieval walls of the town. Similarly, most of the large private residences in the comune flank the narrow streets of the old quarter. The Natisone River cuts a deep path around the southeastern edge of the old town. On hot summer days, young residents bathe along the rocky banks of the river in various states of undress, much to the delight of the soldiers housed in nearby barracks. A high bridge, Ponte del Diavolo, spans the Natisone and connects the center of the comune with settlements to the south. Rising to encircle the old quarter are new apartments, a hotel, and other recently constructed commercial structures. Beyond the medieval walls lie a hospital, a home for the aged, military compounds, a railroad station, and communal soccer fields. Still further removed from the urban center are the rural hamlets and the new industrial zone of the comune. Cividale serves as the terminus of a small regional railroad. Trains shuttle between Cividale and the provincial capital, Udine, which is about a twenty-minute ride away. The 1980 census put the population of Cividale and its outlying settlements, including Rubignacco, at just over 11,000.

Political life in the comune is organized around the city council (*Consiglio comunale*) and the administrative *Giunta*. The council is composed of thirty members elected for five-year terms from lists of candidates drafted by each political party. The members of the Consiglio comunale elect the mayor (*sindaco*), who in turn appoints from among the members of the council five to seven members of the Giunta. The Giunta, headed by the sindaco, runs the comune on a day-to-day basis, setting policy for the local bureaucracy and allocating resources. Each member of the Giunta has responsibility for one or more of the functional areas of the local government, including industry and agriculture, commerce, finance, housing, education, public works, health and sanitation, urban planning (zoning, building codes, etc.), and sports.

The election of May 12, 1985, put the Christian Democrats in firm control of the council, the Giunta, and the office of sindaco. The proportional allocation of seats in the council yielded the following alignment:

Seats	Votes	Party	
17	(4,125)	Dc	Christian Democrats
5	(1,224)	Pci	Communist Party
4	(1,002)	Psi	Socialist Party
2	(479)	Psdi	Social Democrats
1	(303)	Mf	Friulian Regional Movement
1	(254)	Msi	(Right-Wing) Social Movement

Ballots were cast for two other parties—Republican (Pri) and Liberal (Pli). They received 206 and 143 votes respectively—not sufficient to secure positions on the council. In the simultaneous provincial elections, a Democratic Proletariat (Dp) candidate was also listed and received a handful of votes from Cividale. The election of one member of the newly constituted Movimento Friuli, the Friulian Regional Movement, is noteworthy. This group is committed to the preservation of Friulian linguistic and cultural identity. Autonomist inclinations are evident in the Mf's meetings and literature, both of which are in Friulian. The group also eschews identifying itself as a political "party," preferring instead the gloss of "movement." Gaining a single seat on Cividale's Consiglio comunale represented an important electoral victory for the movement. Beyond the range of political parties in Cividale there are, as one might expect, tactical and ideological differences within each party, as well as variations in political activism among members. The politics of the comune are focused primarily on shifting alliances among the parties, particularly along the centrist axis (Dc, Pli, Pri, Psdi) and among the "forces of the left" (Pci, Psi, Mf, Dp).

The pressing issues of the mid-1980s in Cividale continued to be further development of the industry, agriculture, and commerce in the area, infrastructural investments, the delivery of public services, the problems of drug and alcohol abuse, and above all, the issue of political patronage. The recent flaunting by the Christian Democrats of their rather significant clientelist powers has frustrated both the Socialists and the Communists, and has frayed the tenuous fabric of cooperation among the three major parties in the comune (see White 1980: 45–62).

Historical Background

Cividale del Friuli has been a major regional center since Roman times. The town (*municipium*) was founded by Julius Caesar on, legend has it, an ancient Celtic settlement. A majestic statue of Caesar stands in front of the administrative offices of the comune. The original Latin name, *Forum Iulii*, has undergone a series of corruptions to yield the modern name of the town and region—Friuli. In the *Lives of Charlemagne*, an intermediate name of the comune is mentioned. "He [Charlemagne] came to the city . . . which pedants call Forojuliensis" (quoted in Thorpe 1969: 165). During the Carolingian period, the settlement came to be called *Civitas Austriae* because of its position as the major outpost on the eastern frontier of the empire. The name Rubignacco also has ancient origins. Many place names in Friuli derive from the combination of a Latin patronymic (Rubinus) followed by a place or property designation (acco)—hence "the place of Rubinus." Other examples of this form include Premariacco, Moimacco, Remanzacco, and Martignacco (Menis 1976: 39). When trainloads of new recruits pass through on their way to the infantry barracks in Cividale, the young Italian soldiers can be heard struggling to pronounce the strange Friulian place names.

With time, and the help of a guide to local art and architecture, one can begin to see the images and designs that demarcate the phases of Cividale's past. Reflected in the construction and ornamentation of the chapels, churches, and monasteries that overlook the waterfalls of the Natisone are various representations of Christian iconography and symbolism, as well as hints of the church's wealth and authority. Beautiful Gothic arched windows and doorways of private residences face narrow streets and passageways. Images of the lion of Saint Mark are cut into walls and monuments. In the old quarter stands an ancient artisan residence that is the oldest structure in the comune, dating from perhaps the eleventh century. There are telltale signs indicating that the crude structure continues to be occupied—utility lines are connected to the side of the building, and plastic flowers dangle from a windowsill. Running in front of this *casa medioevale* is a street named Via della Giudaica, which marks the location of the old Jewish quarter. Apart from the street name, the only remnants of the Jewish community are tombstones inscribed in Hebrew dating from the sixteenth century displayed in the local archaeological museum.

The museum and duomo hold many other captivating artifacts that represent the distinctive symbols of the comune's long cultural history. A mosaic of a sea god, a bust of Jove, and a fragment of a cornerstone with a Latin dedication to the Emperor Caracalla mark the Roman period. Gold jewelry and clasps excavated from tombs of noble families provide evidence of the Longobarda presence. Perhaps the most interesting works on display in the comune are pieces from the eighth century that merge Celtic, Longobardo, and Christian styles in what suggests the first stirrings of a Friulian culture. These figures, images, and ornamentation from the eighth century are carved in panels that adorn an elaborate baptistery, altar, and storage case created for the early religious patriarchs of Friuli. The panels depict biblical scenes such as the adoration of the magi, Christ on the throne, and the visitation of the Virgin and Saint Elizabeth. Observing this rich artistic legacy, one slowly gets a sense of the heterogeneous styles and motifs that were absorbed and combined to yield the elements of a Friulian identity. Cividale's enduring stature as the cultural center of the patria rests on the fact that this synthesis was largely accomplished within the walls of the comune.

Fig. 3. Eighth-century panel depicting magical creatures carved on the octagonal Callisto baptistery.

Friuli

Friuli is nestled in the extreme northeast corner of Italy. It is officially part of the autonomous region Friuli–Venezia Giulia. The region is bounded by Yugoslavia to the east, Austria to the north, and the Venetian provinces to the west. The Adriatic coastline defines the southern boundary of the region. The plain of Friuli is an eastern extension of the northern Italian plain. These fertile lowlands extend north and east from the Adriatic, until they are dramatically interrupted by the southern tail of the Alpine range. The Dolomite, Carnic, and Julian Alps enclose the plain along the northern and eastern fringes. This situates Friuli on the periphery of the northern Italian industrial economy. The region is linked to the rest of Italy, Europe, and the world economy through a well-developed rail and highway network and major deep water seaports in Trieste and Venice. The regional government in Trieste has promoted economic development through the creation of industrial zones such as the one in Cividale, with various tax incentives and subsidies for infrastructural improvements. Many factors have attracted investment by multinational corporations: Friuli's access to northern European markets, its political stability, the availability of electric power, tax incentives, a skilled labor force, and relatively low Italian wages. These investments have fostered an acceleration of economic development in the post–World War II era (see Parmeggiani 1966; Prost 1973: 232–56).

The region has a rather elaborate political history. Roman, Longobardo, and Carolingian social and cultural systems have shaped Friuli. During the Middle Ages, the region maintained a degree of political autonomy under the patriarchal state of Friuli. Cividale was the seat of the patriarchate from 1077 until 1238. As Udine grew and assumed the position of commercial center of the region, the patriarchate was transferred in the early thirteenth century to its new capital in Udine. The region was absorbed into the Venetian Republic after a slow decay and final collapse of the patria in 1420. Friuli, as a province of the Serene Republic, passed to Hapsburg control in 1797 and finally into the newly formed Italian state in 1866. Perhaps the most noteworthy consistency in modern Friulian political history has been its enduring provincial or peripheral status.

Two major geopolitical realignments took place in this century. After World War I, the Italian frontier was extended eastward. As a result, the old province of Friuli gained 23 towns, 593 square kilometers of territory, and roughly 36,000 residents, many of them Slavic- and German-speakers. The region also underwent a name change, becoming the province of Udine in 1921. The second political realignment came in 1963 with the designation of Friuli–Venezia Giulia, with a current population of 1.2 million, as the fifth autonomous region in Italy. The merging of Friuli with Venezia Giulia, essentially the province of Trieste, led to the formation of a strong regional assembly to administer the distinctive social and economic institutions and cultural traditions that coexist along the northeastern frontier.

Friuli, like many border regions, is linguistically complex. A German dialect is spoken in the mountain villages bordering Austria (Denison 1968). In a larger area running along the Yugoslav border, Slovene is the major language. A few kilometers east of Cividale is the comune of San Pietro al Natisone, which is the center of the Slavic-speaking zone in Friuli. Friulian is most commonly heard in the rural districts of central Friuli (Pellegrini 1972–1986; Strassoldo 1987).

Friulian is generally included in the Rhaeto-Romanic division of Romance. It is paradoxically a "dialect of Italy without being an Italian dialect" (Gregor 1965: 3). The core of the Friulian-speaking area falls within what are now the provinces of Udine and Pordenone. A rectangular zone, extending from the Italian-Austrian border south between Mount Peralba and the Pramollo Pass, and running along the Tagliamento and Natisone rivers to the point where the rivers are crossed by the Venice-Trieste highway, generally defines the Friulian area (Bender, Francescato, and Saltzmann 1952). Offical estimates put the Friulian population in Friuli–Venezia Giulia at approximately 520,000.

Standard Italian is the "prestige" dialect in Friuli. It is taught in the schools and is the primary language spoken in the towns and cities of the region. In many important ways the use of standard Italian demarcates the urban and rural worlds. Thus, even in the heart of the Friulian-speaking zone, standard Italian predominates in the urban centers. Further complicating the linguistic picture is the wide use of a Venetian dialect, Veneto, particularly in the western parts of the region and in the south along the Adriatic coast.

The actual linguistic behavior of the most rural folk in and around Rubignacco is varied and often idiosyncratic. The status of Friulian is particularly problematic, as spoken Friulian has become heavily influenced by Italian. Italian roots are freely borrowed and modified by speakers to conform to Friulian conventions. The result of this linguistic evolution is that some Friulian-speaking informants indicate that they have considerable trouble understanding Friulian dialects spoken in rural hamlets only a few kilometers from their natal settlements (Gregor 1965: 2). Ironically, the only informant who spoke a reasonably unadulterated form of Friulian turned out to have been born in Bordeaux of Friulian-speaking parents. Over the course of the fieldwork I found only one informant, a ninety-year-old woman, who could be considered fully monolingual in Friulian. There is also some confusion surrounding the use of another local dialect, Veneto. Many adults who claimed to speak Italian were actually using a Venetian dialect. Only on a few occasions did savvy informants identify themselves as speakers of Veneto. Standard Italian is used almost exclusively among teenagers and young adults, though most understand the Friulian spoken by their parents and grandparents.

In addition to the militant work of the Movimento Friuli to champion Friulian as a living dialect and focus of regional identity, there has been a long tradition devoted to preserving a distinctive Friulian literary tradition. In 1919 the Società Filologica Friulana was founded to promote Friulian poetry, prose, folklore, regional history, and literary criticism. The society periodically issues publications by local writers, artists, and scholars, embracing a broad range of topics from Friulian children's books to studies of local architecture. In its quarterly review *Ce fastu?* the Philological Society continues the self-conscious tradition of Count Ernesto di Colloredo (1622–1692), Pietro Zorutti (1792–1867), and Caterina Percoto (1812–1887) to establish Friulian as a highly expressive literary vernacular (Moretti 1986; Pellizzoni 1987). Thus, Friulian has two separate identities. First and foremost, it is a rural dialect by which the country folk routinely communicate and around which they sustain their ethnic identity. Second, it is a literary instrument cultivated mainly by urban intellectuals whose linguistic interests are bound up with a highly romantic view of country life.

Getting Started: The Early Fieldwork

In the late summer of 1977 I rented a small Renault and began crisscrossing Friuli in search of a fieldsite. Traveling from north to south, I visited German-, Slovene-, and Friulian-speaking hamlets. Within a few days I found a number of suitable sites. My main criterion for choosing a locale was that both agrarian and industrial labor reside within the settlement's limits. From a practical point of view, I preferred a small settlement where I could get to know most of the residents. I also wanted a site where more than one kind of industry—and thus a greater variety of occupational roles—was present. This eliminated a number of single-industry communities in upper Friuli.

By the second week, I had narrowed my choice to two very different settlements east of Udine, not far from the Yugoslav frontier. One settlement perched in the mountains overlooking San Pietro al Natisone;

the other was Rubignacco. Even though the community near San Pietro
did not meet my research criteria, I briefly considered studying it. My
interest in the mountain hamlet may have been more sentimental than
objective. The settlement clings to the side of a mountain, three hundred
meters above the plain. The Adriatic can be seen from the parish
church. In the center of the hamlet is a pleasant country bar which most
residents of the parish frequent during the course of the day. Within a
short time of my arrival, people were stopping to ask why I had come
and engaging in easy conversations about their lives and their community. I imagined that I could set up my typewriter and do much of the
fieldwork from a table in the corner of the bar. The relaxed ambience of
the mountain settlement seemed to lend itself to ethnographic work.

Rubignacco lacked this comfortable atmosphere. Life was more hec-
tic on the plain. During the day, many residents moved in and out of
the hamlet between their farms and outside wage employment. Interviews were more difficult to arrange, and informants seemed more ret-
icent and impatient, in Rubignacco than in the mountain settlement. I
initially thought that these problems could be overcome with time. Although things became considerably easier, it was necessary to maintain
a fairly aggressive approach to the fieldwork.

It was clear that Rubignacco better fit my theoretical requirements,
but the comparison with the mountain settlement was nonetheless important. Only gradually, as the research unfolded, did I realize that by
choosing Rubignacco I had selected an unusual fieldsite. Unlike the residents of typical rural communities studied by anthropologists, most of
the people of Rubignacco have numerous, wide-ranging relationships
that extend outside the parish. Employment, education, cultural diver-
sions, political activity, even courtship, take place at a variety of venues
in Cividale, Udine, and beyond. The hamlet is no longer the center of
social, economic, and cultural activities for the Rubignacchesi. Each
resident has an idiosyncratic set of direct and indirect relationships with
individuals and institutions that, to a greater or lesser degree, differs
from those of neighbors and even members of the same household. This
distinguishes Rubignacco from more remote, rural settlements in Friuli
and elsewhere where residents share a common scheme of daily involvements and experiences.

Nonetheless, there are two sources from which residents derive a
sense of shared identity. The Catholic church has traditionally served as
the preeminent integrative force in the hamlet. Historically, the Friulian
clergy labored to mold not merely the religious beliefs and practices of
parishioners, but also their family, community, and cultural lives. This
activist tradition made the clergy very public and, at times, overbearing

figures in rural society. Although the church still plays an important role in the lives of older Friulian-speaking adults, it has lost much of its sway over younger residents. For these adolescents, and young and even middle-aged adults, identification is no longer rooted in the parish. Rather, the identities of these residents are shaped by a broad spectrum of national and international influences. Most younger Rubignacchesi emulate models coming from Rome, Milan, New York, and Hollywood (Friedl 1964). Increasingly, the Rubignacchesi share a cosmopolitan Italian identity that allows them to move within the national society—to adopt its styles and clichés—while forgoing the distinctive language and customs that sustained their parochial community. The outward orientation and extralocal involvements of residents raise the issue of Rubignacco's status as a "community." Although I will use the term community in the text, neighborhood, locality, or suburb would perhaps better describe Rubignacco as a social, cultural, and economic entity.

An immediate research problem posed by Rubignacco was its lack of an obvious focus of social life—a union hall, church organization, or even a bar—that could serve as a portal through which one could enter the routine of the hamlet. The only reasonable strategy for penetrating the private world of the Rubignacchesi was through a household survey. Going door-to-door, I gradually persuaded residents to agree to interviews. The effort to gain the confidence of the Rubignacchesi was made considerably easier after the research received the blessing of a respected resident of the hamlet. This man, perhaps more than anyone else in Rubignacco, moves easily between the urban institutions of Cividale and the most modest rural households in Rubignacco. His help in introducing me to his friends and neighbors accelerated the process of gaining acceptance and trust within the hamlet. This in turn facilitated the household survey, and made less formal encounters on the roadside, in the fields and vineyards, in front of the church, or in the municipal offices in Cividale more productive.

The survey was designed to begin differentiating various socioeconomic features within the settlement, and in particular to separate the peasant from the working-class segments of Rubignacco. Each household inventory covered basic demographic characteristics (age, sex, and place of birth); languages spoken by residents; productive resources (land, livestock, and equipment); past and current sources of wage income (including remittances); and state benefits (pensions, disability payments, state subsidized loans). The interviews on the one hand yielded a conventional and unremarkable picture of the agrarian sphere, while on the other hand they presented a challenging picture of wage earning (see Holmes 1983). What follows is a brief overview of the agricultural pursuits in the settlement, as well as of the problems posed by the data on wage employment.

The Agrarian Routine

Three major agricultural regimes coexist in the hamlet: cattle and dairy, wine, and cereal production. Virtually all the small farms, few larger than ten hectares, coordinated the three major agrarian activities. Residents live on farmsteads, usually in new or refurbished two-story farmhouses with indoor plumbing and heating. Generally, next to each farmhouse stands a stall or barn where livestock, fodder, and equipment are stored. These stalls are quite old; some were built as many as two hundred years ago. Many of the current proprietors of the well-kept farmhouses once lived as landless tenants in the lofts of these stark structures.

The care of livestock is the first task each morning. Cows are milked and stalls cleaned. On farms with four or more cows the milking is done mechanically; with fewer animals the operation continues to be done manually. The number of livestock raised is largely determined by the amount of fodder produced on the farm. Cattle usually do not graze freely but are kept permanently in stalls. Farmers sell their milk to a nearby dairy and their cattle directly to local butchers. Livestock and dairy production are the most profitable agricultural activities.

Rows of grapevines radiate out from the farmhouses. Vineyards in Rubignacco are roughly one-half to a full hectare in size. Work in the vineyards begins in late winter with the pruning and training of the vines. In March, each plant is cut back, leaving between two and eight branches, each about one meter in length. The vines are then bowed to form an inverted U and tied to wire supports. Before the new growth begins, sap runs from the wounds at the end of each branch; rows of "bleeding" vines sparkle in the early spring light. Once the first leaves appear, the sap ceases and shortly thereafter the vines blossom. The intensive work in the vineyards ends in April. Through the spring, summer, and early fall, the work entails three or four periods of thinning out leaves along with the application of fertilizers, herbicides, and fungicides. During the grape harvest (*vendemmia*) in October, the mature fruits are harvested.

Grapes are squeezed in old wooden presses or in new ones of polyurethane. The juice is allowed to begin fermentation in open fiberglass vats. The remaining grape dregs (*vinacce*) are collected and brought to the state-licensed distillery where they are exchanged for a few liters of local grappa. After the initial fermentation period (about ten hours for

Fig. 4. The grape harvest in Rubignacco.

white wines, three days for red wines), the grape juice is transferred to large oak barrels. Periodically, the fermenting juices are siphoned from barrel to barrel in the wine cellar. The viscous liquid remaining at the bottom of the barrels (*fondi di vino*) is removed and also exchanged at the distillery for grappa. By June the wine is clear, strong, and ready for consumption.

The vintners of Rubignacco produce Merlot, Verduzzo, Tocai, Pinot Grigio, Riesling, and Cabernet. Most of the wine is of poor quality and is sold in bulk directly to local bars. The wines produced on the hillsides surrounding the hamlet are of somewhat better quality. These wines are generally bottled and sold to private customers. Farmers usually retain between one thousand and fifteen hundred liters for their own yearly consumption.

Two varieties of maize, long-eared and short-eared, are produced in Rubignacco. The long-eared maize is planted in mid-April and harvested in October. Most of this maize is processed and made into corn oil; a small portion is retained to make what was for centuries the local staple food, *polenta*. The short-eared maize is planted in June and harvested in October; it is used exclusively for animal feed. Two crops of barley are produced each year and sold to a nearby brewery in Udine. *Erba medica* is cultivated for fodder and fallow. The grass is usually cut five times over the course of the year to meet the ongoing need for fodder. Cereal and fodder cultivation are completely mechanized and require the least time of the various agricultural pursuits in the settlement. The tractors and equipment needed to fertilize, plow, and plant are owned by most farmers. Outsiders are hired to harvest cereal with large combines. Farmers on unmechanized holdings often form reciprocal relationships with farmers on mechanized farms. For instance, the exchange can entail three days of pruning in a neighbor's vineyard for one day's plowing, fertilizing, or planting with a tractor.

Two secondary agricultural operations also take place in the hamlet. Each farmer owns or has access to woodlands in the hills. These areas are important sources of wood for fuel and poles for vineyards, as well as supplemental sources of fodder. An average vineyard annually requires thirty to forty fresh poles to support the grape vines. The woodland plots are divided into a dozen sections, and every year one section is cleared. This system results in a twelve-year cycle of cutting and regrowth. By law, wood must be cut before March 31. Virtually every farm also has a garden and fruit trees that keep its kitchens well-stocked with produce. These gardens are often planted in the midst of the vineyard in the rows between grapevines; from year to year the rows used for the garden are rotated.

The Peasant-Worker Dimension

The agrarian routine was well-defined within the locale and conformed to conventional notions of rural livelihood. However, other material collected in the household surveys undermined this neat, self-contained picture of Rubignacco, though I was reluctant to acknowledge it early in the fieldwork. Data gleaned from the survey showed quite clearly that wage earning was widespread and was pursued largely away from the settlement. Moreover, the firms that historically operated in Rubignacco drafted much, if not most, of their work force from outside the parish. The frenetic comings and goings of resident and outsider alike that punctuated each workday represented a central part of life and livelihood. Yet I continued to cling to research assumptions which were based on a notion of Rubignacco as a more or less bounded social world whose elements could be abstracted and examined in isolation. I was more troubled still by the data that suggested the insupportablity of a clear distinction between working-class and peasant segments of the settlement. The survey showed that over time, members of these households had had a wide range of wage-earning involvements that were pursued simultaneously with family-based farming. I found this difficult to accept, and I doggedly tried to classify households as peasant or working-class. Much of my energy during this early phase of the research was spent resisting precisely the social complexity that makes Rubignacco an intriguing human community.

As I was drawn to a conception, however imprecise, of the peasant-worker phenomenon, it became evident that I was dealing with a type of society and livelihood that was not neatly contained within a discrete locality. Realizing that this type of society was difficult to study from the standpoint of a single settlement, I began to extend the research to areas outside Rubignacco. Household surveys were made of four nearby hamlets, two of which (Prestento and Montina) I suspected might have a more pronounced wage-earning orientation, and two of which (Bottenicco and Moimacco) I suspected might have a more pronounced agrarian orientation, than Rubignacco. I also sought out former employees of Rubignacco's factories, particularly of the silk mill. These interviews took me to various frazioni and working-class neighborhoods in Cividale and more distant rural settlements to the south and west of the comune. The comparative material drawn from these surveys and interviews helped buttress my original insights regarding the specific social formation prevailing in Rubignacco, as well as provoke new ideas regarding the nature of the peasant-worker phenomenon in general. Particularly salient were characteristic male-female relations, social security strategies, patterns of wage earning, and agricultural activities in peasant-worker households. At the same time, key features of the wider worker peasantry seemed to be present in the realms of politics, patronage relations, dependency ideologies, and class dynamics. In pursuing these issues outside of Rubignacco I eventually arrived at a clearer understanding of the social dynamics at work within the hamlet.

With this expanded frame of reference I gained more confidence in the empirical validity of the peasant-worker social formation as a distinct phenomenon. Concurrently, I began to admit to myself a growing skepticism concerning conventional notions of the peasant-to-worker transition (Franklin 1969). The data suggested two interrelated findings: first, that a stable industrial work force can be created in the countryside

Fig. 5. The steel mill within the industrial zone of Cividale.

without inevitably leading to "working class" formation, and second, that the special circumstances that do give rise to working classes devoted permanently to wage earning are often embedded in a peasant-worker milieu. This analysis further revealed the subtle shifting of work roles and identities which are at the heart of peasant-worker life and which are virtually always missed by the census taker and rarely accounted for in conventional rural labor statistics. The intricate strategies employed by these individuals to achieve their livelihood constitute the empirical fabric of the proletarianization process. The macro-level transition of peasantries to working classes is played out in the households of the worker peasantry, often in the face of daunting risk and uncertainty (see Pitkin 1985).

The Cultural Domain

The study became increasingly estranged from Friulian culture as the research on peasant-worker society developed. In casual visits to the local museums in Cividale, ironically where I went to escape the fieldwork, various displays of medieval art caught my attention and emphasized this estrangement. Playful images of mermaids, birds, and beasts carved in a local Romanesque style of the twelfth and thirteenth centuries, mysterious biblical scenes adorning an eighth-century baptistery, stunning gold ornaments and jewelry excavated from a sixth-century

Longobardo tomb—all left me with a nagging sense of unease precisely because of their aesthetic power. The unmistakable mark of an enchanted cultural realm dwelt in the human scale and symbolic vitality of these artifacts, and yet I had not found even the most modest residues of these "enchantments" in the work up to that time among the Rubignacchesi. The unease intensified as I reread Carlo Ginzburg's famous study, *I Benandanti*, of folk religion in the rural districts around Cividale. Here too was evidence—much more recent—of a rich amalgam of distinctive cultural ideas and images that had flourished in Friuli as recently as the sixteenth and seventeenth centuries. Ginzburg's material also provided the key to understanding why such scant traces of these folk beliefs are to be found. He shows that the peculiar naturalistic beliefs of the Friulian benandanti, which he believes embodied fertility cults, were translated through the legalistic formulas of the church's inquisitorial courts into diabolical witchcraft. In a series of more than eight hundred witch trials lasting longer than a half century, folk beliefs were gradually disenchanted and reassimilated to fit the orthodoxies of Catholic dogma and bureaucratic logic. In the dialogue between the inquisitor and the accused I believe we have a precise record of a cultural interchange that depicts with great clarity two divergent cultural idioms and the subduing of one by the other. I suspected that this rationalization and disenchantment were not confined solely to the realm of folk belief, but had been played out in virtually every sphere of cultural life. By far the most radical instance of this cultural reformulation manifests itself in the clash between the bureaucratic logic inherent in local agrarian contracts and the traditional conceptualization of rural social relations.

From early in the work in Rubignacco, I had been aware that agrarian contracts had been widely used to regulate tenant-landlord relationships. The sheer complexity of these agreements is striking. The contracts from earlier in this century enmeshed tenants in virtually every known type of rental obligation, from share rents to fixed cash obligations. Furthermore, these leaseholders were routinely bound by these same documents in very precise wage-labor relations, thereby merging capitalist wage earning and precapitalist *rentier* elements within a single contractual system. If this complexity were not sufficient, numerous terms and provisions also imparted added social ambiguity. For instance, many agreements specified that tenants deliver a series of status "gifts" (the *regalia*) to the landlord at various times of the year, suggesting a lingering feudal quality to the relationships. Ethnographic accounts of former tenants confirmed that an elaborate dependency ideology characterized ties between elites and rural labor on the estates of the Friulian noble families, and that these relationships had significant consequences for the intervening contractual bond. My initial analysis of the documents was devoted almost entirely to questions regarding how the contractual arrangements regulated and changed various productive activities. Only rather late in the study did it become clear that the contracts had played another, far more important, role in the Friulian countryside. As I found new documents from the two latifondi in Moimacco and Bottenicco, and as I examined the historical development of the contractual system from secondary sources, I became convinced that the leaseholding instruments had realigned fundamental *cultural* categories—those that defined social and economic life—and subjected them to new principles of evaluation. These documents, which were prevalent from their origins in the eleventh century until their demise in the mid-twentieth century, can be used to probe the heart of this cultural transformation. Each contractual refinement added momentum to a process whereby the social realm was categorized so as to permit new forms of manipulation and control of the country folk. The contracts gradually superimposed on traditional social relations a "rational" cultural schema, one that substituted for material and symbolic reciprocities and personal piety a new, abstract calculus. This reification of traditional social ties rendered them "economic" and subject to bureaucratic logic and formula.

There was a third arena of rationalization and disenchantment in Rubignacco: the silk mill. Interviews with former employees of the filanda probed the encounters between these women, many of whom were mere children when they first entered the mill, and the petty bureaucracy of the factory. The women's descriptions resounded with anguish and despair reminiscent of that of their Friulian ancestors faced with the alien logic of the inquisitorial courts. The technical and administrative apparatus of the silk mill, like the provisions of the agrarian contracts, operated on principles of measurement and calculation that workers found barely fathomable. Yet their work lives were ruled by these abstractions—work time, wages, production quotas—which were socially expressed in the unrelenting and at times brutal discipline of the factory floor.

FRIULI was never Arcadia, yet it was a place where sublime values, though values at times shrouded in fear and superstition, bound human beings together and gave coherence and meaning to experience. For reasons that we do not understand, a new cultural dogma imposed itself in the late Middle Ages. This dogma relentlessly banished enchanted values from the public sphere, substituting rational formulas that redefined personhood and bureaucratized socioeconomic relations. Its most grandiose expression was the managerial organization of the large agrarian and industrial enterprises that command the contemporary landscape of the patria. Vestiges of enchantment survived nonetheless. In family life, in bonds to close friends, in linguistic and ethnic practice, in devotion to a regional Catholicism, and in private dreams and fantasies, the countryfolk created a modest preserve of poignant intimacies and mystical beliefs. In the strange and beguiling experiences of peasant-workers, we can begin to fathom the enchanted and disenchanted dimensions of the modern world.

Traditional Society and
Its Disenchantments

TO UNDERSTAND the social milieu that gave form and vitality to the medieval images adorning the museums of Cividale, I turned to the work of Marc Bloch. His work is most relevant here in depicting the enchantments of social relations under feudalism. What he portrays is a cultural realm sustained by sublime values and intimate personal ties which were for the most part unimpeded by abstract institutional formulas. As he notes:

> It was an unequal society, rather than a hierarchical one. . . . In an age of disorder, the place of the adventurer was too important, the memory of men too short, the regularity of social classifications too uncertain, to admit of the strict formation of regular castes. (Bloch 1961: 443)

The enthrallments that drew together the lives of lord and peasant reveal not only the essence of feudalism, but serve also as a foil for subsequent social practices and cultural ideals.

The local character of feudalism in Friuli is developed in the following pages through documentary materials drawn primarily from the extensive collection of Gaetano Perusini (1961). These documents—essentially leasehold agreements—are helpful in rendering the nature of traditional relations; more importantly, they permit a portrayal of the eclipse of feudalism and the inexorable reconfiguration of Friulian culture. The agrarian contracts are not mere records of this transformation; they were the actual instruments of rationalization. Contracts overcame the shortcomings of human memory to establish a historical record that could define, regulate, and maintain enduring distinctions among groups of human beings. The development and spread of these instruments advanced a rational order that ultimately translated human qualities into economic potential. Their achievement, to paraphrase Max Weber, was to denude the bearing of man of its inwardly genuine plasticity (1958a: 148).

This chapter specifically analyzes how a new cultural orientation to hierarchy and managerial control developed in Friuli. In this regard the text has comparative significance for rural areas across southern Europe where similar contractually—mediated transformations of rural institutions occurred (Hansen 1977; Silverman 1975; Duby 1968). The theoretical premise of this section is that the emergence and development of contractual relations represented a fundamental cultural breach—not merely a socioeconomic innovation. These contracts came to embody a cultural dogma that displaced traditional bases of social relations with bureaucratic imperatives. Traditional authority and social inequalities in this context had two radically opposed aspects which in practice were rarely disassociated. On the one hand, they could be expressed as highly personal, quasi-familial bonds sustained by faith, trust, and guardianship, and rooted in enduring symbolic, social, and material reciprocities. On the other hand, these ties could also have a coercive aspect, in which case inequality was expressed in outright fear perpetuated through crude intimidation.

The chronological gaps in the discussion that follows reflect areas where the data are weak, my expertise is limited, or both. The arguments presented here are intended primarily to introduce the issues of cultural reconfiguration that are developed in more detail in subsequent chapters, rather than as a systematic history of agrarian contracts in Friuli.[1]

The Feudal Setting

In Friuli—as in other parts of northern Italy—a feudal system arose out of an amalgam of the Roman practices of clientage and Germanic societal elements (Bloch 1961: 178). The Roman legacy on the eastern frontiers of the patria laid the groundwork for this feudal synthesis. Land encircling Cividale was first cultivated during the Augustine colonization with the creation of *L'agro di Forum Iulii*. The formation of the agro required the clearing and subdivision of the land surrounding the Roman settlement into a vast matrix composed of approximately 20 *centuriae*, each roughly 20 actus by 20 actus (740 meters by 740 meters). The centuriae of L'agro di Forum Iulii ran along the right and left banks of the Natisone between two small streams, the Malina in the west and the Iudrio in the east, and southward from the foothills of the Julian Alps in the north to the marshland and sea.

Agrarian production and rural social relations were organized within the Roman villa, a practice which not only orchestrated the colonization of the landscape but also Latinized the indigenous peoples. Most of the rustic villas in Cividale were relatively small, producing for their own internal needs and for local markets. Wine and wheat were the primary products of this system; secondary goods included barley, millet, oats, rye, fava beans, and honey. Livestock were raised along the fringes of the cultivated subdivisions on abundant common pasturage. Agricultural production was complemented by crafts and small-scale industries involved in cheese making, tanning, woodworking, stonecutting, and textiles (Visintini 1980: 74–82). The villas in Cividale were largely under the direct management of their owners, who used domiciled serfs (*servi*) and tenants (*coloni*) to work the land. Coloni often lived in modest cottages clustered along the borders (*limites*) of the centuriae, as their descendants continue to do to this day in hamlets such as Rubignacco.

With the Longobardo invasions in the sixth century, the Roman villas, though by no means eliminated, were gradually displaced by the *curtense* system as the countryside's pivotal socioeconomic institution. Major ecclesiastical entities assumed the organizational initiative in Friuli in the wake of the disintegration of the centralized Roman state institutions. The monastery of Santa Maria in Valle was responsible for the organization and management of the large agrarian operations in Cividale.

The *curtis* was composed of the padronal household, peasant quarters, and modest farm structures surrounding the land under direct cultivation of the lord. Independent farmsteads operated by various categories of "free" and "dependent" labor were typically dispersed in nearby rural settlements and managed by more indirect methods. The architecture of the manorial settlement consisted of storage areas, livestock stalls, facilities for olive pressing, wine cellars, rooms for wool processing, and serfs' quarters. Artisans generally lived alongside serfs but had access to their own subsistence plots as remuneration for their skilled labor. The manor's social and economic life was overseen by a very powerful manager, the *gastaldo*, who made the day-to-day decisions concerning operation of the manor.

Another important organizational system—one with a distinct Germanic flavor—consisted of *arimannie*. The arimannie originally functioned as agricultural-military units with common rights over open territories consisting of woodlands, pastures, and arable. These lands formed hereditary grants to groups of soldiers who assumed obligations to provide military service on horseback and pay modest levies to their Longobardo lord. The lands of the arimannie were cultivated under various communal arrangements, often using the pooled labor of its members. These members, known as *arimanni*, were "freemen" forming a community of "neighbors" (*vicini*) bound together by oaths and ties of kinship and sharing responsibility for the internal administration of the community. The thirteen arimannie in Friuli formed the *presidio* of the *Ducate longobardo*. The duchy was established in 568 and continued under a succession of thirty-five dukes who ruled from their capital in Cividale. One of the thirteen affiliated arimannie was located in Rubignacco. The social and territorial integrity of the arimannie was loosely maintained through the thirteenth century within the later Carolingian system and under the patriarchal state (Perusini 1961: 100–107).

With Charlemagne's conquest of Cividale in 776 and the subsequent integration of Friuli into the Carolingian system, two prominent trends developed. The first was for ecclesiastical entities to accumulate—by way of donations, grants, and seizures—ever larger amounts of productive property. This expansion was most pronounced in the case of the office of the Patriarch of Aquileia, which became the most powerful political force in the region and eventually the seat of the feudal or patriarchal state. Some of the first documents we have from Friuli deal with these transfers of property. For instance, in a missive dated December 21, 811, Charlemagne granted to the Church of Aquileia the properties, "villas, courtyards, vineyards, pasturage and woodlands," of three rebellious Longobardo noblemen who had been executed for their wayward political insurgency.

The second major trend was the shift in agrarian management from the operation of a more or less integrated curtense system to a decentralized system based on small farmsteads (*masi*). The subdivision of large manorial properties required new forms of management. This trend is revealed in documents from a somewhat later period. In an important document dated October 7, 1062, Friderunda, the abbess of the monastery of Santa Maria d'Aquileia, ceded farmsteads to 273 freemen. The agreement made by the abbess (who was, as it happens, the sister of the patriarch) is one of the earliest descriptions of a long-term tenant arrangement. The document discloses the emerging managerial procedures applied to new and preexisting peasant tenements, as well as the lingering characteristics of the classic manorial economy. It specified that the freemen affiliated with the monastery received for twenty-nine years:

> houses and household goods with vineyards and arable land, pastures, and woodlands . . . under the condition that they make efforts on behalf of the abbess with the purpose of living in the [houses] and cultivating the [lands] so that they be enhanced and not damaged. [They also agree to provide] after every grape harvest the third part of the wine which came to the tap ready to drink. Everyone who has one whole field of vineyards must [also] give as

a fee at the grape harvest two loaves of bread, two measures of wine, and two measures of meat. [Each tenant] must also provide one day's worth of work for the vineyard, one for the pastures, and one for the storage facility [of the monastery]. In addition each must agree to transport annually six cart loads of goods from Cervignano to Aquileia. The tenants will have access to common lands on which to graze their livestock or on which to plow within the borders therein marked. The abbess promises not to make any extra demands. For those who violate this agreement there will be [unspecified] penalties. (Quoted in Perusini 1961: 98)

An inventory made for the same monastery about a century later lists more than 300 leased properties scattered in twelve villages in Friuli. For approximately 140 of these properties, rents were calculated in fixed quantities of wheat, millet, sorghum, fava beans, cocks, eggs, wine, and small sums of cash. A few of these arrangements required of the tenants only modest labor services during the hay and flax harvest, along with haulage of harvested crops and a fixed cash payment. Finally, about 100 of the properties were ceded to skilled craftsmen, including grain processors, tanners, masons, carpenters, soldiers, shepherds, and messengers, presumably as payment for their services to the lord (Perusini 1961: 98).

By 1077, when Emperor Enrico IV assigned to his faithful patriarch full feudal investiture with ducal prerogative over all the territories of the Friulian counts, the independent peasant farmstead, the *maso*, was firmly established as the primary productive unit in the region. The maso was of variable size, typically eight hectares of scattered parcels of arable, pastures, woodlands, and swamp, with or without farm structures. The maso's boundaries rarely were distinct. When a peasant dwelling was present, the maso was referred to as *loco et foco* (with place and with fire), indicating that resident tenants worked the land. The term *sedime* was used to refer to the house, stable, sheds, courtyard, and vegetable gardens on improved masi. The work force for these properties was composed of "free" or "dependent" tenant farmers known as *massari*, who often held perpetual leases requiring annual payments in cash and in kind (Brozzi 1980: 113; Cammarosano 1980: 128; Perusini 1961: xv).

Though the massari were the most numerous and most ancient, there were three other related and perhaps overlapping forms of tenant status that were present under Frankish rule—the *censuari*, the *livellari*, and the *enfiteusi*. Those segments of the rural populace occupying various types of the agricultural holdings (*censi*) under the control of the patriarchate were known as censuari. The unifying characteristic of this diverse category of labor was that members of the censuari owed rents, labor, and fealty directly to the patriarch—usually in perpetuity. The livellari seem to have been composed of "free" tenants who had rights over a specific parcel of land, the *livello*, often under long-term or perpetual leases with fixed rents. Enfiteusi appear to have labored under circumstances that were very similar to, if not indistinguishable from, those of the livellari. Property was conceded to livellari and enfiteusi by noblemen, religious entities, and private owners, with the obligation to clear and improve the land, and sometimes to erect farm structures. However, the enfiteusi were probably lower in status. It is known that in subsequent centuries enfiteusi arrangements were often used by ecclesiastical and private owners as quasi-charitable concessions to the poorest segments of the countryfolk. These major categories of labor were, at best, poorly differentiated, and they hardly convey the nuances or, in Marc Bloch's words, the "intricate dishevelment" of feudal status distinctions in the region.

Feudal patterns of overlordship are often seen as syntheses of Roman, Germanic, and Carolingian institutions, suggesting a coherent and uniform restructuring of society. It is perhaps more accurate—in the Friulian case—to view suzerainty in terms of a jarring coexistence of heterogeneous local traditions. In particular, the lack of an overarching state structure to regularize human relations meant that social life was defined and regulated through verbal and written agreements and overlapping customs, as well as ad hoc interpretations of rights and obligations among various ill-defined categories of human beings. Consensus on basic societal assumptions was weak, particularly as one moved from hamlet to hamlet or district to district.

> Imagine the problem confronting a man in the early ninth century, trying to determine differences in legal status among a group of assorted human beings. . . . In the same region at more or less the same date, we almost never find two manorial surveys (*censiers*) employing the same criteria. Evidently, to contemporaries the structure of the *society in which they lived did not possess clearcut contours*. (Bloch 1961: 255, emphasis added)

The confounding character of feudal social relations can be analyzed from two complementary perspectives. The first, outlined above, views these relations as the outcome of a gradual political decentralization which led to a weak institutional integration over the countryside. The second perspective, to be developed below, views these same relations as the outcome of flexible social arrangements which permitted highly personal and specific interpretations of ties among various categories of human beings.

Social Bonds

Marc Bloch captures, in the following passage, the elusive character of dependent status that prevailed in areas such as Friuli during the Middle Ages. He accomplishes this distillation of feudal social relations by contrasting the Roman concept of society out of which feudalism issued with the medieval concept.

> The abstract concept in Roman law which made the *colonus* (a free man by personal status) "the slave of the estate on which he was born," in short the dependent not of an individual but a thing, became meaningless in an age too realistic not to reduce all social relationships to an exchange of obedience and protection between beings of flesh and blood. (Bloch 1961: 257)

This cultural realm was populated with beings who were for the most part naive about regularizing legal codes like those that fused the Late Empire. Here, human relations were created by moral obligations and animated by the power to instill fear and dread.

What is striking about these relationships is the degree to which they could vary to meet essentially local needs. Social status as a legal abstraction, though not entirely forgotten, was subject to modification by powerful individuals. The most distinctive aspects of social relations were their highly personal nature and strong affective character rooted in loyalty and subsistence guarantees. At the center of this value sphere were the ideals of vassalage which—enshrouded in the dogma of the medieval church—served as the defining ideology of social life. These elegant ideals specified a code of conduct and devotion that bound together human lives in a system of long-term symbolic and material reciprocities.

The ideals of vassalage reached their most ardent form as a moral code regulating the relationship between lord and military retainer. The basic assumptions of companionage were more pervasive, however, serving as the rationale for virtually all social practice. The codes of vassalage extended down to the relationship between lord and peasant, though in less elaborate form. "Because the serfs were the 'men' of their lord, it was often said of them that they lived in his 'homage' " (Bloch 1961: 161). Through servile homage expressed in agricultural, military, bureaucratic, or other forms of service, a serf was able to improve his material wealth to the point that he might have his own vassals and tenants laboring on his land. Unlike the homage between freemen, which was often ceremonially enacted, the homage between lord and peasant was implicit, though modest rituals were occasionally used to ratify alterations in these status circumstances. Companionage came to be superimposed on hereditary status, providing a reward arrangement that could modify conditions of legal dependence for the countryfolk. An individual's social status in the feudal world was reckoned in terms of two often contradictory dimensions: heredity and service. Over many generations the potential for achieved status eroded distinctions among hereditary categories, leading to confounding social complexity. The central ideal of the society, vassalage, served paradoxically to modify the basic social relations at the heart of feudalism, thereby perpetuating ongoing patterns of differentiation.

This process of status modification can be glimpsed through documentary sources, specifically wills and papers relating to donations and sales of property. A lord transforming the status of one of his dependents is well illustrated in a document dated February 25, 1261, that also makes parenthetical reference to the ritual by which this type of change was customarily enacted.

> Tomasuto feudal lord of the castle of Porcia for the salvaging of his soul and that of his ancestors emancipates Gisla his servant and leaves her free from any servile condition as if she had been given into the hands of a priest and brought three times around the altar.
> (Quoted in Perusini 1961: 101)

The transaction is couched in a moral motive that relieves a spiritual burden on the lord and his ancestors while emancipating the serf "as if" a priest had ritually untied the servile bond. Even more interesting is a document from Cividale dated 1263 that transformed the servile tie of two serfs into a tie of vassalage. The two are referred to as *masnada servi*, literally "crowd of serfs," which suggests that they were most likely part of a group of domiciled dependents. The document also depicts an apparently common situation, one in which members of servile groups had rights over income-producing property.

> Asquino, feudal lord of the castle of Varno emancipates two of his masnada serfs with their heirs and their goods among which are 18 campi (approximately 6 hectares), 1/10 income produced from 8 units of land and 1 woodland which they had rights to while under servile conditions and which are given to them as a feudal holding.
> (Quoted in Perusini 1961: 102)

With these simple entries the status of the two serfs was permanently transformed. However, while renouncing the servile bond, the lord was creating a new bond ratified by the reclassification of property. This social maneuver created ties of companionage not merely by emancipating the peasants, but by rebinding lord and peasants through the granting of lands.

Mentioned in a roughly coeval document is a modest and rather common ceremony through which status obligations were transferred from one lord to another. The ceremony took place the day after the sale of a maso and the brother and sister who worked the holding under servile obligations. The seller and the two serfs each ceremonially presented to the hand of the lord of the castle of Maniago a clump of hay taken from the thatched roof of the peasant cottage. In the first instance, the old lord ritually transferred ownership of the property to the new lord; in the second instance the peasant siblings ritually transferred their servile homage to their new master. It is particularly noteworthy that even in the legal documentation of these social transactions, reference is made to the symbolic idiom that pervaded social relations as well as to the rituals that sanctified these ideals.

Through these very modest social manipulations, the overwhelming majority of which were not recorded, social change occurred. From locality to locality, these manipulations proceeded at different rates and were directed at meeting different local circumstances. The lord's ability to interpret status relations in terms of manorial custom, largely unhindered by codified legal apparatus, gave impetus to this gradual modification and redefinition of rights and obligations. Certainly by the thirteenth century, the results of this slow transformation were unavoidable facts of social life in the Friulian countryside. By far the most significant consequence of this social flux was represented by an ever-growing class of peasants, among whom such distinctions as "free," "servile," and "formerly servile" became increasingly difficult—if not impossible—to draw. Even members of such autonomous groups as the arimanni were confused with servile groups and in some cases fell under feudal suzerainty (Perusini 1961: 105).

What emerged under feudalism was a social world, the outcome of old and shifting hereditary bonds of dependence between social groups, and highly personal bonds entered into for the purpose of mutual assistance in the face of social and economic decentralization and endemic political instability. The result was a maze of imprecise, overlapping, and varied rights and obligations that linked one class to another and which for the most part defied legal codification. One striking aftermath of this societal momentum was that conditions of dependence varied dramatically over time and through space. "Nothing varied more from manor to manor according to locality, nothing exhibited more diversity, than the burdens of tenancy" (Bloch 1961: 249). Moreover, the persistence of ancient social categories long after the exact legal meaning of the terms had been forgotten demonstrates the degree to which social continuity and coherence had been eroded. Yet at the same time, what animated the medieval social milieu was precisely the fact that human beings learned to forge social ties more or less unhindered by abstract institutional formulas. What guided social life was the immediate urgencies of production, protection, devotion, and faith. Social relations were experienced in direct human ties and rendered meaningful through symbolic ideals and manorial traditions. Again to quote Bloch, the "far-reaching restriction of social intercourse" yielded a "mentality attached to things tangible and local" (1961: 443).

The Emergence of Contractual Relations

Little by little, feudal relations came to be disenchanted in the face of an emerging world view based on a radically different set of cultural assumptions. Weber diagnoses this process of disenchantment in terms of the advance of a rational metaphysic oriented to practical mastery of the socioeconomic sphere. Rationalization is a multidimensional concept in Weber's sociology, one far from free of ambiguity (Bendix 1965). Wolfgang Schluchter (1979) has distinguished three usages of "rationalism" in Weber's work: first, as the capacity to control the world through calculation and empirical knowledge (scientific-techno-logical rationalism); second, as patterns of meaning that involve the intellectual elaboration and deliberate sublimation of ultimate ends (metaphysical-ethical rationalism); and third, as the achievement of a methodical way of life through the institutionalization of interests and meaning (practical rationalism). The contractual system that emerged in Friuli came to embody elements of these three aspects of rationalism.

Beyond question, the persistence of a literate Latin tradition that used agreements rendered in "black and white" to establish the legal contours of relationships among individuals and institutions gave impetus to this rationalization and cultural reconfiguration in the patria. The revival of written instruments promoted formulas for the abstraction and manipulation of social practice. "It led to a recognition that the realities of social life were something that could be described methodologically, and consciously worked out" (Bloch 1961: 108; see Clanchy 1979).

What follows is a retracing of the incursion of rationalism as reflected in the development of these documents.

In some of the earliest documents from Friuli, two related organizational challenges were met using written instruments. First was the requirement to extend managerial control and oversight beyond the periphery of the manorial settlement to newly cleared peasant farmsteads. Second was the shift in traditional obligations from direct labor services to payments in kind. These very practical achievements provoked a fundamental breach in the conceptualization of social relations. Written contracts could bridge organizational exigencies, where face-to-face interaction and control were attenuated (as seen even in the document drawn up by the abbess of Santa Maria d'Aquileia and quoted above). This ability to delineate increasingly impersonal social ties was antithetical to the traditional social order rooted in intimate and quasi-familial relations. From this dubious innovation a panoply of disenchantments was unleashed.

By the late thirteenth century, documents appeared that were virtual prototypes of the agrarian agreements that were to align rural life for the next six and a half centuries. One very modest document dated March 5, 1292, shows an early figuring of the contractual relationship. The patriarch, Raimondo, rented to one Dominico Pevono three fields of approximately one hectare in total size for a ten-year term. The tenant was obliged to pay each year at Santa Maria di Agosto six *staia* (one staio is approximately 73 to 80 liters) of wheat, half his harvest of wine, and another tenth of the tenant's share of the wine in the form of a tithe. The short agreement also specified that the tenant must hoe the vineyards three times per year (Perusini 1961: 102). This contractual prototype abstracted a relationship that was essentially economic—based on a differentiation of material interests—in which the individual peasant was a rent payer and the patriarch a rent receiver. There was no evidence of labor services as such as part of the arrangement, and rent was computed solely as a fixed quantity of wheat and a share payment of wine. Included was a simple managerial directive, which required the tenant to care for the vineyard by periodically hoeing it, and which further specified when rents were to be delivered. Finally, the relationship was temporally limited to a ten-year period. The agreement thereby disengaged a series of economic obligations between lord and peasant from the wider sphere of potential material and symbolic reciprocities. This conceptualization of the bond between the two parties not only circumscribed a limited set of obligations; it prefigured a new rationale of hierarchy and inequality rooted in an abstract economic calculus (Clanchy 1979: 46, 235–36; Dumont 1980).

It can safely be inferred that these early agreements were not intended to precipitate radical social change; on the contrary, they attempted to meet new and changing circumstances by setting forth in writing what were the preexisting local traditions. Yet as time passed, the contracts were increasingly often used to define obligations and duties that went beyond traditional norms and customs. The ability of these documents to address very specific socioeconomic problems—where few precedents obtained—was the source of their unusual utility.

The Repertoire of Utility

By the fifteenth century in Friuli, there was a widespread reintegration of productive relations through which the diverse status obligations of various categories of free and dependent labor were transformed to "simple rents" regulated by contract. The social bond between peasant and lord was largely replaced by an economic relationship between lessor and lessee that was defined and mediated by contractual provisions. Contracts provided an administrative framework for the vicarious organization and management of agricultural production. The leasehold instruments also served as mechanisms for addressing very specific socioeconomic problems and challenges in ways that transcended local tradition. Bureaucratic principles came to displace customary arrangements in the organization of life and livelihood on the larger agrarian holdings in the patria. In the surviving documents, the terms and provisions that bureaucratized the tie between tenant and lord are unmistakable. In an analysis of the contents of 93 documents made by Gaetano Perusini (1961: 4–93), as part of his study *Vita di popolo in Friuli: Patti agrari e consuetudini tradizionali*, the range and precision of issues covered by the agreements is evident. The inventory of contractual utilities summarizes the various social and economic concerns that were administratively addressed in the sample.

Among other things, in this compendium of functions it is clear that the unity of the traditional agrarian cycle has been fragmented and reconceptualized. Productive activities were categorized within this contractual framework on the basis of specific managerial ends and inherent characteristics of particular crops, maintenance routines, and administrative procedures. For each subsystem of activity, rules were delineated—whether for the application of manure, the conservation of seed, the care of silkworms, the maintenance of irrigation canals, the protection of property, or the division of the harvest. A measure of circumspection was crucial to categorizing and regulating these managerial subsystems. Even in the earliest contractual provisions, the potential

Contractual Format

Types of Rent
  Fixed In-Kind
  Crop Sharing
  Cash
Parties to the Contract
  Fathers and Sons
  Brothers (and assorted affines)
  Single Women
  Conjugal Pairs
  Strangers
Duration of the Contract
Modification of the Contract
Transfer of Contractual Obligations
Renewal of the Contract

Managerial Provisions

Standards for Crop Rotation
Care of Vineyards and Woodlands
Care of Silkworms
Planting of Trees and Vines
Maintenance of Irrigation Canals
Rules for Using Pasturage
Application of Manure
Off-Farm Wage Labor
Subleasing Agreements
Management of Seed
Procedures of Threshing Grain
Procedures for Pressing Grapes
Procedures for Harvesting Cereal
Payment of Rents and Taxes
Division of Grape and Silk Harvest
Sale and Transportation of Crops
Protection of Property
Use of Tools and Equipment
Improvement of Farm Structures
Habitation of Farmhouse
Changes in Land Use

outcomes and mishaps of agrarian livelihood, and their impact on the parties to the agreement, are anticipated. Foresight came in this way to be institutionalized in the logic of agrarian production (see Bourdieu 1979: 8). Thus, we have in paradigmatic form an example of how rationally-based cultural assumptions were introduced and operated in the agrarian realm. In this embryonic stage, rationalization proceeded along two axes: first, through the bounding of discrete spheres of activity or responsibility; second, through the specification of rules that operated within these spheres.

One rather lengthy contract from the early sixteenth century (1505) depicts the way rental and managerial elements were routinized in a single agreement. The most mundane procedures of agrarian production are abstracted in the document. Despite the use of the personal pronoun (provision 2), the needs of the tenant and owner are depersonalized and rendered as a series of divergent interests expressed in contractual provisions. The concerns of the owner were represented in standards of performance required of the tenant within various subcategories of agrarian and management duties (provisions 2–10). The traditional round of labor activities is projected into a contractual framework in which tasks are enumerated and the conditions of their performance specified. The concerns of the tenant are also contractualized, though in less explicit and on less favorable terms (provisions 6, 11). The final provision of the contract (provision 11) reflects the critical reworking of social relations from a feudal to a rentier system. It indicates that the disenchanted bond linking rural work force and owner was contingent on the execution of contractual provisions. Failure to satisfy these requirements was grounds for severing the social tie.

What does this modest document achieve? It is not merely a projection of customary obligations into a literate medium. Rather, the contract represents a fundamental *translation* of human potential and productive arrangements by a new social grammar. The new grammatical rules centered on a rational delineation of social categories and managerial principles. Social ties were rendered in this contractual framework as material interests subject to legal contingencies, while the rules for operating the farmstead were expressed in a series of managerial directives. Through this *indigenous* institutional framework, traditional relations were refashioned and new economic potential was unleashed in Friuli. Human lives could be conceptualized and manipulated through these contracts in ways that would have been incomprehensible to earlier generations of feudal overlords. The shifting loyalties and duties that sustained the medieval realm succumbed to impersonal legalities. Refinement of these basic contractual innovations continued for the

Contract from Laipacco, 1505

1. A piece of [arable] land along with three pastures, a farmhouse, and a courtyard in Laipacco are leased to three brothers.

2. The tenants will give ⅓ of the cereal harvest, ⅓ of the bean harvest, a large pig [of 200 pounds], ½ of the [2nd quality] wine, and ½ the vinnace [grape dregs]. The peasant will also have to pay 20 staia of wheat and 12 staia to my [the owner's] demand. I [the owner] do not want more than 8 fields (campi) planted with miglio and Arab wheat, that is to say 8 campi of secladici or rotation crops which in the preceding years had not been cultivated. It is up to the tenant to decide [where and when] to plant miglio or Arab wheat.

3. The tenant. . . will obtain permission from the owner to cut the crops and the owner can send cutters who will be paid by the tenant.

4. The hay and remains of the harvest will be used in common to feed livestock and cover [the roofs] of the houses.

5. If the owner chooses, the harvest will be divided and stacked in the fields. The tenant assumes the obligation to prepare the land for seeding in the right places and at the right time and to have available at any given time draft animals for pulling two ploughs.

6. The tenant will have to cultivate one field of sugar beets and one field of flax [lino] whose products will go entirely to the owner, who will provide the seed. The tenant has the equal right to cultivate one field of sugar beets and one field of flax [for his own purposes].

7. The tenant must deliver all products to the house of the owner. He [the tenant] will not be allowed to start the grape harvest without permission [of the owner]. He will plant the trees and vines that the owner gives him without compensation. Every year he [the tenant] is obliged to carefully hoe the soil beneath the vines on two occasions and cultivate them according to their needs. The tenant is obliged every other year to repair the irrigation ditches, or more often if needed. The owner keeps all the mulberry [leaves].

8. The tenant will not be allowed to let livestock graze on the [owner's] land nor his [the tenant's] land nor anyone else's. He should remove the weeds in the pasture and build ditches where they are needed.

9. The tenant will not be allowed to build without [the owner's] permission. Instead, he will have to haul materials to finish off the wall of the courtyard, and if the roofs or stables are to be built [or rebuilt], he [the tenant] will haul materials and help in the construction along with a carpenter [sent by the owner]. There will be no compensation for transporting.

10. The tenant will have to haul two cartloads [of goods] to any place in Friuli should the owner request it.

11. At the close of the rental, if the above-mentioned terms are observed, it is understood that I [the owner] will lease them [the tenants] the same property without altering any provision in any way or having added anything to them for a period of another five years, provided that all the brothers stay together and that they maintain two good plough teams. Further, the tenants must not lease fields from any other owners with the exception of pasturage [which they are permited to rent].

Source: Perusini 1961: 42–43.

next four and a half centuries, culminating in a bureaucratized social formation that relentlessly conceptualized human relations in terms of an abstract logic. Nevertheless, remnants of symbolic meaning continued to be projected by the countryfolk into the realm of production on the latifondo and even in the rural factory well into the twentieth century.

The rationalization of rural life has been discussed to this point as the consequence of local conditions and circumstances. To be sure, external forces which contributed to this cultural transformation also impinged on the modest farmsteads, hamlets, and estates. The most prominent of these exogenous factors was the assimilation of Friuli into the Venetian Republic. This development is relevant here insofar as it fostered the commercialization of the rural economy. The emergent logic of risk and reward inherent in market production served as a powerful impetus for the further rationalization and bureaucratization of country life.

The Commercialization of Agricultural Production

By the time the Venetians took control, however indirectly, of Friuli, the social prerequisites were in place for a wide-ranging dissolution of traditional cultural ideas and social practices. The element that was missing was the market orientation that could endow social relations with an all-embracing logic—what Marx refers to as a "second nature."

Commercial pressures encroached on the patria as a result of important changes happening within the Serene Republic during the latter part of the sixteenth century. While it is indisputable that Venetian development was in many respects eccentric, its very limited interdependence with rural areas (terraferma) was particularly unusual. As a tenth-century observer commented, "These folk do not plough or sow or gather grapes'' (quoted in Duby 1974: 152); instead, Venetians provisioned their city through trade and seamanship. The agricultural dilemma for Friuli and the rest of the terraferma was reducible to one mercantile fact: Venetian seamen were able to transport grain over a thousand miles of sea for about the same cost as transporting over fifty miles of land (Lane 1973). This made Friuli more remote in mercantile terms than, for example, the ports of Greece, Sicily, or North Africa, where the fleets could be dispatched to purchase grain. Venetian merchants had so perfected this system that they were actually able to supply wheat to settlements on terraferma when shortages occurred. ''In a record twelve months, 1511–1512, ships brought 60,000 tons of wheat to Venice, enough to feed more than 300,000 people, more than twice its own population'' (Lane 1973: 306). It is no wonder, then, that this scheme depressed rather than invigorated the development of food production in the Venetian hinterland. Only in the second half of the sixteenth century did this provisioning arrangement begin to falter and conditions in the countryside begin to change.

The growth of the Ottoman Empire and the rise of Constantinople as a major urban center created a serious commercial rival for Venice in the eastern Mediterranean. Grain from many of the republic's traditional ports of call along the eastern littoral of the Mediterranean became increasingly difficult to secure. As a result, the price of wheat in Venice rose dramatically, tripling between 1580 and 1591 alone (Lane 1973). Contemporary observers had anticipated these supply problems and proposed that Venetian hydraulic expertise be applied to the drainage of vast marshlands in Padua, Treviso, and Friuli to create new farmlands and hence domestic sources of grain. A governmental commission (*Provveditori dei beni incolti*) had been established as early as 1556 to develop such a program. The commission met with only limited success, however, and the burden for land reclamation was ultimately borne by consortia of private entrepreneurs.

The Venetian ''flight from the sea'' and colonization of terraferma effectively met the city's need for grain. By 1595, 30 percent of Venice's annual wheat supply was coming from sources within the Republic. The ensuing commercial development of agriculture in the hinterlands made Venice virtually self-sufficient in production of grain by the mid-seventeenth century. Indeed, the new sources of supply were so secure and the quality so high that Venetian bakers in 1601 could favorably describe the grain as their own. '' 'We are now being given . . . grain from outside that does not produce such good results as ours,' by which they meant *padoan*, *trivisan*, *polesene*, and *friul* grain'' (Braudel 1972: 423). The price of domestically grown grain had a clear impact on newly colonized areas. Wheat's price in the main market in Udine exhibits a significant growth after showing virtually no change for a century (1400–1500). By contrast, from the first half to the second half of the sixteenth century, the average price of wheat increased more than 150 percent. During the same period, the average price of wine increased 75 percent. These price gains stimulated not only Venetian investment, but agrarian entrepreneurship by Friulian merchants and nobility.

The extent of commercial penetration is reflected in the expansion of Venetian ownership of Friulian lands. In less than a century (1636–1722), property owned by Venetians increased from approximately 23,000 hectares to 43,000 hectares (Gaspari 1976). By the early eighteenth century, approximately 174,000 hectares of property were registered in Friuli, of which 44,000 were controlled by Friulian nobility and 43,000 by Venetian citizens. These statistics may even underrepresent the extent of investment and commercial penetration. First, Venetian ownership was concentrated almost exclusively in productive property amounting to 48 percent of the total land under cultivation (Gaspari 1976: 118). Second, Venetians purchased not only Friulian lands but also the aristocratic titles that went with them; therefore, their property may have been categorized as Friulian rather than Venetian. Third, by the seventeenth century, the Friulian aristocracy, particularly in Udine, mimicked Venetian styles of investment and improvement of farmland and thus fostered commercial development. The shadow of this market calculus moved over the consciousness of the countryfolk and gentry alike through new standards for calculating rents. Curiously, the rental arrangements which came to manipulate commercial risk and uncertainty were in themselves *pre*capitalist.

As early as the fifteenth century, the highly localized and idiosyncratic mix of fixed in-kind and cash obligations began to give way to an increasingly standardized figuring of rents, known as *partitanza*. Partitanza arrangements typically specified a fifty-fifty division of major cereals and wine. For minor cereals the peasant usually retained two-thirds of the harvest while paying the owner the remaining third. Special contractual agreements known as *soccida* were also adopted to govern more complicated issues involved in the share-raising of livestock. Partitanza was gradually modified in western Friuli, making the system almost indistinguishable from the Tuscan form of sharecropping, *mezzadria* (see Kertzer 1984; Silverman 1975). To the east, including the area around Cividale, contractual evolution yielded a different leaseholding system known as *affitto misto*. Affitto misto incorporated fixed in-kind and share rents with cash payments, and often incorporated wage labor provisions (to be discussed in chapter 4). The rental provision (2) in the contract of 1505 discussed earlier appears to represent the shift from partitanza to the affitto misto system.

The enthrallments which in the Middle Ages had tied peasant and lord together in enduring material and symbolic reciprocities were increasingly displaced by economic formulas during the early modern era. The essence of this transition on the eastern fringe of the Friulian plain was expressed in the formulation of affitto misto. Each type of rent included in these agreements represented an administrative allocation of both productive and market risk. Under affitto misto, rents were established for each crop according to its particular risk characteristics. The vagaries of agricultural production, along with the uncertainties of market price, were ''rationally'' distributed between the parties to these agreements: Share rents divided both types of risk equally between tenant and owner; fixed in-kind rents shifted all productive risk onto the tenant; fixed cash rents shifted both productive and market risk entirely onto the tenant (see Roseberry 1976; Scott 1976). The commercial orientation of the Friulian *latifondisti* was not toward ''profit'' per se, but toward systematically deflecting various forms of risk onto leaseholders. The outcome of this institutional arrangement was, from the standpoint of the gentry, to insure that their revenues and hence their lavish lifestyles were preserved from year to year. For the hapless tenants, the formulas created chronic and often unmanageable uncertainties that exposed them to potential economic ruin.

The social and economic innovations and entrepreneurship that marked the early phases of Venetian domination began to falter as the sixteenth century wore on. The truncated commercialization of the agrarian economy, though fostering increases in cash cropping and the growing encroachment of market relations, did not yield large-scale capitalist enterprises based on wage labor. The Friulian plain, depleted of its population, continued to be cultivated by small tenant farmers operating under the standards of partitanza and affitto misto. The development of a contractual system had, nevertheless, accomplished three major ends: first, the displacement of feudal social relations and the substitution of ''economic'' ties binding workers to landowners; second, the formulation of increasingly ''rational'' and precise contractual obligations that enhanced managerial mastery of agrarian operations; and third, the adoption of rental formulas to allocate commercial risk and reward. Only in the late eighteenth and early nineteenth centuries, with the rebound of population and the gradual reorganization of larger agrarian operations, do these various tenurial elements coalesce in a clearly defined social formation. The final section of this chapter is devoted to a brief introduction to the type of social formation that developed on the large estates of eastern Friuli.

Bureaucratic Capitalism

The transformations of agricultural production in early modern Europe fostered an orientation about which Herman Rebel recently noted, "Increasingly and inexorably, personal, social and political success went to those who managed to combine traditional feudal authority with the pursuit of market advantages and profitable enterprises" (Rebel 1983: 21). This hybrid scheme has been widely discussed, most notably in the Eastern European literature, under the rubric of "feudal capitalism." Werner Stark characterized this type of transitional social formation for seventeenth- and eighteenth-century Bohemia in these terms: "Seigneurial enterprise in that period was internally, in its social structure, feudal, but externally, in its relationship to the market, it was capitalistic" (Quoted in Rebel 1983: 21). The organization of Friulian agrarian production with its feudal residues and commercial elements might seem, at first glance, to fit neatly within the formulation of "feudal capitalism." Yet if one carefully examines the internal operations of agrarian enterprises in Friuli from the sixteenth through the twentieth century, that they were only superficially feudal becomes increasingly evident. Indeed, in chapter 4 it will be argued that the lingering feudal idiom formed an intriguing facade; a facade, however, that resonated with new rather than ancient meaning. The more compelling interpretation is that commercial forces introduced distinctive organizational principles, particularly to the latifondi on the Friulian plain. As suggested above, these new organizational principles translated traditional productive bonds into "economic" relations subject to "rational" calculation and manipulation.

Herman Rebel has advanced the idea of "bureaucratic capitalism" as an alternative to "feudal capitalism" in order to explore the impact of commercial and state influences on the internal organization of the peasant "housecommunity" in Upper Austria. His analysis emphasizes how social relations in the peasant household were bureaucratized by Hapsburg administrative policies on the one hand, while individuals simultaneously adopted a voluntaristic economic rationality to pursue their material goals on the other. In this work, the general concept of "bureaucratic capitalism," as inspired by Rebel, will be used to analyze the Friulian rural experience. The notion of "bureaucratic capitalism" will be modified, however, in ways that further adapt the concept for social and cultural analysis.

Evidence of a slow reawakening of the agrarian economy began to appear in the eighteenth century. One indication of this renewal was the founding of the Friulian Agrarian Association by a group of large landowners. The association met in Udine to discuss a variety of agricultural matters and to evaluate and promote new farming techniques and managerial practices. The findings of the group were disseminated among its members in the form of published proceedings. Venetian authorities subsidized the activities of the association, consulting it on issues of agrarian policy as well as providing funds for grants and prizes to encourage further innovation and development.

A more fundamental indication of institutional change came in the administrative reorganization of the large estates. The reappearance of full-time managers as part of the petty officialdom that directed major operations on the Friulian plain marked the critical change around which bureaucratic capitalism coalesced. The gastaldo oversaw the daily routine of the estate, scheduling various operations of the agricultural cycle and advising tenants on proper farming practices. These estate managers generally had responsibility for recruiting and removing tenants, surveying lands, drafting contracts, collecting rents, and keeping various records that tracked the agrarian operation from year to year. During the late nineteenth and early twentieth centuries, the petty bureaucracies of these latifondi expanded, as bookkeepers, accountants and lawyers assumed many of the increasing record-keeping responsibilities of the gastaldo.

Coincident with the emergence of these specialized personnel was the reciprocal tendency for the owners to remove themselves from the day-to-day administration of their enterprises. In many instances, the owners and their families were in residence at their rustic Friulian villas for only a few months of the year, preferring instead the cosmopolitan life offered by Venice, Milan, or Udine. By and large these families, with their aristocratic pretensions, were no longer oriented toward direct agrarian entrepreneurship, but toward sustaining their ostentatious styles of consumption and leisure. Nevertheless, the urgency involved in maintaining these grandiose lifestyles often provoked the gentry to make ruthless demands of their workers.

The increasing disengagement of ownership from agrarian management pushed the development of the latifondi further down the path of bureaucratization and created a third social category—the managers. The relentless division of productive activities into narrower systems and subsystems of responsibility required increasingly precise arrangements for evaluation, whether for digging ditches, planting vines, feeding silkworms, fermenting grappa, or even presenting ''customary gifts.'' The expertise of the petty officialdom of the latifondi was used to refine and maintain these reified organizations. The lawyer transcribed agrarian responsibilities into a legally binding format, while the bookkeeper measured and calculated the performance of various agrarian operations. The surveyor classified land according to its quality, parceled out tenant farmsteads, and maintained estate boundaries. The gastaldo coordinated the overall agrarian operation, dictating proper farming techniques and overseeing the daily conduct of the estate's personnel. In this way, rational principles came to define the spectrum of social roles and their particular jurisdictions within these bureaucratic domains.

THE decay of feudalism yielded a novel cultural dogma, one that used rational "economic" ideas to delineate new organizational principles, social categories, and productive formulas. The preeminent institutional focus of this new dogma on the Friulian plain was the latifondi, which became the epicenters of a local form of bureaucratic capitalism. The reified rules that defined and regulated the "outer life" of these estates were embedded in the terms and provisions of agrarian contracts. The resulting institutional structure of these agricultural enterprises had three interwoven bureaucratic elements:

1. A managerial stratum composed of a petty officialdom interposed between owners and tenant laborers. These salaried specialists were responsible for planning, overseeing, scheduling, and recording the routine of the estate.

2. Legally binding written contracts that defined impersonal productive relations. Each agreement specified the precise rights and obligations of tenant and owner, as well as the procedures by which various responsibilities were to be executed.

3. Rational formulas for the administrative allocation of risk. Rather than figuring rents on the basis of traditional notions of equity or reciprocity, this system relied on a formal scheme for distributing risk according to market fluctuations and the vagaries of nature.

Thus, within the agrarian operations in eastern Friuli, basic cultural assumptions were fundamentally reworked. Human capabilities were translated through legal instruments into economic potentials. The symbolic ties and reciprocal obligations that bridged social inequalities in the feudal realm were displaced by an impersonal bureaucratic hierarchy in the early modern era. Enchanted views of social hierarchy were perpetuated, nonetheless, primarily within the framework of patronage. Despite the persistence of a feudal idiom on the latifondi well into the twentieth century, the structure and underlying logic of these operations were new. Chapters 4 and 5 will return to these issues, concentrating in more detail on the baroque institutional principles that regulated the petty bureaucracy of Friuli's agrarian operations from the late nineteenth through the early twentieth century. Through archival materials and ethnographic accounts, the social world of the latifondi will be reconstructed from the perspective of the various categories of individuals who lived and worked in the agrarian realm. By scrutinizing the peculiar and often contradictory ways tenants, managers, and proprietors interpreted this social environment, it is hoped that the reader will gain a sense of the actors' experience and the nature of their day-to-day performance. First, however, the text turns to the issue of peasant-worker society and culture. Chapter 3 introduces a theoretical perspective on the Friulian countryside which contextualizes the bureaucratic development of the latifondi within a broader social formation. Only on this wider plain can we observe how rationalization, spawned within the latifondi, reconfigured Friulian religion, politics, ethnicity, and folk consciousness.

Peasant-Worker Society

WITH the earliest stirrings of industry in the cottages and workshops of the European countryside, an intriguing interchange commenced that wove an intricate social fabric spanning the agrarian and industrial realms. Labor was mobilized in novel ways, and new assumptions came to define social ties, yet many of the participants in this ongoing upheaval maintained identities and values rooted in the traditions of country life. In this interstitial environment, a society was created, one that merged disparate economic, political, and cultural elements in a beguiling and often contradictory fashion. Perhaps because conventional sociohistorical analysis depends so much on a clear demarcation of agrarian and industrial societies, we have difficulty probing the dynamics and even elucidating the characteristics of the peasant-worker social life (Williams 1973). To begin with, this society is difficult to locate—it can be neatly situated neither in a peasant district nor in a working-class neighborhood. Peasant-workers are preeminently sojourners who traverse regional and national frontiers as easily as they trespass the conceptual boundaries fabricated by social scientists.

The empirical problems posed by peasant-workers are complex and refractory, basic to the very nature of country life. Worker peasantries appear to develop out of the exigencies of rural livelihood which favor the integration of a variety of productive involvements rather than the creation of narrow occupational identities. Concentration of capital, the presence of a significant land-poor as opposed to landless population, and endemic under- and unemployment, served as the structural preconditions for this adaptation (see tables 3.1 and 3.3). A Friulian labor career in the early twentieth century could cover episodes of tenant farming, agricultural wage work, local factory employment, seasonal and long-term labor migrations, and retirement back into peasant-farming, now underwritten by the welfare state. Livelihood in this context is not merely an individual concern; it is generally part of broader household strategies sustained by a common commitment to a family-based agrarian holding. From the standpoint of the rural household, members are deployed over the course of the domestic cycle into agrarian and industrial wage work, mining, construction, domestic service, and a range of scavenging activities. Bonds among family and kin serve as the critical interface between peasant-worker livelihood and social organization.

The failure of sociohistorical research to address the integrative character of peasant-worker livelihoods and to conceptualize peasant-worker activity from the perspective of the rural household has led to a fragmented understanding of the phenomenon (see R. Bell 1979: 227–29). Typically, peasant-workers appear in the literature as cottage industrialists, part-time farmers, return migrants, guest or undocumented workers, and transient day laborers: more often, they are simply classified as either workers or peasants, with little or no regard to the agrarian pursuits of workers and the wage-earning pursuits of peasants (see Franklin 1969: 65; Roseberry 1976: 46; Sozan 1976: 199).[1] To overcome this empirical dilemma, the peasant-worker phenomenon is defined here in broad terms which allow the consolidation of heterogeneous laboring groups into a single theoretical framework—emphasizing the diversity of wage involvements on the one hand and the unifying influence of rural households on the other. In this definition, worker peasantries are composed of individuals who, through their productive activities, create links between agrarian households and the wage nexus. And the empirical core of the phenomenon is enacted by peasant-workers who, in their efforts to secure a livelihood, continually craft relationships that span small-scale agrarian and wage-earning activities. Rubignacco has been swept by these crosscurrents since the first peasants ventured out to seek their fortunes along the narrow byways and crowded docksides of Venice.

The anomalies of peasant-worker life extend beyond the contours of livelihood well into the arenas of religion, ethnicity, and politics. Peasant-workers are still eyed with sympathy and lingering suspicion by Cividale's political leaders, a number of whom were interviewed regarding the electoral orientation of the rural population. Perhaps the most interesting response came from a shrewd regional official of the Christian Democrats. The Dc is widely viewed as having carefully and effectively maintained Friuli's peasant-workers as a pillar of its electoral dominance. Ironically, this senior official dismissed the idea that the peasant-worker population was a major force. He emphatically claimed that there were few—if any—of these people left in Friuli. (Unfortunately, his reasons for making this interesting assertion could not be elicited.) However, two other local politicians, a Socialist and a Communist, were willing to comment in some detail on the historical development and political orientation of Friulian peasant-workers.

The Socialist Party official, with a picture of Sandro Pertini (former Socialist president of the republic) hanging on the wall above his head and three Catholic medals dangling from his neck, portrayed the peasant-worker in these words:

> This figure [contadino-operaio] still exists and has become stronger with the mechanization of agriculture. In the past, this type of agricultural operation required many hands. They were composed of little pieces of land upon which big families had to struggle to survive. Mechanization of agriculture and new industrial opportunities led young peasants into wage employment. Many left agriculture for industry, but many others . . . held onto their property. They did not want to sell out to bigger operations. They continued with great sacrifice to operate these small farms. Thus, ''part-time'' work was born. They managed both a full-time worker's job and the demands of their farmstead. The peasant-worker is conservative because he does not want to lose his land. He does not understand that it is *not* economical for him to have a small farm with only two cows. He sticks to the land that he inherited from his father and grandfather.

In a bar frequented by other party members, a Communist official depicted the peasant-worker in less sympathetic terms:

> The peasant-worker is typical of all of Friuli and a big part of Veneto. This figure has been one of the reasons for the existence of the conservative consensus. The recent development of industry in Friuli began in the 1950s. The development has been based on low salaries and old technology. This situation often occurs in agricultural regions. . . . Where this type of industrialization takes place, where the agrarian economy is based on small ownership, factory work becomes integrated with agricultural income. So much so, that we also observe a [reciprocal] transformation of farming, the introduction of maize monoculture, and the adoption of new farming methods that correspond to industrial development and simplify the agrarian operation. . . . These people have not been expelled from their land. But I have to say this, these peasant-workers provoke divisions in the working class. As a former union leader, I know the peasant-worker is more prone to absence. He is absent when he has to harvest or when he has to till the land. The [traditional] factory worker is more devoted. He is tied to his work and stays at his place. This has produced huge conflicts. The peasant-worker did not lose when he entered the factory, he acquired a privilege. Because the industrial worker has only the income from the job, he is more willing to fight. The persistence of the peasant-

worker has maintained the social consensus for the Christian Democrats.

Both the Socialist and Communist politicians identified an economic rationale that perpetuates worker peasantries, and both acknowledged, albeit superficially, its political consequences. Analyses like these two, which emphasize the economic foundations of peasant-worker society, tend to obscure far more complicated dynamics that animate this realm. Indeed, the more deeply one probes these economic motives, the more one is struck by how they reflect powerful cultural sensibilities. These sensibilities represent a fundamental orientation to the modern world that induces a more intriguing cultural experience than any of the political leaders in Cividale was willing to admit. Only through an assessment of the largely concealed and unvoiced cultural stance of peasant-workers can we fully grasp the peculiarities of their economic and political life.

Precisely because rural wage earning emerged in Friuli within an ancient cultural context, a new analytical emphasis is required—one that addresses these enduring cultural sensibilities. Peasant-worker society in Friuli, as in the rest of Europe, is embedded in the traditions of the countryside. The various struggles that unfold in this milieu are played out against rural sensibilities and outlooks which have an intricate historical character. By contrast, the consciousness of urban working classes tends to be divorced from rural traditions and tied to the immediate social urgencies that define the workers' contemporary existence (D. Bell 1986; Bourdieu 1979; Habermas 1974; Kertzer 1979; Willis 1981). Thus, capturing the nature of peasant-worker life requires a thorough portrayal of historical continuities and discontinuities that frame peasant-worker experience, most notably in terms of religion, politics, ethnicity, and individual identity. The Friulian peasant-worker brings to the factory, workshop, or construction site not merely a preoccupation with his farmstead, but a distinctive regional language, fidelity to ethnic practice, Catholic faith, and a morality through which he interprets the world and understands his position in it. The analysis that follows begins with an evaluation of the social and economic dimensions of peasant-worker society and then progresses to a depiction of the distinctive cultural commitments that sustain this social realm.

Status and Livelihood

Peasant-worker livelihood and social relations had been fully assimilated among the various social groups then extant in the rural districts of Cividale by the early decades of the twentieth century. Though many of these rural groups had ancient origins, their internal dynamics had been recast by the imperatives of the developing wage and industrial economies. The identities of these peasant-worker groups were based on the characteristic productive exploits, personal aspirations, family relations, community involvements and political predispositions of their members. Specifically, the social organization of Rubignacco and surrounding rural districts has historically rested on a substratum of productive roles and social statuses. From the late nineteenth to the mid-twentieth century, seven major statuses served as axes on which rural society developed. These social groups have persisted for generations, yet with the passage of time their internal makeup has been reworked, their productive activities modified, and their relationships to each other realigned.

The period from 1900 to 1960 underscores the bewildering complexity of this type of society. The interplay among ancient and modern, agrarian and industrial, local and extralocal elements in the day-to-day lives of the Rubignacchesi is staggering. Indeed, representation of these Byzantine social elements can be achieved only in a crude and incomplete fashion. Fortunately, this former world can still be probed through the ethnographic accounts of older informants; the span from 1920 to 1960 is particularly alive in the minds of many residents. Their reminiscences provide a picture of the peasant-worker groups that prevailed in and around the hamlet; these narratives also introduce a crucial tension between the culturally defined groupings and the subtle ways in which the Rubignacchesi enlivened them. Not only did the Rubignacchesi defy the narrow statistical rubrics that census takers, economists, and sociologists impose on rural life, but their behavior overflowed the cultural categories that the rural folk themselves used to make sense of their social world. Their reconstructions of this past reality resist efforts to narrowly define or overly abstract peasant-worker society. The material from Rubignacco demonstrates how individuals maneuver within this matrix of economic roles and social statuses, and how the contours of peasant-worker society are thus established.

Liminal, Transitional, and Phantom Groups

The concept of "liminality" has been used by Victor Turner (1967) to denote an ambiguous condition in which an individual is positioned between two statuses—the "interstructural position." Liminality is used in this work to capture the contradictory and at times paradoxical quality

60

of the social groups that compose peasant-worker society. Members of these liminal peasant-worker groups continually move back and forth across the threshold—the limen—that divides the world of the peasant and the world of the worker. Yet this movement and repositioning does not generally result in a full shift from one to the other identity; only under special conditions is this total transition accomplished. One point needs to be emphasized: Although this liminal status appears ambiguous to the observer, the experience from the participant's standpoint is likely to be entirely coherent. What the anthropologist perceives to be a "split experience" is in fact a relatively unified cultural orientation.

In two earlier works (Holmes 1983; Holmes and Quataert 1986), the basic premises of peasant-worker livelihood were outlined and its historical development analyzed. The most significant findings of these earlier studies were that a stable industrial work force can be created in the countryside without inevitably leading to "working class" formation, and, furthermore, that the special circumstances that *do* give rise to working classes devoted permanently to wage earning are often embedded in peasant-worker social formation. Under the transitional conditions that will be discussed below, the intricate strategies employed by these peasant-workers become the fabric of the proletarianization process. In these circumstances, the macrolevel transition of peasantries to working classes is mediated within the households of the worker peasantry, often in the face of daunting risks.

Finally, there is a third group—in reality a "nongroup"—that haunts this social milieu. Often segments of peasant-worker society are uncritically identified with a particular occupational category, be it migrant, rural worker, or tenant. The mistaken inference fostered by census and other forms of survey data is that each occupational role defines a discrete social group. Through ethnographic analysis, we can demonstrate that occupational roles are typically only an *aspect* of peasant-worker livelihood, rather than an exclusive productive pursuit. Hence, a simple one-to-one correspondence between work role and social identity is at the very least flawed. Although these phantom groups continue to impede a full elucidation of the peasant-worker phenomenon, they nonetheless suggest why this type of society has been misapprehended in the sociohistorical literature.

This chapter's aim is to demonstrate that peasant-worker society is an enduring phenomenon with its own distinctive characteristics and dynamics. Specifically, the chapter is concerned with outlining the links among the various forms of peasant-worker livelihood, a specific type of social organization, and a distinctive cultural experience.

Cossans: The Underlings

The *cossan* status, more than any other in Rubignacco, typifies both the liminal and the transitional potentials of the groups that compose peasant-worker society. Cossan (or *sotan*) can be glossed in English as "underling," and historically the term has been used to designate the poorest and most marginal inhabitants of the Friulian countryside. The archaic cossan groups were composed of dependent laborers with lingering ties to land; these statuses originated in the realm of the feudal manor and Roman villa. "Cossans" came to be used in the modern era to refer to destitute populations camped outside the gates of cities like Cividale or on the outskirts of rural settlements like Rubignacco (Barbina and Battigelli 1980: 346–47).

Within the memory of residents of Rubignacco, the cossans primarily constituted a very marginal tenant status. Members of this group typically rented rural dwellings—often little more than pathetic hovels—with tiny subsistence plots. From a few rows of maize, these families fed themselves and, when possible, raised a calf or perhaps a small pig. The livestock was not intended for household consumption but was to be sold at the end of the contract year to help defray rental obligations. Under the terms of these agreements, the cossan family was also required to provide labor on the demand of the landlord, for which members were paid a meager sum. This productive arrangement left the basic subsistence of the cossan family very much in doubt and pushed family members into relationships with their landlords that resembled debt-bondage. To forestall starvation and eviction, the cossan usually resorted to transient off-farm employment. To be sure, wage work was difficult to find, often involving long treks to and from worksites. Here, too, payment was in doubt, wages were minimal and, at times, rations of flour or grain were substituted for cash. The uncertainties of tenancy and off-farm work largely defined the fate of this segment of the rural poor. The rental arrangements ensnared the cossan family in a web of cash and labor obligations that severely taxed their meager resources and threatened their survival. It is hardly surprising that pellagra was rampant among these countryfolk in the pre–World War I period.

The composition of the cossan status fundamentally changed in the post–World War I period from a liminal peasant-worker group to an emerging segment of the working class within a rural ghetto of Rubignacco known as Lazaret or le baracche. Lazaret was originally an army barracks that was converted into a military hospital toward the end of

World War I to treat soldiers fighting east of Cividale at the infamous battle of Caporetto (Kobarid). Immediately after the hospital was closed in the early 1920s, the encampment was invaded by homeless and destitute squatters—the cossans. The municipal authorities assumed control of the structures shortly thereafter and converted them into a public shelter for the poor of the entire district of Cividale. Lazaret thus became the focus of poverty not just for Rubignacco but for the entire comune. "*Lí, c'era proprio il centro della miseria di Cividale.*" Nevertheless, the fact that the cossans could secure shelter, however rudimentary, without entering into a relationship that simultaneously bound their labor to a landlord fundamentally altered the conditions of cossan status.

Cossan families living in Lazaret had four basic productive pursuits: (1) adult males worked as day laborers, taking virtually any available job in agriculture, construction, and, when possible, at the local factories; (2) children younger than twelve were organized into groups of beggars who ranged through the rural frazioni and urban *quartieri* of Cividale; (3) households were organized to scavenge for firewood that was carted and sold door-to-door as fuel for urban dwellers; and (4) members engaged in petty theft, usually involving the surrepetitious harvesting of grain or potatoes from the fields of *fittavoli, contadini,* and *padroni* alike. These activities reflect the precarious economic position and marginal status of the Lazaret cossans. In fact, the plight of these families was tacitly acknowledged by other residents of the hamlet. Though bitterly resented, the thievery was tolerated and the authorities were rarely called in to prevent the offenses or punish the participants.

The cossans, in their final incarnation, were able to stake out new productive involvements that moved them from the peasant-worker milieu into the transitional realm of the proletariat. Despite the squalor and poverty in the ghetto, residents could circumvent dependency relationships, permitting them a measure of autonomy in fashioning their livelihoods. Using their wits and guile, the cossans became increasingly committed to wage earning, and by so doing furthered their integration vis-à-vis class-based identities. New social and political identifications surfaced in the barracks with surprising rapidity, once the threat of contractual entanglements was removed. The first communist cell there was established in the 1930s, and members of fascist organizations were also prominent in the ghetto during its early history. The process of working class formation in Rubignacco will be examined more thoroughly in chapter 7.

Famei: Domestic Service

A group that often drew its members from cossan families—but which differed markedly in terms of its members' roles—was the *famei*. This group, unusual by Italian standards, was composed of male domestic workers who were housed with peasant families in Rubignacco. Young famei boys of six or seven years of age were sent to live with contadini in need of extra labor. Once assigned to a host family, a lad would remain on a more or less permanent basis, eating, sleeping, and working side-by-side with other household members. These boys and men performed basic domestic chores—"like a housewife"—and were also required to work alongside the contadini in fields and vineyards. A former famei described his status in blunt terms: "I was a slave for thirty years." A dismal wage was, however, paid for these services, usually to the parents of the famei.

Most famei were drawn from the overburdened households of the rural poor, making their social reproduction directly dependent on other groups like the cossans and agricultural wage workers (*braccianti*). As these other groups declined during the 1950s and 1960s, the famei were eclipsed. Government conscription since the late nineteenth century also altered the fate of this group. Compulsory military service redeemed many of these young men from their bondage, and those who returned to Rubignacco after their service were generally unwilling to resume the burdens of famei status. By 1960, only a few aging famei could be found laboring in the peasant households of the hamlet.

A less formal arrangement existed for young girls who worked for contadini. These female workers were less likely to become permanent members of the host family. Typically, they worked in the farmsteads and fields of their employers before and after school, spending nights away from home only during the peak periods of the agricultural year. The income from their labor, like that of their brothers, was paid directly to their fathers. After leaving school, these young women often sought employment as domestic servants or as full-time wage earners at Rubignacco's silk mill.

Braccianti: Agricultural Wage Laborers

The complicated relationships between the ways in which individuals derived their livelihoods and the social groups with which they came to be identified are reflected in the dynamics of the braccianti segment of peasant-worker society in and around Rubignacco. In simple terms, the braccianti were agricultural wage workers. However, the highly liminal nature of this population makes it difficult definitively to categorize the braccianti as a distinct social group. Only by placing the braccianti in the context of the wider peasant-worker framework can their social composition be assessed.

Braccianti were most frequently used by tenants and landowners to supplement the permanent work forces of the agrarian operations on the eastern fringes of the Friulian plain. For instance, braccianti were often hired by smallholders with farms as small as two or three hectares for a day or two per week during the agricultural year. The peasant would set aside a variety of tasks that needed heavy inputs of labor for the periods when the worker was to be employed. Similar relationships developed between braccianti and tenants on large integrated tenant farmsteads.

During peak periods of the agricultural calendar—planting, harvesting, and the forty days of the silk cocoon cycle—work would dramatically expand and the need for braccianti would become pressing. Virtually every agrarian operation recruited help at these critical times. Compensation for agricultural laborers was minimal. Early in this century, the traditional rate of pay was one lira per day; during the harvest, modest rations of flour, a piece of salami, half a pack of cigarettes, or similar handouts were routinely substituted for cash payments.

Peak agricultural periods also coincided with a dramatic multiplication of the number of braccianti in the region to tens of thousands of workers. Yet these extraordinary numbers misrepresent the braccianti as a distinct and cohesive group, as most of these wage earners were drawn from other peasant-worker segments. The cossans regularly sought this type of employment. Perhaps the most significant source of rural wage labor was the peasants living in the poor mountain districts that ring the plain. Contadini would pour onto the lowlands from their tiny holdings (*fazzoletto di terra*) to work the harvest as well as provide the regular day or two of labor per week to tenant and peasant farmers. Even workers from local factories frequently engaged in agricultural wage work to enhance their own livelihoods or to assist family or friends in cultivating their fields. In fact, the silk mill closed for a month during the most intense phase of the silk-raising cycle, freeing workers to tend cocoons in their home districts.

One other very important source of agricultural wage labor was the tenant population who worked on large and small holdings alike. Under the terms of virtually all tenant contracts, families were obliged to provide labor to their landlords on demand. Specifications governing rates and conditions of agricultural wage labor were an integral part of the contracts by which tenants gained access to land. In this way, the vast tenant population on the plain was tied directly to rural wage-earning schemes.

Although the braccianti represented an important cultural category for the Rubignacchesi, from an empirical standpoint it is clear that agricultural wage labor was rarely conducted independently of other productive involvements. Hence, full-time braccianti represented only a tiny and often transient segment of a diverse worker peasantry who engaged in agricultural wage labor during the course of any given year. In interviews with scores of older residents of Rubignacco and adjacent settlements, I did not come across a single individual who had pursued agricultural wage labor as a sole basis of livelihood. Yet the vast majority of these same informants had been engaged in one of the forms of agricultural wage work described above at some point during their labor careers. Even in the late 1970s, the Rubignacchesi would refer to agricultural wage earners, who continued to be employed on a casual basis, as braccianti. Only when I interviewed these workers did it become evident that rural wage work was merely an aspect of a much wider peasant-worker livelihood that embraced such pursuits as peasant farming, work for the regional railroad or a local trucking firm, pension income, and the like.

Thus, the braccianti in Rubignacco constituted something of a phantom group, whose numbers are easily misconstrued. The behavior of the braccianti was far more important in revealing the intricate productive relations of worker peasantries, than in defining a distinct social group within this society.[2]

Fittavoli: Tenancy and Wage Labor

In order to probe the nature of tenancy in Rubignacco and its environs, it is essential to trace how fittavoli were both tied to and insulated from other groups in rural society. Some of the smallest tenant holdings in Rubignacco operated on the marginal land of independent farmers. These peasant farmsteads were of modest size, ranging from five to ten hectares. One or at most two hectares would be set aside and rented to fittavoli. The proprietor would choose either cash (*affitto intero*), share (mezzadria), or a mix of cash and in-kind payments (affitto misto), and specify the duration of the lease, which was usually one year. The owner also obligated tenants—as part of these leasehold agreements—to supply labor on demand. This labor would be compensated at an agreed upon rate. The advantages of this type of arrangement for the farmer-landlord were obvious. On the one hand, the owner obtained tenants to work land that might otherwise be underexploited; on the other hand, he secured a reserve pool of workers to provide supplemental labor for the cultivation of land directly under the owner's management. This put a premium on fittavoli with many family members who could not only work the rental plot, but also provide additional labor to meet the needs of the proprietor. Fittavoli were so conscious of the necessity of providing labor that they were often reluctant to send their children to school for fear of angering the owner. This type of leasehold arrangement established circular relationships in which payments for tenants' wage labor were used to defray rental obligations to the landlord: "This is how they [the fittavoli] swallowed the rent."

The pressures on small tenants were formidable. They faced the classic problems concerning rents, debts, market uncertainties, and the vagaries of nature. However, with the intensification of competition among tenants seeking access to land, new problems were created and old ones compounded. An extreme overabundance of labor during the late nineteenth and early twentieth centuries rendered tenant families vulnerable to displacement by other tenants who were willing to accept higher rents, lower wages, or both. This bidding up of rents and down of wages undermined many tenant operations, pushing the marginal fittavoli toward the involuted productive involvements of the cossan group.

The experiences of fittavoli living on large estates were somewhat different. The tenant family rented an integrated farm (*podere*) with pasturage, vineyard, and arable, covering as much as ten hectares or more. Tenant families on these *poderi* often numbered twenty or more members and inhabited modest living quarters which were rented as part of the tenancy agreement. Often these living quarters amounted to little more than a loft suspended over livestock in a barn (*stalla*). Tenants, under these agreements, contributed their own tools, equipment, and draft animals. Although these poderi were potentially more productive operations, it is unclear whether the fittavoli were significantly more secure than their counterparts on small tenant farms. In one case, a family had continuously maintained its name on the same podere from the eighteenth to the mid-twentieth century. However, stories also abound of terminations and evictions, particularly in the early decades of this century.

Wages and Rents

The integration of wage earning and tenancy reached its most developed form in the contracts that governed the relationships between tenants and owners on large noble estates. A 1925 agreement entitled "Farm

Leasing and Sharecropping Contract'' (''*Contratto di affittanza mista e mezzadria*'') contained a detailed specification of rents and labor obligations. The agreement covers an integrated podere of approximately twelve hectares. (The entire contract is reproduced in chapter 5.) Embodied in this document is a merging of peasant and worker obligations in a formal, legally binding arrangement. The terms of the document specify means for translating the tenant's family labor into wage labor—mediating the precapitalist rentier orientation of the podere and the agro-business orientation of the wider estate. The translation created

RATES OF CARTAGE AND RENDERING OF LABOR
BETWEEN PARTIES, 1925

Male labor tasks for November 1st to April 1st	6.00 [lire]	
Male labor tasks for April 1st to November 1st	8.00	
Female labor tasks for November 1st to April 1st	3.00	
Female labor tasks for April 1st to November 1st	4.00	
Plowing with four animals per day	30.00	
Plowing with two animals per day	15.00	
Harrowing with two animals [per day]	15.00	
Planting with four animals [per day]	30.00	
Planting with two animals [per day]	15.00	
Conveyance of various goods on behalf of the company		
with two animals (for the outward journey only) per km		1.00
with one animal (for the outward journey only) per km		.75
For the above-mentioned transport surpassing ten km six lire shall be provided for food.		
Cartage of sand, gravel, [roofing] tiles, bricks, lime and lumber for construction or repair of farmhouse and owner's building:		
gravel, sand, stones		
from Natisone and Torre per cubic meter		10.00
from nearby streams [Maluia, Grivo, Ruch] per cubic meter		5.00
bricks, tiles and lime per cartload		
with two horses	15.00	
with one horse	10.00	
[Cash and In-Kind Rents]		
Wheat	28.0 q.li.	[2,800 liters or 28 quintals]
Maize	3.0 q.li.	[300 liters or 3 quintals]
Cash	818.00 [lire]	

wage differentials for men and women, and seasonal variations in rates of pay. The tenant's horses, tools, and cart were also transformed under the terms of the agreement into the petty capital needed to fulfill the tasks laid out in the contract. With a very limited series of provisions, contracts like this one managed to realign productive resources between the tenants' sphere and the agro-business sphere on these latifondi.

Contadini: Independent Peasant Cultivators

The relative status of independent cultivators (contadini) living in Rubignacco depended directly on the amount and quality of land they owned (see table 3.1). There were fewer than ten independent peasant farms operating in the hamlet before 1960. Three of these were sizable, ranging from seven to ten hectares; the remaining holdings were of five hectares or less. A third group of landowning cultivators lived outside the hamlet in the foothills surrounding Rubignacco. These contadini regularly made the trek from the farmsteads in the hills to their scattered dwarf holdings on the plain.

Contadini on the larger independent farms generally had tenants working small parcels of land. They hired braccianti periodically, and typically had famei living in their households. On more modest farmsteads, peasant families sought to work their lands with as little outside help as possible. Nevertheless, they too usually engaged braccianti dur-

TABLE 3.1
DISTRIBUTION OF LAND IN FRIULI, 1961

Size of Holding	Number of Estates	Total Area
Less than 1 hectare	19,695	10,478
1 to 2 hectares	17,808	26,852
2 to 5 hectares	30,840	101,064
5 to 10 hectares	14,784	103,432
10 to 50 hectares	7,772	123,495
50 to 250 hectares	262	26,302
250 to 1,000 hectares	62	30,988
Over 1,000 hectares	47	147,253
Total	91,270	569,864

Source: Gaspari 1976: 255.

ing harvest, planting, and other periods of intense agricultural work. It was not uncommon also to find famei in these very modest peasant households. The nonresident contadini with dwarf holdings in Rubignacco were generally involved in a range of other productive pursuits. They frequently combined herding in the mountains, collection and peddling of firewood, agricultural day labor, and other forms of side-employment with the cultivation of their land on the plain.

The economic strength of the three substantial peasant farms made the heads of these households the leaders (*caporioni*) of the hamlet. As heads of households and caporioni of the settlement, they enjoyed local influence and responsibility. Their interests and concerns were generally familial, revolving around property, marriage, inheritance, and reputation. The caporioni sat in the front pews during mass; they were allies of the priest and strong financial supporters of the church, providing an annual share of their production to support the parish. These prominent families formed the social core of the rural settlement, and some have retained their proprietorship for more than two centuries. The outlook of these middle peasants was parochial—rooted in an economy and tradition that was immovable and relatively inert. As the following account attests, these families tried to preserve social boundaries between themselves and other segments of peasant-worker society. The daughter of one of the caporioni gave a melancholy reminiscence of a thwarted romance from the mid-1920s.

One San Martino [St. Martin's Day] I went to the festival in Cividale with a chaperon, always with a chaperon, you know. We never went dancing without a chaperon. My mother was not willing to accompany us that night, but my aunt offered to go. We arrived in Cividale. We were just girls. A young man came to me. He was a handsome young man, handsome was he, handsome, he was a handsome man from Prestento. We danced together that night [due to the oversight of the chaperon]. Later he came to visit me at my house. I entered the house with this man, you know, and as we entered my father immediately departed for the stable. [When I saw him leave] I said to myself, "It does not go well." My father stayed in the stable the entire time, all the time the young man remained. He was a handsome brown man, a handsome brown man. After he left my father returned from the stable and so said my father, "Look, you are not going to take any *barufans* [ruffians] into this house." The young man never came back. I let him go wherever he wanted. [Later] he went to America [to find work]. He went to America and died there.

Although the men from Prestento had a reputation as brawlers, the father was objecting to something more basic. The "handsome young man" was a peasant-worker with little property. Thus, the father's disapproval of the romance was an expression of his objection to the man's status more than to his character. As we will see later, however, there were circumstances that arose even within the households of the caporioni that required them to accept wage earners as marriage partners for their daughters in order to preserve these operations.

The seasonal ties between the contadini and the wage economy were fairly straightforward. Smallholders, particularly the nonresident cultivators, again regularly supplemented their livelihoods with rural wage earning, while the large independent peasant proprietors in Rubignacco regularly took on hired hands. These same contadini were tied to and dependent on the wage nexus in more remarkable and compelling ways. For instance, two of the independent farmsteads operating in Rubignacco just prior to World War II were newly created. Both of these peasant holdings were established by families whose members had worked overseas for extended periods of time, in one case in the Italian colonies of North Africa and in the other in western Australia. Wages earned at great distances from the patria permitted these sojourners to accumulate modest savings and thereby accomplish an eventual repeasantization on their return to Rubignacco, as the following case demonstrates.

Beneath the rustic demeanor of many contadini is a striking worldliness. In the lengthy account of one of these rustic sojourners, we can begin to see their intriguing orientation to livelihood, and assess the nature of peasant-worker sensibilities. Perhaps most important in this latter regard is the "comparative perspective" which results from the varied roles and locales through which peasant-workers move during the course of their vagabondage.

My father first went to America where he worked as a manual laborer. From there he went to Australia [c. 1910]. I was born in Australia [in 1915] and I came to Friuli when I was eight years old. My father was the youngest of four brothers. They were very poor peasants in Friuli. They had only one or two campi [approximately one-third to one-half hectare]. . . . Everyone worked the land. [He curses the small size of the holding.] My father left because of the poverty. They could not all live on the land; there were too many in the family. The brothers sold the land and divided the proceeds. Two brothers used the money to go to France; one eventually returned to Friuli, the other is still in France. Another brother found a job with the communal government while my father of course went to America. In America he got a job as a seaman and sailed to Australia where he decided to jump ship. He got papers from the Italian consul and started to work as a woodcutter but soon he heard about opportunities in the sugarcane fields of the northwest land. The government gave free virgin land. If the homesteaders cultivated it the land was theirs. Work gangs would clear the land and establish individual farms. They made good money. People who were careful could save some money, but it took lots of work. My father sent money to Mother in Friuli so that she could purchase passage to Australia and join him. . . . He would say "We worked but we earned." The cutting of sugarcane was done on contract. The more you worked the more money you made—the contract was always respected. My parents quickly became prosperous enough to begin hiring people to work their own farm [he used an Italianized English term, *la farma*]. They had a nice freestanding farmhouse by a river with more than fifty hectares of land. I went to school for two years there and I spoke English quite well. When we returned to Friuli the children would laugh at us so we stopped speaking English. My parents were very upset. . . . My father decided to return because he was ill, tired of work and very homesick [the father died shortly after arriving back in Friuli]. My mother did not want to leave. In Australia my father was a "nigger" but I was an Australian. I was one of them but my father wasn't. . . . Little had changed in Friuli when we arrived here [in 1923]. With the money from Australia my father purchased this farm of five hectares; thus we had status in Rubignacco. Here the padrone had the power—contracts were not respected. If you [a tenant] did not pay you had to leave on San Martino. There was little poverty in Australia. We could have one kilogram of meat per day. Here you could not be certain of meat once a month. Jobs were just not available in Friuli. A household considered itself lucky if one member worked and that one for five or six months per year. You had to sweat to sell your livestock even at very low prices. Workers could not be buyers and everything was a great misery. The luckiest were those at the cement mill, they worked year round. But still they would die of silicosis. In those days they had hand operated furnaces, they had to tend open fires with long prongs. Life was better in Australia in regard to everything, not just money. We had a comfortable house—it wasn't cold. . . . There was a lot of work. We worked but we earned.

As a young man the informant was drafted into the Italian army for a very different sojourn—one that took him to Greece, then Croatia, and finally to the Russian front. He was captured while retreating along the Don near a city called Popfka in January of 1943. For the next three years, he labored in Siberia as a prisoner of war "in the cold and with hunger. . . . Was it cold!" He displays no ill feelings about the experience; indeed, he seems to have developed a certain warmth, if not affection, for his Russian captors. Nevertheless, he lost part of his foot to frostbite, which made him eligible for an Italian military disability pension. Today this robust fellow works the same farm his father purchased more than sixty years ago, and collects social security benefits. He still ponders the enigmatic cultural encounters of his youth. He was eager for me to interpret the mysterious meaning of "week-ends" and "picnics" that still haunts his recollections of an Anglo-Australian childhood. I tried my best to unravel these mysteries, with little success. In response to my limp efforts at interpretation, this remarkable man just shook his head and repeated wistfully and without a trace of irony, "A wholly different life. . . . A wholly different life."

The daunting itineraries through the wage-economy followed by Friulani to establish independent holdings in their home districts are by far the most dramatic expressions of the fusion of peasant traditions and outlooks with a wage-earning orientation. There was, however, a wide range of more subtle interactions fashioned by residents, continually drawing together diverse socioeconomic practices to create and recreate peasant-worker social relations. For instance, pressing social problems that were reconciled by extending ties outside the parochial peasant sphere arose even on the oldest and largest independent farmstead in Rubignacco. In one particular case, a caporione family faced the classic peasant quandary of not having a male heir. The situation was resolved around 1947 by marrying one of the family's three daughters to a worker who assumed responsibility for the operation of the farmstead. The new husband had been raised in a tenant family and hence fully understood the demands of the agricultural regimen. However, he continued to maintain his off-farm employment even after the marriage, thereby establishing an ongoing peasant-worker dynamic within the rural household. Although the marriage of a worker to the daughter of a wealthy peasant family in itself represented an unusual social arrangement, it nonetheless suggested the innovative relations fashioned by contadini to meet the challenges and opportunities posed by country life.

In sum, the difficulties, misfortunes, and calamities that punctuated peasant life also defined the motives, character, and duration of involvements with the wage economy. Land hunger; periodic crop failures; difficulties posed by illness, disability, and old age; fluctuations in household size and composition; disputes over land, inheritance, and the operation of agrarian holdings were, alone or in combination, able to insinuate crises that strained and distorted peasant livelihoods and social relations. The wage nexus offered contadini a way to resolve, however imperfectly, the agrarian predicaments that have shadowed rural households in Rubignacco for the last millennium.

Operai: Industrial Wage Work

Male workers (*operai*) in the vicinity of Rubignacco had a number of major employment alternatives: two cement works, the tannery, the brick factory, and numerous small construction firms. Working women had only one major industrial employer, the silk mill (see table 3.2). These factories were basically involved in the extraction and primary processing of raw material. The brick factory (*fabbrica di mattoni*) provides a good example of the organization of these primitive industrial entities.

Clay was quarried from large open-air pits directly behind the brick kilns. Workers excavated the raw clay and carted it to huge mixers under the wood roof of the factory. From the mixers, the processed material was poured into molds and left to dry. The dried bricks were then fired in enormous ovens and when "cooked," they were removed and allowed to cool. The factory employed from thirty to forty workers, and the owner personally managed the operation. The manufacture of brick

TABLE 3.2
FRIULIAN INDUSTRIAL WORK FORCE, 1890–1961

Date	Total industrial work force	Workers in heavy industry *	Workers in textiles	Workers in construction
1890	24,555	1,190	13,242	2,532
1914	27,165	1,769	15,665	3,361
1927	49,307	4,857	16,664	4,739
1937–1939	55,074	5,319	13,691	7,676
1951	60,016	7,351	12,582	8,803
1961	80,759	15,073	6,967	16,842

Source: Parmeggiani 1966, 149–53.
Note: Reprinted by permission. From Douglas R. Holmes and Jean Quataert, "An Approach to Modern Labor: Worker Peasantries in Historic Saxony and the Friuli Region over Three Centuries," in *Comparative Studies in Society and History* 28, no. 2 (Cambridge University Press, 1986): 191–216.
* Includes metallurgy, casting and machine industry.

Fig. 6. The abandoned brick factory of Rubignacco.

was an uncomplicated process requiring little skill. In fact, most work roles were interchangeable and productive activities easily rotated among employees. Operation of the factory was seasonal, contingent on warm weather for the quarrying of raw clay. The work itself was physically arduous, as work areas were open to the elements, exposing employees to extremes of heat and cold. Pay was very low, and harsh conditions were an unremitting dimension of industrial work. Workers readily accepted these grim circumstances, and many saw themselves as "privileged" to have any type of regular employment at all. In many cases, though usually not at the brick factory, workers were forced to endure humiliation and brutality in order to gain and maintain their jobs. It was not, however, the conditions of employment, but the conditions of unemployment, that were the central defining features of industrial life. Looming insecurities posed by job loss rendered workers defenseless and pliant in these early factory settings. At the cement mills, the employees had a saying: "Either fire and smoke or the door." Indeed, unemployed men clustered at the gates of the cement mills in anticipation of a worker's termination or injury on the job. Similarly, destitute parents arrived at the silk mill early each morning to plead with the owner to hire their daughters, many of whom were mere children. The only conditions worse than those experienced in the workplace were those posed by unemployment. The disturbing dilemma pervaded the outlook of the operai. These urgencies created situations in which land-

75

Fig. 7. Retired brick worker with his wife.

holding, however fragmentary, became a critical adjunct to long-term industrial work.

For the poorest workers, particularly those in construction, unemployment was the corrosive norm. Workers in small construction firms faced seasonal layoffs in late fall with only occasional work during the winter and early spring, depending on weather conditions and building activity. Local jobs were difficult to find even in summer. During hard times, one rural household composed of a father and five sons, all of whom were skilled masons, survived with rarely more than one member employed at any given time. Year in and year out, from the 1920s through the 1950s, the family eked out a meager subsistence by cultivating a few scattered fields totalling less than a hectare. They further supplemented their livelihood by gathering wood and engaging in occasional agricultural wage work. I asked one member of the family if they were forced to cultivate their few small fields in order to survive. The elderly man responded by cursing the question: *"Urco boia, altro che."* A former cement worker was asked if his family could have gotten by without the few goats they tended. The answer was the same—the informant cursed the idea as unthinkable. In yet another instance, a former brick worker was asked:

Q. Did people in the factory also do agricultural work?
A. We were forced to. How could eight of us [in the family] live on a wage? [From planting to harvest time] we would rise at 4 A.M. and work the land. We went back to the fields after returning from the brick factory. It was work without consumption.

In what amounts to an inversion of the strategies used by the contadini, the operai sought to protect themselves from the chronic insecurities posed by wage employment through the maintenance of a subsistence plot. Workers and their families achieved a measure of protection from the low wages and under-or unemployment through common ties to a modest agrarian holding.

In the midst of these uncertainties, a few workers maintained periods of unbroken employment. Skilled workers like the *maestre*—the highly experienced spinners—at the silk mill were apt to have long periods of continuous tenure. A few of the maestre had worked at the mill from the early 1920s, when they were eleven or twelve years of age, until its closing in the early 1950s. The unusual technical skills of these women and the dependence of their employer on their specialized abilities largely account for their job security. Nonetheless, during the first half of this century the lot of the vast majority of workers, skilled or not, was circumscribed by the paucity of local employment opportunities. Only the broader opportunities and intrigues of the world economy allowed these operai to circumvent the predicaments posed by the political economy of their homeland.

Peasant-Worker Sojourners

The scarcity of local employment made labor migrations a particularly compelling alternative for operai. A government office, the *Ufficio di collocamento*, served as a clearinghouse for both local and extralocal employment. Operai and other segments of the rural work force frequented the office to scrutinize boards on which jobs were posted. Employment opportunities ranged from the coal mines of Belgium to the sugarcane fields of Australia. By means of labor contracts secured through the office or through informal contacts and connections established by family and friends, waves of workers set out for distant job venues (see table 3.3).[3] Virtually every middle-aged and elderly worker I interviewed had at least one episode of employment outside the region or nation. These odysseys beyond the borders of the patria exposed Friulian workers to living conditions that differed markedly from those they knew in their homeland. Many of these operai, unbound from Friulian social restrictions, never returned; others retreated home, overwhelmed and perplexed by their peregrinations; still others returned with new ambitions and new perspectives on their homeland. This latter segment of worldly sojourners used their rural households in Friuli as bases from which to embark on repeated journeys. Thus, as William Douglass points out, these migrants were not permanent departees, though their absences may be measured in years; rather, their migrations were intrinsic parts of their lives (1983: 163). The pursuits of these sojourners tied their households and hamlets to urban industrial centers of Western Europe and the frontiers of North Africa, the New World, and Australia. These departees created an axis of peasant-worker society along which a diverse succession of relationships was forged. In distant worksites, circumscribed by unfamiliar cultural assumptions and

TABLE 3.3

POPULATION OF FRIULI, RESIDENT AND TEMPORARY ABSENTEE, 1871–1961

Date	Resident population	Temporary absentees	Absentees as percentage of total
1871	506,924	31,099	6.1
1881	528,559	32,489	6.1
1901	614,270	28,781	4.6
1911	726,445	110,497	15.2
1921	817,058	73,424	8.9
1931	787,598	84,667	10.8
1951	795,568	76,940	9.7
1961	767,908	97,155	12.6

Source: Panizzon 1967, 93.

Notes: Reprinted by permission. From Douglas R. Holmes and Jean Quataert, "An Approach to Modern Labor: Worker Peasantries in Historic Saxony and the Friuli Region over Three Centuries," in *Comparative Studies in Society and History* 28, no. 2 (Cambridge University Press, 1986): 191–216.

In 1921, there were minor changes in the provincial-national border. There was no Italian census in 1891 or 1941.

by alien social and political practices, the sojourners fashioned ties that either reinforced the *liminal* or precipitated the *transitional* potential of the operai.

In his conversations in crowded barracks or in interchanges among comrades in multinational work gangs, the *operaio* learned to evaluate opportunities for subsequent migrations, and to reassess conditions in his homeland. A simple visceral calculation guided his journeys from outpost to outpost of the world economy. In the words of one informant, "Can I fill my belly as a worker should? . . . Will I have enough [money] left over to send home to my family?" Though he might be thousands of miles from Friuli, the sojourner's preoccupation was with the fate of his rural homestead and his abiding responsibilities to its survival. These fundamental social commitments set the peasant-worker apart from the working classes with whom he intermingled and from whom he would otherwise be indistinguishable. Rather than seeking protection and security through the collective action of political parties and worker organizations, the peasant-worker was committed to a *household union* sustained by bonds of family interdependence and common social welfare. Out of these primary imperatives emerged a practical consciousness, expressed in domestic solidarity, capable of bridging separations over immense distances and long durations. The operaio tenaciously retained his Friulian identity. He faithfully sent

Fig. 8. Retired coal miner with his grandchildren.

79

home remittances; he continued to transmit detailed instructions on planting and harvesting, the purchase of a calf, the sale of a pig, the construction of a new shed. He lined his walls with photos of family and postcards of Friulian landscapes and landmarks. He also sent home passage so that his wife, fiancée, brothers, cousins, or nephews could join him in the foreign land and partake of its riches. Above all, however, he planned to return home, perhaps first only through intermittent visits, but with the ultimate aim of resuming permanently his roles in a Friulian rural household. Caroline Bretell's description of *saudade*, the nostalgia or yearning for one's natal village experienced by Portuguese migrants, approximates the sentiments of these Friulian sojourners (1986: 263).

Yet at the same time, along the margins of these interactions, the metamorphosis from peasant-worker to working class identity was often completed. The sublime hold of the homeland on the peasant-worker could weaken in the face of expanded opportunity in the new migrant outpost, the promise of regular employment, the potential for promotion, the availability of affordable housing, or the allure of new consumer goods. The romances spawned in frontier saloons, boarding houses, and dance halls, or on street corners, had a similar effect. Unanticipated pregnancies, marriages, and new familial obligations drew the wayward peasant-worker increasingly into the orbit of working-class family, neighborhood, and identity. As overseas communications and gift exchanges faltered, the transition to the new status in a new land was completed. Perhaps the most poignant expressions of the last vestiges of peasant-worker identity were the promises—endlessly deferred—to return home the following year.

Padroni: Agrarian and Industrial Ownership

The padroni were members of a group that mirrored the complexities of the entire social system. From the perspective of the Rubignacchesi, padroni could be small peasant landowners who lived in close contact with their tenants and rural laborers and who were active participants in the social life of the hamlet. Living outside the settlement were the middle-class professionals who owned property in Rubignacco. The pharmacists, merchants, doctors, and lawyers residing in Cividale often owned income-producing property in the rural frazioni of the comune. Ownership of plowland, pasturage, and vineyard formed an important bridge between the urban elites of Cividale and outlying hamlets like Rubignacco. These relationships were, however, more economic than social. Whereas peasant proprietors were intimately involved in the day-to-day life of the hamlet, the urban absentee owners were removed from these routines. The interests of these town dwellers were represented by accountants and bookkeepers who managed the ties between rural and urban spheres.

The case of the grand padrone who reigned over entire settlements was different still. Here the great villa dominated the landscape. The power of the padrone imbued the architecture and the formalities of daily routine of the estate, even though the owner might spend only a few months of the year in residence. A retinue of servants, cooks, coachmen, and gardeners maintained the lavish living quarters, landscaped gardens, and stables, and a gastaldo managed the agricultural operation. As overseer of tenant life and work, the gastaldo recruited and removed tenants, drafted contracts, and collected rents. Although the management of these great estates was almost exclusively in the hands of agents and retainers, ownership was nonetheless seen in extremely personal terms. Tenants and employees were keenly aware of the virtues and vices of their noblemen and noblewomen, and the nuances of managerial decisions were interpreted in terms of the character and temperaments of the overlords. Punishment and reward, blessing and threat were routinely conveyed to the work force in the name of the noble family. The personification of ownership was misleading. Ownership of these large-scale operations was, in fact, usually vested in an economic abstraction, most often a partnership or other form of incorporation. Hence these estates were technically agro-businesses, despite the overlay of regal pretensions.

Industrial ownership had many features in common with the property relationships prevailing in agriculture. The owners of the two small industrial operations in Rubignacco—the silk mill and the brick factory—lived in close proximity to the factory and its work force. The owner-manager organized production, hired and fired employees, set wages, purchased equipment, kept the books, sold the output and, from these activities, reaped profits or absorbed losses. Most of all, these padroni were active participants in the daily operation of their factories; they were compelled to understand the subtleties of factory operation and routinely made decisions that affected the factories' future. The intimacy of this relationship is evident in the architecture of the silk mill and brick factory (see Guiotto 1979; McDonogh 1986).

Overlooking the weathered wood walls of the brick factory was an austere building that served as the home of the owner and his family. Without the ornamental shrubs and bushes that ringed the red brick house, it would have been indistinguishable from the other working structures of the factory. From the second floor of the house, the padrone could gaze over his modest industrial domain. A similar proximity existed at the silk mill, where the owner's palatial eighteenth-century villa was attached directly to the mill. A passageway connected the owner's living quarters to the management offices directly under the floor of the main spinning room. In both the silk mill and the brick factory, the owners were inseparable from the operation of their respective domains. Their characters were stamped on the productive process and their temperaments affected relationships with the workers.

Ownership of these small firms was generally held by family partnerships. Familial tensions regularly intruded on the running of these organizations, and, in cases where disagreements among partners could not be managed or resolved, the firm was often closed or sold. Without partners actively contributing their own labor, these small industrial firms were difficult to maintain as going concerns, particularly during hard economic times.

The two cement works represented the large industrial operations in the vicinity of Rubignacco. These concerns employed hundreds of workers and had full-time managers. Their huge furnaces produced cement for national markets, and the works were capable of generating substantial profits for their owners. Here too, ownership was vested in a corporation. These padroni were outside the social system of Rubignacco and, to be sure, their relationship to Friulian society was based on purely economic interests. Though these interests had form and substance in the factory and its labor force, ownership was impersonal, mediated through the legal abstractions of the corporation.

IN THIS overview of peasant-worker society, I have tried to portray the internal composition of its constituent groups, their intriguing interactions and interdependencies, and their elaborate ties to other types of rural and urban societies, whether within or at a great distance from the homeland. The analysis has yielded a portrayal of a type of society better conceptualized in terms of enduring social flux than of rigid structures and fixed conventions. Individual peasant-workers and members of their households, through their pragmatic maneuvers within the socioeconomic crosscurrents of their rural districts, nearby urban centers, and the wider world economy, enliven peasant-worker society and perpetuate its liminal and transitional potentials. The intermingling and shifting dependencies among these diverse peasant-worker groups expose the underlying dynamics by which wider societal conditions were forged. These complicated interactions also frustrate an overly rigid analytical separation of the various segments of peasant-worker society.[4] The cultural forces at play in this social realm, however, have not been fully explored. The final section of this chapter will reintroduce the axis of cultural enchantment and disenchantment in order to analyze individual experiences within the peasant-worker milieu.

Peasant-Worker Culture and Experience

In my interviews with Friulani in rural districts and urban neighborhoods, I did not encounter a single, overarching cultural orientation. I discovered, on the contrary, a compendium of outlooks and voices. Yet as time wore on, I began to see that this diversity was largely created from a common set of elements assembled by individuals in novel ways to yield a rich variety of experience. Moreover, within this social landscape, a number of pivotal arenas of shared activity did yield a common dimension of experience for participants, but by no means a uniform outlook. The four notable arenas were the farmstead, the latifondo, the factory, and the church. The denizens of the latifondi and the factories faced the quandary of wresting meaning from social environments in which traditional cultural assumptions had been distorted or where few cultural precedents applied. To introduce these issues, the analysis will turn first to the cultural perspectives of the peasant-worker sojourners. These individuals, perhaps more than any others in this type of society, experienced the cultural contradictions of peasant-worker life in radical terms. Hence, in representing the cultural dynamics that affect this realm, the experiences of the peasant-worker sojourners provide a crucial point of departure.

In the accounts of elderly peasant-worker sojourners in particular, I occasionally stumbled on narratives that seemed fantastic, even bizarre. My initial response was to dismiss these strange tales as fabrications. In fact, I thought some of the narrators were deranged. What I found unsettling was the way informants would shift from what appeared to me to be very realistic, commonsense depictions of their life experiences to portrayals that were filled with magical content. The effect of this "unexpected juxtapositioning" was surreal (Clifford 1981: 540).

One narrative was particularly riveting. The informant was an elderly man who, at the time of the interview, was in his late eighties. He recounted his early exploits at my request. As a young lad, barely in his teens, he had labored with construction gangs in Germany. After returning to Friuli during World War I, he set out again in the early 1920s on a far more ambitious odyssey to the oil fields of Tampico. While in Mexico, political unrest broke out, and he and his Italian comrades found themselves in the middle. The Italians decided to make their way north from Tampico and escape across the border into Texas. At the Rio

83

Grande crossing, they were caught in a serious skirmish in which one of their compatriots from Naples was killed. That night they were attacked and all their money and clothing were taken. In the morning they counted forty bodies in the river. Once across the border, the informant and a few of his friends sought passage to Cuba, where they worked for a time before returning to Italy. The discussion moved from the issues of the informant's wage-earning pursuits to an account of family life and agrarian routines in Friuli, and finally to local folk beliefs, at which point he recounted the following experience.

> One day I went with my son and nephew into the forest. My son walked on ahead with his cousin and called out, saying, "Father, look at this!" It was a *garbon* [a mythical serpent]. It was enormous—almost a meter thick [in diameter]. I said, "You kids go away." As I approached the beast it whistled three times and my hair stood on end. I hit it [with a pole]. I hit it again and again until it was dead.

The old man still regrets that he did not bring the corpse of the garbon to the municipal offices for verification. It annoys him that people continue to doubt his magical tale. He ended by saying whimsically, "I have seen things that are most incredible." Thus, in the course of this interview, the elderly peasant-worker moved from a highly "realistic" account of his travails in the New World to an imaginative rendering of a mythical experience in the forests of his homeland (see Comaroff and Comaroff 1987: 193; Taussig 1980: 14–22).

It is evident from this informant's account, like those of many other peasant-worker sojourners, that he was able to apprehend and deftly pursue opportunities offered at worksites from Central Europe to the New World. He adapted to the conventions of the wage nexus and understood the various risks and rewards inherent in its "rational" systems. A different cultural logic, however, guided his experiences in the enchanted enclaves of the patria. His experience in the homeland was framed by a sublime orientation to the world rooted in ancient sensibilities that social scientists generally abstract as "ethnicity." In reality, these sensibilities are an amalgam of the routines and dramas of family life, fluency in an obscure dialect, preference for a simple country cuisine, participation in a regional variant of Catholic ritual, lingering memories of beguiling folklore, a familiarity with rustic architecture and the layout of rural settlements, a keen understanding of the agrarian cycle and the nuances of seasonal changes, knowledge of local flora and fauna, and images of a much-loved, rolling landscape.

Up to this point, I have portrayed the rationale for peasant-worker livelihood and society—at least from the standpoint of the actors—in terms of the shifting interplay of social and economic motives. It is clear that fundamental cultural motives modulated the social and economic imperatives. In this case, one can view the rural household of the peasant-worker not only as a bastion of social and economic security but also, and perhaps more importantly, as a haven in which vestiges of enchanted cultural values and intimacies are preserved. A commitment to this style of life is, for the individual, in reality a commitment to a Friulian cultural identity. What has changed is that the cultural identity, which in the remote past was implicit, now must be actively reaffirmed and reconstituted. Hence, the surreal incongruities in peasant-worker life come from a struggle in which the individual participates in, and may even have a shrewd understanding of, alien social environments and patterns of activity. However, identity is largely removed from these engagements, creating a paradoxical form of alienation by which the individual views the wage-earning experience as merely instrumental in maintaining a distinct Friulian identity and framework of meaning. The enduring irony here is that to secure and maintain a modest preserve of enchantment, the peasant-worker is required to journey to the very heart of disenchantment.

The cultural orientation of these peasant-workers also has unexpected political consequences. Its most characteristic manifestation is an inability or unwillingness of individuals to politicize events or conditions except when they are put in the traditional idioms of religion or patronage. In a troubling account—one that verges on black comedy—related by a jovial man in his late sixties, this type of political indifference is expressed. This man, like many Friulian peasant-workers, had journeyed back and forth during the interwar period between German construction jobs and his farmstead in the patria. His macabre account concerns his efforts to continue these sojourns during World War II. In the dimly lit kitchen of this man's modest farmstead, he recounted his seasonal routine. "From spring to fall I was abroad [all'estero]. Construction stopped with the cold weather. I brought home some money, made another child and away again [in the spring]." The war presented staggering challenges to this routine. It meant that the peasant-worker had to avoid being drafted, find work in wartime Germany, then escape back across the border into Friuli while dodging Nazis, Fascists, and partigiani. Despite these obstacles, the fellow found work building airfields, roads, and military installations, and managed, when he had made enough money, to return to his crude hideouts in the forests of the patria. Unfortunately, this quixotic fellow was captured by the Germans. At this point, the account became thoroughly bizarre. "They de-

Fig. 9. Retired mason.

cided to execute me. . . . You know those Germans sure know how to
scare a guy." In the face of this strange story, I began to wonder if I
was being mocked or if the informant was a lunatic. I asked for clarifi-
cation. He responded, "Yes, they executed me. I was very frightened."
I politely tried to listen to the rest of his story, which involved his exploits "after being executed." He claimed to have found his way back
to his Friulian hamlet where he hid for many months. He repeatedly
punctuated his account with the phrase, "those Germans sure know
how to scare a fellow." The narrative moved into what seemed to me
to be a nonsensical dimension, when the informant related that after
hiding out for a number of months in the forest, he heard from a friend
that one could earn "a tiny bit more money if you were willing to work
for the Germans." That was enough of an enticement for this fellow.
Undeterred by his earlier encounter, he decided to return to German-

controlled territory, where he labored on a military installation in the Alps that was eventually captured by the Allies. By this point, I had completely dismissed the informant's account and I was ready to depart. As this very kind man said farewell to me at the door, I noticed in the sunlight through his open shirt a star-shaped wound in the middle of his chest. Confronted with concrete evidence that confirmed the eerie tale of execution, I began to rethink the significance not only of this man's experiences but also of accounts of other sojourners that I had discounted as exaggerated or inconsistent. Though the narratives of most peasant-worker sojourners interviewed were hardly as disjunctive as the two just described, they nonetheless resonated with a similar cultural experience.

No claim is being made that either of these two elderly informants is in any way "average." They are no doubt marginal, though endearing, figures. What is being suggested is that their accounts depict, albeit in heightened terms, an orientation to the world that is central to the lives and experiences of peasant-workers, particularly those who engaged in repeated and long-term sojourns. This cultural orientation entails an aloofness, if not an active disengagement, from the complex social and political experiences that surround and define wage labor in capitalist societies. Though these individuals participate in various forms of wage earning, often for extended periods of time, their identities are tied to a separate cultural experience; in this case, one steeped in the traditions of the Friulian countryside. This cultural stance contributes to the uncanny ability of these individuals to move across hostile borders, traverse war zones, survive revolutionary uprisings and various types of labor unrest, earn their wages, and return home relatively unscathed. Even when they are unavoidably entangled in the much-feared apparatus of the state, like the hapless fellow just described, they interpret the experience in terms of intense personal struggle, as opposed to attaching political significance to their fate. One is struck in their accounts by the superimposition of modest human sensibilities onto the panoply of international upheavals.

Finally, an obvious complementary dimension appears in this analysis. The nature of peasant-worker experience and outlook suggests why the powerful appeal of working class politics and culture has such a limited impact on their lives. Rather than transforming their personal experiences into collective action through guilds, unions, political parties, or other voluntary organizations, peasant-workers struggle to avoid precisely these types of involvement in order to maintain their commitment to the interests of a rural household and their fidelity to Friulian culture.[5] In a small factory on the outskirts of Cividale, two workers may sit side by side, doing precisely the same job. Yet one might have an identity rooted in the peasant-worker realm, the other in the realm of proletarian politics and culture. Only by tracing the productive involvements of these individuals, probing their patterns of identity, and analyzing their life experiences can we differentiate these radically different—though in the case of the peasant-worker, largely concealed—cultural orientations. Much of the rest of this work is devoted to portraying this peasant-worker cultural orientation and experience in two very different social arenas—the latifondo and the factory.

THIS chapter has investigated the basic characteristics of the peasant-worker realm. There exists a broad area of social life and cultural experience that is at best poorly understood using conventional approaches to rural society. Members of a diverse set of social groups in and around Rubignacco struggled with common socioeconomic and cultural imperatives which both defined and enlivened peasant-worker society. These struggles yielded a society best conceptualized in terms of an enduring social flux. Shifting socioeconomic ties developed that crisscross the rural districts of Friuli and extend beyond the borders of the homeland to distant frontier outposts and industrial centers.

The cultural orientation of the Friulian sojourner is emblematic. The experience of these individuals is ambiguous and contradictory from the standpoint of most theoretical perspectives. In Michael Taussig's words, these sojourners are the most liminal of beings: "Neither what they are, nor what they will become" (1980: 103, 113). Seen in the peasant-worker context, however, the cultural stance of these sojourners gains coherence and meaning. To put it in radical terms, the peasant-worker engages the modern world in order to retain vestiges of the ancient cultural sensibilities of his patria. The peasant-worker can earn wages at the same steel mill, construction site, or coal pit as a worker, or till the same land as a peasant, yet the nature of his experience is fundamentally different. His understanding of the factory, the latifondo, the city, the state, national politics, religion, family, friends, and self are relativized by cultural ideals preserved in the routines, language, and intimacies of a modest Friulian farmstead.

Choosing the latifondo and silk mill as the settings in which to develop the analysis further shifts the focus of the study to the agrarian and industrial fringes of this society. It also introduces somewhat more subtle theoretical issues. In making a case for the distinctive nature of peasant-worker society, it is important to investigate how this nature manifests itself in what otherwise would be construed as peasant or working-class settings. Assessing the value of the peasant-worker framework requires not only the depiction of a distinctive type of social and cultural realm, but the elucidation of this realm more thoroughly than other descriptive models of rural society generated from the perspective of either the peasant or the worker. The challenge of the following chapters is to illuminate life in the rural factory and on the agrarian operations in Friuli from the standpoint of the peasant-worker theory. A parallel challenge enhances this examination of peasant-worker society, but also stands as an important discussion in its own right; an exploration of the latifondo and the silk mill requires the portrayal of Friulian identity, ethnicity, sex roles, politics, Catholicism, and folk religion. It is no accident that these issues are crucial to the development of a general Friulian ethnography—as well as to the specific theoretical issues raised in this text.

The Latifondo

THE VILLAS are surprisingly inconspicuous. If you drive down the streets of Bottenicco or Moimacco, it is easy to miss the structures around which the life of the latifondi revolved. Concealed behind high gray walls are the architectural remnants of what were the focal points of rural power and influence. Formal gardens, tastefully unkempt, ring the rustic villa in Bottenicco. Its main residence is an imposing building with an austere facade. Aesthetically, it is a crude relative of the extravagantly scaled and ornate estates that dominate the Venetian and Lombardian countrysides. Inside, the rustic Friulian villa is dark, dank, and airless. Sheets cover what little furniture remains. Unflattering portraits of twenty or so of the minor grandees who ruled this domain line the walls of the library where six centuries of estate records are stored. Bundles of documents are piled indiscriminately in cabinets that surround the archive. The provenance of the papers is haphazard. Documents from the fifteenth century are bound with eighteenth-century papers. Hidden in these notations, rendered in bedevilled dialects and impenetrable handwriting, are secrets of this social world.

The disposition of working buildings around the villa is similar to that of the small factories in Rubignacco. Next to the gatehouse and the family chapel stretches a long, two-story warehouse filled with equipment and machinery for processing wine, threshing grain, plowing fields, and pruning groves and vineyards. Adjacent structures served as vast storage areas for silk cocoons and huge oak barrels of wine and grappa. Passageways connect storage areas, greenhouses, and now-vacant worker dormitories. Within the complex of buildings is a small office directly across from a side entrance to the villa. An old desk strewn with paperwork, a few wooden chairs, a clock, a calendar touting a new Swiss herbicide, and shelves of black-bound ledgers, identify the office of the estate manager, the gastaldo. Scattered in apartments and farmsteads beyond the walls of the estate are former personnel of these agrarian domains. In their recollections, as well as those of current caretakers of the estates, resides an understanding of the latifondi different from that conveyed by the documentary record.

These formidable agrarian institutions embody a distinctive bureaucratic dimension of peasant-worker society. The latifondo may seem at

Fig. 10. The count's villa in Bottenicco.

first to be an unlikely place to begin a detailed examination of the peasant-worker realm. Yet there are significant precedents for this approach. The rural laboring groups that populate the large estates of Latin America, Asia, and Africa have been the focus of some of the most forceful theoretical efforts to address, in some cases rather critically, the peasant-worker phenomenon (Mintz 1974; Mintz and Price 1976; Roseberry 1976; Stoler 1985; Taussig 1980). One finds, particularly at the fringes of these agrarian operations, wage-earning strategies fused with family-based peasant agriculture. Eric Wolf refers to the "double lives" of these peasant-workers "with one foot in the plantation way of life, while keeping the other foot in the peasant holding" (Wolf 1959: 143; Stoler 1985: 11–12). Pedro Carrasco points out that plantation work can be temporary "duty or an occasional source of income that will perhaps be used . . . to maintain an autonomous cultural system that is quite, if not totally, foreign to the plantation society" (1959: 53). Sidney Mintz has proposed, equally significantly, that these types of peasant-worker involvements represent an enduring state, in his words, a "flux equilibrium," as opposed to an ephemeral transition (Mintz 1959: 43; Stoler 1985: 11–12). The feature that distinguishes the Friulian latifondi from plantation systems elsewhere is the degree to which peasant-worker dynamics were central to the *formal* organization of these operations.

91

"Rational Matter-of-Factness" and Peasant-Worker Culture

Chapter 2 examined how a modern cultural metaphysic became ingrained in the social life of the Friulian countryside, displacing the enchantments of feudalism. Yet the latifondi continued to retain precapitalist characteristics well into the twentieth century. The technical definition of these operations is open to question: Were the latifondi rentier systems or agro-businesses? Did they use dependent labor or wage labor? Though their socioeconomic character was equivocal, their cultural character was not. It was the rationalizing compulsion, expressed in bureaucratic organization and management, that embodied the commercial "spirit" on these large estates.

This chapter begins with an assessment of the latifondi in terms of the workings of these managerial entities during the late nineteenth and early twentieth centuries. An analysis of the ongoing elaboration of the contractual instruments themselves, and the insights and interpretations of former inhabitants of these agrarian enclaves of peasant-worker society, serve as points of departure for the chapter. These data permit a glimpse of the peculiar cultural impulses that dominated the social life of these large estates, which Weber refers to as "rational matter-of-factness," and what Marx calls "second nature." The daily routines of these agrarian operations were impelled by a powerful legal-bureaucratic logic that clashed with the traditional sensibilities of the countryfolk. The engagement involved two very different visions of social order—one embodied in law and accountancy; the other expressed in the idiom of patronage.

Contractual Realities

Encoded in contractual provisions and regulations governing the operation of these estates were the cultural formulas and nomenclature that expressed the local dialect of Friulian capitalism. Contracts constituted the pivotal institutional apparatus for the calibration of human relations and potential and their transformation into abstract utilities. Conveyed in these contractual instruments was a cultural rationale that became, in Weber's words, "the subjective meaning-complex of action." Although the contractual system represented a monolithic presence in the realm of the latifondi, the terms and provisions of the documents did not mechanically generate social practice. The people in these domains confronted and manipulated these abstractions, often in a contrary manner that mixed conformity with opposition.

Contracts were drawn between male representatives of closely related domestic units, usually fathers, sons, brothers, or cousins, and the *signor*. Legal formalities aside, the contract was binding on an entire household, often numbering twenty or more members.[1] The leasehold agreement had a direct impact on the composition and dynamics of these households. The contracts had their most pronounced effect on the size of tenant household units and their internal authority relationships. The necessity to supply large amounts of labor put a premium on families with many members. The first question put to the representatives of a family seeking a tenant holding, either by the padrone on the small independent farmstead or by the gastaldo on the latifondo, went directly to this issue of family size.

> When the fittavole goes to have himself seen, this father [head of the household] would say, "I would like to come to your estate, into your house and work in your fields." He [the padrone or gastaldo] would ask, "How many children have you? How many children are you there?" The more children the more likely they would be taken, the sooner they would be given a podere. . . . They looked for big families with many children because the babies, by the time they were five or six, could begin to supply their arms to the owners.

In this way, the initial procedure by which a tenant secured a holding was exposed to a series of preliminary evaluations and calculations.

The tenant household diagram is based on the description of a former tenant whose family occupied a large farmstead during the early 1930s. This household reflects the basic principles of family organization prevailing on the latifondi around Cividale from at least the mid-nineteenth century until World War II. The family constitutes the "patriarchal" tenant household of Friuli. However, the household was actually based on a cooperative fraternal core, rather than on a patriarchal hierarchy. The patriarchal ideal was maintained nonetheless, even though the presence of a single patriarch might represent only a short episode in the domestic cycle of one of these large domestic units. The five brothers who made up the fraternal core ranged in age from late teens to late twenties; thus, the unit was still growing as members married and children were born. In 1933 alone, three children were born to the household. A manager of one of the estates commented on the demographic orientation of these families: "The numbers of family members would never decline. [The family] would never let that happen."

Once the contract was extended to the family, the authority system of the estate was linked to the authority relations within the tenant

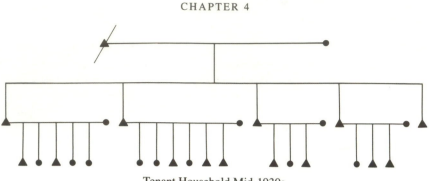

Tenant Household Mid-1930s

household. This contract essentially endowed the *capo*, the male head of household, with the power of the signor. "The owner gave a lot of weight to him [the capo of the family], because he was the one who had to lead, to hold the reins. . . . The capo was always an important person; he was feared and respected." The personal style of these capi was often tyrannical. The capi are invariably described as tough, physically imposing figures: "The capo of the family was like a god to them; he controlled everything; he kept the keys to the storehouse." An insightful priest, however, modified this by saying, "There were the great patriarchs—but poverty was the [real] authority."

The case on which this section focuses is drawn from archival materials retrieved from files of the latifondo located in Bottenicco. The documents cover the period 1897 to 1903 and trace the fate of a single tenant family headed by the conjugal pair Giuseppe S. and Andriana N. The first handwritten agreement, dated September 2, 1897, is structured along lines virtually identical to those of other coeval contracts from both of the estates studied. The only unusual aspect of the agreement is that it is drawn between the proprietor and a married couple, rather than a single male capo or a group of closely related male kin. The document displays the striking mix of terms and provisions characteristic of the affitto misto agreements contracted during this and subsequent periods. It defines four major types of tenant obligation, including rents, customary "gifts," pseudo–wage work, and other forms of labor. The contract not only allocates productive risks and rewards; it specifies procedures for improvements of land and farm structures, and it defines various managerial responsibilities. The parcels of land that made up the modest podere of 2.27 hectares are contractually classified in terms of their use, size, location, and respective cash rents. The agreement was renewed with only minor changes for the next six agricultural seasons.

KINGDOM OF ITALY

Province of Udine   District of Cividale

Cividale, on this day, Sunday, 15 fifteen August, 1897 ninety-seven. Between Count G., son of the late N., landowner of Bottenicco of the first part, and S. Giuseppe, son of the late Antonio and N. Andriana, daughter of the late Antonio, farmers also of Bottenicco of the second part, the following stipulations are concluded:

Private Lease Agreement

1. The abovementioned Count G. offers, submits and for the right of simple rent grants to the previously mentioned Andriana N. and Guiseppe S., a married couple, who for the same right of simple rent accept and receive the real estate described later under the following terms and conditions:

2. The Lease will have a term of one year commencing 15 October 1897 for the land and on the following 11 November for the house and will terminate on the same respective anniversaries in 1898.

3. The annual payment of rent which the Lessees undertake to pay jointly to Count G. and at his domicile in Bottenicco is the following:

    (a) Wheat, healthy, clean, dry, and well sifted, during the month of August 1898, hectoliters 6.50, six and fifty liters.
    (b) Rent for the land, Lire 70.00, seventy.
    (c) Rent for the house, Lire 150.00, one hundred fifty.
    (d) Chickens, one pair.
    (e) Capons, one pair.
    (f) Wine and ''zarpe,'' one-half.
    (g) Cocoons, one-half.
    (h) Mowing the meadow called Malina, not part of the leased land, drying the hay and transporting the same to the Lessor's house, free of charge, together with other Lessees.
    (i) Cutting trees in the woods of Marnis and Prestento, not part of the leased land, and transporting the cut wood to the Lessor's house free of charge, together with other Lessees.

4. The Lessees are obligated to give their work, free of charge, as field hands as well as with cart at the request of the Lessor, and failing to do so, when the Lessor himself requests, they will pay as indemnity Lire 2.00 two each day and Lire 6.00 six for each cartage.

5. This lease is made and accepted in whole and not in parts and the Lessees undertake the joint obligation to pay to the Lessor the agreed amount of rent regardless of any misfortune, foreseen or unforeseen.

6. In case of repairs to the farmhouse or new buildings to erect, the Lessees will transport, free of charge, sand, stones, materials, lumber, and everything else needed for such work and one of them will lend his help as a day laborer free of charge.

7. The Lessees must protect and preserve the entire stretch of land leased to them; if any damage to the Lessor should result from unlawful easement, the Lessees will be obliged to inform him immediately, and under pain of penalty to compensate for damages which may have been caused.

8. The Lessees cannot sublease in whole or part of leased estate.

9. The tithe and all other customary canons which burden or could burden the rented estate must be fulfilled by the Lessees.

10. The house and land described below are leased in the order and condition defined by the surveyor Giuseppe R. to whom the Lessees are obliged to refer for the settlement of the farm account.

11. The Lessor does not assume any obligation for the improvement of the arable land, but this must be settled at the end of the lease with the new Lessee.

12. The cost of the lease and of the survey of order and condition are charged to the Lessees.

13. For the purpose of registration, the rent amounts to Lire 260.

Description of Leased Real Estate

Tax District of Bottenicco

Nos. 2500, 2501	House, veg. garden, arable, wooded	Rod. 7.24 Lire 41.48

Tax District of Moimacco

No. 80	Arable, wooded vineyard called Voi	Rod. 4.51 Lire 15.01
Nos. 2150, 2283,673, 674,1649, 2462, 2320, 886	Meadows, pasture and "zerbi," of which the tall trees of robinia are reserved for the Lessor	Rod. 10.97 Lire 11.74
	Total	Rod. 22.72 Lire 68.23

There are 22.72 Rod. equal to hectare 2:27.20; Revenue Lire 68.23.

Read, approved, and signed by Count G., marked with a cross by the Lessees because they are illiterate.

[signature] Count G.   Cross [X] of Giuseppe S.
Cross [X] of Andriana N.   [signature] Giuseppe R. - Witness
   [signature] Pietro G. - Witness

Recorded in Cividale on 2 September, 1897
Private. . . . . . ?. . . . . . 31. . . . . . ?. 128
. . . . . . two and forty centesimi
L. 2.40   The Registrar
             [signature illegible]

Rents

Just about every known form of rental payment is included in this modest document. A fixed in-kind payment (6.50 hectoliters) is listed for wheat; a fifty-fifty division is required for wine, *"zarpe"* (probably grape dregs), and silk cocoons; and cash payments are computed for the farmhouse, its adjacent property, and small parcels of vineyard, arable, pasture, and woodland amounting to just over two and a quarter hectares. Customary "gifts," in this case a pair each of chickens and capons, are also listed as contractual obligations. The rent for wheat, as was typical of industrial crops, is the only payment computed as a fixed volume of the farm's production. The conventions of tenant social and productive life were ruled by a logic embedded in this assortment of rents and contractual provisions.

Each rent achieved a different utilitarian end. The six and a half hectoliters of wheat (provision 3a) represented, from the owner's standpoint, a guaranteed quantity of a crop for which the yields varied substantially from season to season. As I suggested in chapter 2, computing the rent as a fixed in-kind quantity shifted all productive risks to the tenant household. Fixed in-kind rents were also applied to maize and sorghum on adjacent farmsteads. For wine and silk cocoons (provisions 3f and 3g), which required careful attention and, in the case of the silk cocoons, *bozzoli*, frenzied periods of work, the risk and reward were evenly divided. As the gastaldo of one of the estates put it, "The bozzoli were like gold." In fact, the entire annual expenses of the Bottenicco estate could be met solely from the income derived from the production of raw silk. It is not surprising, then, to find the pertinent rent for this valued commodity calculated to motivate the tenant to use the greatest possible care in its production.

By far the most onerous rents were the cash payments for house, garden, and farmland (provisions 3b and 3c). These large cash obligations formed the so-called oppressive pacts, which exposed tenants to the full brunt of market as well as productive risk. Because of risks arising from price fluctuations in agricultural commodities and uncertainties surrounding crop yields, both of which the tenant family was forced to bear in full, income from this type of leased property could in any given year fall below the rental charge. Under these conditions, tenants were forced to sell the harvest from other parcels of land to cover the outstanding cash obligation. If this was not sufficient, they were often compelled to dispose of property or livestock—referred to by tenants as "eating the cow"—or to have the remaining charge carried over to the next year. The formulation of these cash rents exposed the tenant to chronic and often unmanageable problems with debt. Other more modest cash obligations, such as registration fees for the contract itself and for land surveys (provision 12), as well as "the tithe and all other customary canons" (provision 9), further contributed to financial insecurity for the leaseholder.

The intriguing inclusion of the traditional "gifts" (provisions 3d and 3e) that made up the regalia (or *onoranza*) as explicit contractual provisions appears fanciful indeed. These gratuities historically represented the ritual tie between lord and peasant. The items that composed the regalia were delivered to the nobleman's kitchen on specific festival days of the Christian calendar, or on demand of the lord when he was in residence. Despite the minor nature of these obligations, this feudal vestige was very much resented by the tenants, because the signor or his agent could demand the most prized of the tenants' petty products. In this case it was chickens and capons; in other contracts, it was eggs, turkeys, hens, and even such things as handmade brooms and brushes. "It had to be the best." Yet a counterflow, ritual or otherwise, was no longer expected. The signor's right to these "gifts" constituted a perpetuation of the customary authority that permitted the lord enormous discretion to make material demands of his tenants as he saw fit. Hence, the regalia resonated with invidious status implications for the tenant, and symbolized an enduring subordination to the personal authority of the lord, which was directly at odds with the reciprocal rights implied by the contract.

Pooled Labor and Pseudo–Wage Work

A series of terms are written into the contract that relate to wide-ranging labor obligations of tenants and, once again, to the peasant-worker dimension of the tenurial system. These obligations can be viewed either as a form of labor service paid for the right to lease the farmstead, or as part of a parallel relationship that bound the off-farm wage labor of tenants. For the purposes of this analysis, the latter position will be emphasized. Nonetheless, it is important to keep in mind the dual character of this labor, for it enmeshed the parties to these agreements in relationships that were inherently ambiguous and confounding to the researcher.

Two provisions (3h and 3i) mediate the shift of family labor from the tenant farmstead to the pooled labor among tenant households used for working the land under the direct management of the latifondo. These terms specify that tenant labor from a number of poderi was to be combined for the periodic cutting and transporting of hay to feed the owner's livestock, as well as for the felling of trees to supply wood and fuel for the owner's vineyards and household. Both terms state specifically that no compensation is involved.

Provision 4 achieves a similar translation of family labor from the rentier system of the podere to the wage work of the latifondo. The tenants were required to supply their own carts and mules to work as field hands on demand of the owner. This provision is intriguing because of the manner in which the work of field hands was evaluated. The provision makes clear that no money is to be paid for the work, yet the labor is clearly calculated in the form of a wage. The indemnification of the labor, two lire per day and six lire for each cartload, constitutes what might be called a "pseudowage." In other words, the tenant was liable to pay a wage, presumably for the substitution of his or her labor by another field hand. Through this odd arrangement, a precise wage rate was attached to labor, even though an actual payment was made only when the labor was *not* provided.

Provision 6, pertaining to work involving repairs and improvements of the farmstead, had a similar impact. Hauling construction materials and supplying the labor necessary for these projects were, under this provision, to be performed by the tenant "free of charge."

Through these four provisions, the estate secured from tenant families three types of labor: corvée labor for various harvest operations, a pool of field hands virtually available on demand, and transient day laborers for modest maintenance and construction projects. What makes this arrangement particularly interesting is that the unpaid labor was required under the terms of the "tenant" contract. Hence, to lease a farmstead, the tenant family had to submit to various demands on their labor distinct from those necessary for the operation of the leased podere. Again, this gave the labor the dual character of rent service on the one hand and wage labor on the other. It should be emphasized that these forms of wage labor were defined by contractual provisions—they did not require a self-perpetuating "labor market." Rather, this type of wage work, like other productive activities on the estate, was a contrivance of the contract.

Provision 8 had a related, albeit negative, impact on the formation of productive relations. The term was simple enough; it forbade the sublease of lands held by the tenant family. The effect of this provision, aside from affixing responsibility squarely to a single family unit, was to prevent the formation of sublease arrangements that had the potential for creating alliances among rural laborers beyond the confines of the tenant household. Contractual terms such as provision 8, directed at isolating tenant families, became more precise under fascism, as will be seen in a contract to be examined in chapter 5.

Managerial Authority—The Gastaldo

With a single contractual provision (provision 10), management of the operation was established. Giuseppe R., a surveyor, filled the position of gastaldo. Traditionally, the gastaldo was either a surveyor or a book-keeper, often from a peasant family. However, individuals with formal training in agricultural techniques and management began to take over these jobs on the latifondi around Cividale by the 1920s. The gastaldo's position required that he reconcile the abstract provisions of the contract with the social and productive realities of the estate. He was responsible for hiring and removing tenants and agricultural workers, organizing the various types of "tenant" labor described above, drafting contracts and maintaining account books, surveying and classifying estate property, and deciding on crops to be planted by tenants as well as the timing for other important agricultural procedures. The gastaldo was also respon-sible for managing all the nontenant lands under direct cultivation of the estate. As overseer, he saw to it that the terms of the contracts were fulfilled, and as mediator, he bridged the "great [social] distance" be-tween tenant and owner.

One of the successors of Giuseppe R. described for me the responsi-bilities of the gastaldo on this same agrarian operation in Bottenicco. The following excerpts are from two long interviews that cover the gas-taldo's recollections of his own experience over a thirty-year period un-der a succession of grandees (latifondisti) and his understanding of con-ditions and practices that existed before he took over. One of the most disturbing aspects of the gastaldo's role was the conflicting loyalties that the position demanded. During the interviews, the informant slipped back and forth between articulating the signor's problems and articulat-ing the corresponding tenant dilemmas.

Q. Was there fear and reverence [*timore reverenziale*] for the Count?
A. Certainly there was!
Q. What about the gastaldo?
A. I think so. I never had difficulty cooperating with the employees. I have always been respected. One is respected on the basis of his respect for others.
Q. What was the difficult part of the job?
A. There were parts that were very difficult—the eviction of ten-ants, the reclaiming of land. Having to take land from the people

who needed it to live was a hard thing to do. Mediation between tenant and padrone was very troublesome. There were many times I was tempted to quit because of this, but I had a family to support. . . . The tenants had absolutely no dealing power. It got to the point where a tenant was evicted for not saluting [taking off his hat] to the Count. Tenants could be kicked off for any reason; the padrone did not have to justify his acts. The country-folk were very *tense* and would even worry about the Count's face and expression. A tenant could be ruined by the bad mood of the owner.

Managerial supervision was also embedded in the documents themselves. Provisions were routinely included that defined, with various degrees of specificity, appropriate and inappropriate agricultural techniques. The following provisions appear in a contract dated 1906 from the estate archives.

The Lessees are not allowed to sow medic, nor clover directly under the grapevines or under the mulberry trees, but should keep a distance of three furrow widths on each side of the plants.

The Lessees are obliged to work, fertilize and improve the leased land as is expected from considerate and skillful farmers. Furthermore, the Lessees will not sell hay, nor sorghum, nor straw, because everything must be used to fertilize the land leased in this agreement.

It was not always clear who had responsibility for the management of the podere. The capo of the family was invested with legal accountability for running the farmstead; however, his latitude for making independent decisions was circumscribed by various contractual provisions as well as by the gastaldo's judgment. Looming in the background was the ever-present possibility that the padrone would intervene directly with little or no regard for contractual provisions, tenant rights, the judgment of the gastaldo or, for that matter, common sense.

The fittavoli were caught between the risks and constraints inherent in the contract and the whim of the count, who was a fanatic about the smallest sums of money. "In matters pertaining to the estate he [the count] would cut the lira (*spaccava la lira*)." Yet there were also episodes that suggested a detached concern on the part of the owner for his tenants and staff. On one occasion when the gastaldo himself fell behind on a loan from the bank, he was astonished to find that the owner had, unbeknownst to him, interceded and paid the debt. On other occasions the count simply cancelled the debt of a tenant because of some momentary sympathy for the family in question. The signor could also involve himself with great subtlety to mediate disputes within and between tenant families, when he saw fit. The gastaldo summarized his reflections on the old agrarian order:

> So much depended on [the owner's] mood. Certainly, it is so much better now and I would not like to go back to those times. Even if I could be thirty years younger—I would not go back.

Finally, provisions 5 and 7 established stark responsibility in the event of misfortune—both "foreseen and unforeseen"—that might befall the tenant operation, along with an obligation to protect the podere from potential damage resulting from illegal easements on tenant lands. The tenant family bore virtually the entire burden for every disaster that might occur, and were forced to accept responsibility for protecting the tenant holding from misuse by outsiders. World War I created precisely this kind of "unforeseen" devastation for Friulian tenants.

Double-Entry Accounting

Subsequent renewals of the agreement between Giuseppe S. and Andriana N. and the count were very similar to the original contract. During the first few years of the twentieth century, a larger parcel of land was added to the agreement and the cash rent correspondingly increased. Otherwise, the terms of the agreement for 1903 were identical to those for 1897. Yet an added dilemma appears in the tenurial documents that altered the position of the tenant family and ultimately led to its ruin.

The accounting statement embodies a different representation of the formula that dominated tenant life. It depicts the accumulated outcomes of the risk arrangements specified by the tenant contract over time. Again, these mere notations on paper represented an austere presence in the minds and lives of the fittavoli. The two columns of numbers, headed simply "debit" and "credit," hark back to one of the most powerful innovations of the northern Italian commercial revolution, double-entry accounting. Like the contract, the balance sheet served as an instrument for reifying social relations in the agrarian world. This particular document represents the closing of the account between tenant and owner after the termination of their contract. During the early spring of 1903, the count brought suit before the local magistrate in Cividale to have Giuseppe S. and Andriana N. evicted. The eviction proceeding will be discussed after examining the account records—that

STATEMENT OF ACCOUNT [FOR] TENANT FARMER GIUSEPPE S.,
SON OF THE LATE ANTONIO AND ANDRIANA N.,
A MARRIED COUPLE OF BOTTENICCO.

Agricultural year 1902–1903		Debit		Credit
Carried forward on 11/11/1902	Lire	152.23		
Rent payment				
Wheat, hectoliters 6.50 @ Lire 18.00	Lire	117.00		
Cash for meadows	Lire	70.00		
Cash for house	Lire	150.00		
Cash for Braida dei Larghi	Lire	158.00		
Chickens, one pair @ Lire 1.80	Lire	1.80		
Capons, one pair @ Lire 5.00	Lire	5.00		
Eggs, 20 @ 7 centesimi	Lire	1.40		
Payments				
Tenant credit from 1902 statement delivered to Antonio and Pietro S.			Lire	12.00
Payment on account (October 17, 1903)			Lire	175.00
Wheat, hectoliters 6.50 @ Lire 18.00			Lire	117.00
Chickens, one pair @ Lire 1.80			Lire	1.80
Eggs, 20 @ 7 centesimi			Lire	1.40
Total Debits	Lire	655.43	Lire	307.20
Total Credits	Lire	307.20		
Remaining tenant debt on 11/11/1903	Lire	348.23		
Paid on account (June 14, 1903)	Lire	140.23		
		208.00		
Less sum for improvements		30.00		
Remaining debt	Lire	178.00		

is, in reverse sequence—because only by exploring the problems revealed in the bookkeeping statement can the eviction be understood.

The document covers the period from Saint Martin's Day, November 11, the traditional day for the settlement of tenant accounts, 1902, to the following Saint Martin's Day of 1903. The first entry is an outstanding debt carried forward from the prior agricultural year, amounting to 152.23 lire. This entry is followed by a debiting of all the rent charges for the 1902–1903 agricultural year. These debits are surprising insofar as *all* the rents are expressed in monetary terms, not just those computed as cash obligations. The in-kind rent for wheat is stated as 6.50 hecto-liters, multiplied by 18 lire, a price per hectoliter, to yield a debit of 117 lire. In another document from this estate, a provision states that any part of the in-kind payments not delivered will be charged to the tenant at an "official sale price," which presumably approximated the market price. The cash payments for meadows, house, and farmland follow, amounting to 70, 150, and 158 lire respectively. Most surprising of all is that the regalia is also expressed in monetary terms. Each item of this traditional payment is multiplied by what appears to be its market price to yield a cash payment. The status gifts embodying the regalia—chickens, capons, and eggs—are fastidously transformed into debits of 1.80, 5.00, and 1.40 lire respectively (see Bourdieu 1977: 173 for a similar example).

The credits on this balance sheet begin with a small carryover of 12 lire. That is followed by payments made on October 17, 1903, that covered part of the tenant's cash obligations and all the rent for wheat, chickens, and eggs. A similar cash payment is also listed, dating from the preceding June 14. After totaling all the debits and subtracting credits, including a sum for farm improvements, the tenant family was left with an outstanding delinquency of 178 lire on Saint Martin's Day, 1903, when the farmstead passed back to the owner.

An ominous document, titled "Acknowledgment of Debt," was drafted on the preceding day, November 10, when it became clear that the tenants were unable to meet their final contractual obligations. It reads, in part:

> Following the closing of the final farm account between Count G., son of the late N. of Bottenicco, and Giuseppe S., son of the late Antonio, and N. Andriana, daughter of the late Antonio, a married couple, also of Bottenicco, it resulted that the said married couple N–S are debtors for rent in arrears on 10 November of the current year, that is as of today, in the sum of Lire 178 . . . which they obligate themselves to pay by the day 28 . . . of the current month without exception.

This rather substantial debt was paid off even before the deadline demanded in the document. A receipt in the count's archives, dated November 22, 1903, states "On this day the undersigned received from Giuseppe S. the balance of his debt defined as Lire 178. In trust. [The count's signature]." There is no direct evidence to indicate how the tenants met this outstanding debt. The usual procedure was for the tenants immediately to sell their share of the harvest. Although this resolved the tenants' contractual obligation, it invariably threatened their basic subsistence. In this particular case the point was moot, insofar as the eviction had by this time been technically executed.

The bland formula of double-entry bookkeeping added distress to the outlook and existence of fittavoli. Recurrent problems with debt compounded the uncertainties of the tenancy arrangement. The distinction between the tenant's share of production and rental payments was clouded by the carryover of outstanding charges from one agricultural year to the next. Tenants routinely sold what the contract implied was their "share" of the harvest, to cover their prior years' cash obligations to the owner. "The fittavoli had to sell [their crops] at very low prices. . . . You had to sweat to sell the crops. You had to take what they [the owners] would give you." In more extreme circumstances, tenants sold land and equipment to meet their obligations. Ironically, the primary reason for the fragmented composition of many leased poderi (see the 1922 contract in chapter 5) was that the farmsteads themselves had been created from small parcels of land forfeited by prior generations of debt-ridden tenant families. The only alternative was for family members to seek wage work outside the estate. "My father worked eight to ten hours a day [as a laborer] just to pay the rent for house and meadow." As we have seen, wage work was difficult to find, pay was low, employment was often seasonal and job security was, at best, tenuous. Tenants employed the extreme procedures of selling property and adding ever-increasing hours of wage work to resolve the abstract imbalance between columns of numbers headed "debit" and "credit." Often, as in the case of Giuseppe S. and Andriana N., the efforts were in vain.

These involuted productive circumstances had their most devastating impact on the basic subsistence of fittavoli. It is recalled most vividly by former tenants in terms of diet. "We ate bread only twice a year!" The monotonous staple of corn mush (polenta) provided the caloric base of the rural diet, yet its nutritional flaws exposed the countryfolk to the chronic dangers of pellagra. For many fittavoli, impoverishment was so extreme that a watered-down form of polenta known as *xuf* was used to extend the maize supply during the seemingly endless hard times. When the gastaldo said "the land gave very little," he was no doubt referring to the fertility of the soil—"the first nature." It was, however, through the social workings of the agrarian system—"the second nature"—that the meager products of the land were eroded to inhuman extremes for those who worked it.

Evictions

Severance of the tenant-landlord relationship required its own legal formalities, from which we can infer the stark political nature of agrarian social relations. The sterile procedures of eviction reveal how the internal organizations of the latifondi were far from autonomous, but were vertically linked to the legal-bureaucratic apparatus of the comune, province, and state. The Italian Civil Code and provincial ordinances empowered local judges, magistrates, bailiffs and police to enforce contractual arrangements at the behest of proprietors or their agents. The precise inequalities established on each estate through contractual formulas were generalized throughout the region by the regularizing power of the administrative system. This marriage of contractual provisions and civil administration created an enduring medium of class division in the rural districts of Friuli. The articulation of the petty bureaucracies of the latifondi with the legal-political apparatus of the liberal state represents the type of class system that Antonio Gramsci calls "civil hegemony" (1978: 12; Anderson 1976).

The termination document (*sfratto*) drafted by the bailiff of the Royal District Court of Cividale at the behest of the count reads in part as follows:

> With my office I hand deliver to the said Giuseppe S., son of the late Antonio, and Andriana N., daughter of the late Antonio of Bottenicco, this Act of Notice of Lease Termination intending that on the day of 11 of November 1903 the land shown on the map of Bottenicco [five parcels are listed] and on the map of Moimacco [nine parcels are listed] for a total of hectares 3.437, return to him [the count] free of people and things.

Although termination proceedings were accomplished before a local court, the *pretura*, they did not represent an advocacy arrangement in which the tenant's interests were represented. Rather, the procedure was uncontested and the tenants, as in this case, usually were not even present. In reality, termination was automatically granted (*"punto e basta"*) at the owner's request. An elderly priest described the situation in these terms:

> The threat of eviction hung over the peasant's head. Eviction was at the owner's wish. . . . It was not fair. There were no means available [for fittavoli] to defend themselves. Their lack of education and sophistication limited their ability to take [legal] steps.

The priest offered help but it was very difficult [for the clergy] to act directly.

A retired Communist Party official gave a similar account:

A little mistake, an incivility [*sgarbo*], a rise in the rent or because the padrone did not think the land was worked in the best possible way [and the family was evicted]. In the month of May they would be given the order to leave by San Martino. They would have to leave and look for another padrone. So these people moved from hamlet to hamlet. They had no protection.

A writ of assistance is appended to the eviction papers by which the Chancellor of the Court directed the bailiff to execute the termination notice. The document closed with a procedure for eviction if enforcement was needed.

We command all Judiciary Officials as they are requested, and to whom it may concern, to execute this Notice, to the Public Ministry to help you [the bailiff], to all Commanders and Officers of the Public Forces to help you with this when they are legally requested to do so.

This decree empowered police authorities to assist the bailiff, if necessary, in evicting the tenant family. Thus, the power of local judicial and police authorities directly supported the padrone in the execution of the eviction writ. Again, the Communist informant described how the evictions were carried out by the authorities:

If a family got eviction papers they put everything onto their carriage and looked for another podere. There were public officials who evicted fittavoli. When the time came they had to be out or the officials would throw their possessions into the street. If they owed money [these officials] would forcibly take the furniture and sell it for the [outstanding] debts.

As the gastaldo succinctly put it, ''Evictions were easy.'' Within a decade provisions like the following began to appear in contracts which made explicit what had been traditional practice: ''Any failure to fulfill the established conditions and especially the lack of punctual payment, even in part, of the rent will give the Lessor the right to immediately terminate this lease.''

An interview was conducted with one of the padroni, now in his late seventies. The signor's family was one of the largest landowning families in the area, and the family had also founded and operated one of the local factories. This particular informant had as a young man earned a colorful reputation as a playboy. It is said that he spent, or perhaps misspent, his youth in the casinos, bars, and hotels of the South of France. More relevant to this study was that he had also been trained as a lawyer and had practiced law in Cividale. All in all, this gave him an unusual perspective on the workings of rural society and the local legal-political system. What was, however, most compelling about his perspective on pre–World War II society was that it so closely paralleled accounts of priests, former tenants, estate managers, and others. His account was most helpful in confirming the documentary evidence and informants' reminiscences about legal practice in the pretura. The most noteworthy comment by the signor came in response to an intentionally naive question. He was asked if tenants could contest their evictions or bring suit against their padroni over violations of contracts. He responded with a deep-throated, menacing laugh. Not only was the question grotesquely naive, it was laughable. Thus, the cultural assumptions that regulated contractual relationships on the latifondi basically diverged from, for example, Anglo-American notions of contractual norms (see Durkheim 1933). Rather than serving as instruments to protect the interests of the contracting parties, the agreements formalized social inequalities. Again to quote the gastaldo: "The contract did not imply equal status between the two sides. The owner could break [the terms of the agreement] at any moment."

Patronage—The Barbed Hook

In the shadow of the legally circumscribed routines of proprietors, managers, and tenants, there was a veiled arena in which a clientelist idiom was invoked to guide social action. The natures of these social frameworks were in many respects antithetical. Contractual principles were delineated to establish unequivocal rules for social interaction, while in the clientelist medium, shifting rights and obligations were open to ongoing redefinition and reinterpretation. Vestiges of a classical form of patronage could be found on many Friulian estates during the early decades of this century. More significant, however, was the use of the dependency ideology couched in the idiom of clientage to manipulate—most often in a secretive and illicit fashion—relations in the shadow of the rationally organized rural institutions. This section is devoted to examining the clientelist ties spawned along the disenchanted fringes of rural bureaucracies, the "evil flowers" of rationalism. Both empirically and ethically, these are troublesome issues to uncover and analyze. As will be seen in chapter 7, I was more successful in probing these questions among the personnel of a rural factory in Rubignacco, where the codes of shame and secrecy have begun to lapse. Nonetheless, it is reasonable to introduce this issue on the terrain of the latifondo, where these relationships were first gestated and where their powers were first exercised.

Patronal ties develop in social situations where moral pressure is invoked as a counterweight to material inequality. "Confronted with a stronger man the weak may adopt a posture of deference, may give way, and then salvage what he can by exerting moral pressure—pressures of acceptance, deference, friendliness, of godparenthood; even to try to control the prepotence of his acknowledged superior" (Davis 1977: 132). With the projection of a familistic idiom of godparentage, tenants in the rural districts of Friuli hoped to gain security and to restrain the excessive and arbitrary demands of their overlords. In theory, the economic ties between tenant and owner were transformed by affection and intimacy, which sustained a patronal bond. As Sydel Silverman puts it, "The two families linked by such [patronal] ties interact frequently, in an intimacy that imitated familial affection" (Silverman 1975: 90). However, the ideals of patronage—faith, trust, guardianship, and devotion—go much deeper. They have historically represented for the countryfolk standards by which equity and justice were reckoned. Patronage circumscribed an ethical framework, sanctified by Catholic dogma, that largely defined morality in rural society.

There is no doubt that classical forms of patronage did develop in rural districts of Friuli, particularly among tenants and small to medium-size landowning families, where the parties were directly involved in the working of the land.

> Fittavoli who pleased the lord in every possible way were in a position to receive the padrone's godparentage for their children . . . those who were considered honorable, "*ben volus*," by the proprietor. Large families were particularly well regarded. It did not happen often, but it happened. The padrone would send his wife to the tenant family [after the birth of a child] and she would offer to be the [child's] "*santola*" [godmother]. . . . The tenant family gained "*bravura*." The wife of the padrone had more contact with the tenant family. A woman is always a woman. She [often] became close to the tenant's children. The padrone would keep an eye on the *figlioccio* [godchild]; the relationship between the landowner and the capo of the family was like *compari*. [They lived] only a few meters from each other. . . . There was little distance.

Even on large estates, intimacy and trust developed that could sustain "lopsided friendships."

> There was a padrone for whom the tenants would have built a monument. He was like a father. The workers were very thankful for this man. He had a good gastaldo—"*un fiore di galantuomo.*" The lord visited the peasants, he was hearty, polite and he would acknowledge [the needs] of the tenants. He was not overly demanding. In economic matters he was generous.

Although more or less "classical" forms of patron-client bonds persisted in the rural districts of Friuli, these *relations* did not operate as a major integrative force in the countryside. Rather, the *ideology* of patronage served as a powerful metaphor for legitimizing the domination of the landowning gentry.[2] The moral force of the ideology derived from the fact that the principles of patronage encompassed much of the traditional Friulian social ethic. The use of the familial idiom translated abstract power relations into language and symbols accessible to the Friulani. However, the manner in which the ideology was invoked led to the degradation of the moral fabric of patronal relations.

It was common for proprietors of small to medium-sized operations to be addressed by their tenants as "*santolo*" or "*santul*" (the Friulian form), whether or not the owner was the actual godparent. Similarly, on the large estates the gastaldo and other members of the estate's petty officials were also addressed as "santolo" by the heads of tenant families, in which case the usage was entirely figurative. Thus, the term "santolo" was most often used to convey the superior position of one individual to another, rather than to depict any underlying sentimental tie. Deference was paid to the powerful out of respect, fear, and—to a certain degree—awe. Respect and obedience were expressions of the dependent position of a powerless individual, and only in a secondary sense can they be viewed as deliberate efforts to manipulate the sentiment of overlords and overseers.

With the lopsided friendship or godparentage that enlivened the patronal relationship came the hope on the part of the client of some modest and generally ill-defined amelioration of his or her material circumstance. The substance of the counterflow from patron to client is the test of the integrity of the bond.[3]

> The padrone was santolo for many children. It was important for the tenant family to have him as santolo for their children.

[The relationship] worked to bind the peasant to the lord. It was a hook for the purpose of forcing the people to work hard. The hook was barbed!

Q. Would the lord help if your child was ill?

A. Hardly, hardly, hardly . . . they [tenants] asked [for help] but it was not forthcoming . . . [that is] if they asked at all. If one child died another was born.

A priest in Cividale commented on the general situation that prevailed between tenant and lord during this period:

Feudalism died slowly as the people tried to emancipate themselves. The padrone held the knife by the handle and [protective] social laws were lacking. The laws of the state did not interfere. Old-fashioned liberalism was something that worked on behalf of the owners. Their freedom to act reached horrible heights. For the tenants it was always debt, debt, and never credit. The actions of the owner were essentially madness.

Often the only hope held out to the tenants for the reciprocation of their loyalty and service was through the posthumous cancellation of all debts that was occasionally willed upon the death of the padrone.

The most critical determinant of the viability of the patronal arrangement was the size of the enterprise, and hence the degree of inequality between the parties. The prerequisites for clientelist ties were more likely to emerge on the small estates, less so on the grand noble latifondi: (1) the frequent interactions and intimacies between potential patrons and clients that Silverman stresses, and (2) the opportunities for would-be clients to exert "moral pressure" on powerful individuals, as Davis emphasizes. In the first instance the marked separation, both socially and spatially, that prevailed on the large estates made interactions rare and intimacies unlikely. Rarely were counts directly addressed by tenants. The extent of their interaction generally amounted to little more than bowed heads and the muted salute, "*Sior Paron*," as the nobleman's carriage passed. In the second instance the bureaucratized nature of the tenurial system preempted the exercise of moral influence by tenants over their grandees. Even on small estates, "economic" pressures could disrupt or preclude an enduring patron-client framework. When small independent farmers received as many as five bids for a single tenant holding, as they did during the early decades of this century, competitive forces overwhelmed the sentiments of patronage.

111

Black Clientage

What is significant about these rural social relations is not that patron-client ties were poorly developed in the countryside, but that the clientelist idiom and social equation had been corrupted. Not only did most tenants and workers lack the power to bargain an amelioration of their social and material circumstances; proprietors and particularly their agents were in a position to extend their coercive demands beyond most legal and moral bounds. Patronage, stripped of its sense of moral guardianship, became merely an instrument for the powerful to wring submission and dependence from the powerless. "There was much fatalism. The countryfolk had their backs bent under a weight they had to carry. They became resigned to it."

Endemic unemployment, combined with an enormous landless and land-poor population, created the kind of social dynamic, which David Gilmore (1977) calls "primary structure and process," that breathed life into a black dimension of interclass relations and promoted heightened abuse and coercion (see Pitt-Rivers 1954: 204). This *black clientage* depended on pervasive insecurity for its authority. The more extreme the insecurity, the more likely a clientelist idiom would be used by the powerful to strong-arm the weak. The veneer of guardianship gave way to a stark view that held that the countryfolk were inherently inferior and unworthy and that abusing them was not a serious moral issue.

It was the rationalized organization of the latifondi, and of the local factories and government agencies, that empowered petty officials to exercise this type of power. Paralleling these bureaucratic social structures was a shadowy realm in which illicit relationships were created and manipulated.[4] Officials, by virtue of their formal positions, could extort concessions, bribes, and the like from underlings and those dependent on their special administrative services. Their power, though illegitimate, was exercised with a significant measure of autonomy protected by codes of secrecy and bonds of complicity. Many of these petty bureaucrats operated not as mere surrogates of the proprietors, but as entrepreneurial agents acting in league with them or in ways that were carefully concealed from them. Thus, the rational organizational makeup of these institutions defined a veiled social realm where the most sinister "traditionalist" codes and practices endured unhindered by moral restraints or legal control (see Blok 1969; Schneider and Schneider 1976). Some of the most egregious of these practices were exercised by managers and proprietors of the rural factories surrounding Rubignacco.

Patronage and Its Disenchantments

Capitalism as a cultural force in Friuli was driven by an insensate logic that imparted specific institutional imperatives. Market dynamics were experienced most immediately by the fittavoli in the organizational apparatus of the latifondi, rather than in the embrace of a "commodity fetish" or in the axioms of a "market mentality." The rationalizing compulsions that were first observable in the region in the early sixteenth century continued to encroach on rural institutions in the early decades of the twentieth century. The four basic procedures by which social relations were calibrated on the latifondi included (1) the circumscription of discrete spheres of human life and activity; (2) the assignment of roles, usually in hierarchical relationship to one another, with associated rights and duties; (3) the delineation of measures, susceptible to mathematical calculation, to audit productive aspects of human performance; and (4) the specification of arrangements to enforce the rules that governed these disenchanted domains.

The rendering of social bonds as utilities, largely unbound by moral constraint, created new kinds of distress for the countryfolk. By invoking the symbolic vestiges of guardianship, managers and overseers defiled the moral basis of the social order. The anomic relations that emerged were stripped of guardianship and empowered by the pervasive insecurity of the countryfolk in order to extort concessions from them. Thus, folded around these rational organizations, such as the latifondo, were illicit relations antithetical to the formal rules of bureaucracy and yet entirely dependent on these entities for their perverse power.

Bureaucratization of rural social relations had very specific cultural consequences. The moral fabric of patronage—faith, trust, equity, guardianship, and devotion—could no longer sustain a public ethic. These moral values were not eradicated; rather, they retreated to the rural districts of the region, and particularly to the life, language, ethnic practices, agrarian routines, and social intimacies of the family farmstead. Within these refuges, Friulian culture could be enacted relatively untainted by disenchanted formulas. Steadfastness to these bastions of rural identity is what gives peasant-worker life its distinctive character and enduring meaning.

Agrarian Politics

THE ORGANIZATIONAL imperatives and interpersonal manipulations
that dominated life on the latifondo, spilled over during the early decades of the twentieth century into the arena of politics. A reform movement, orchestrated by an activist segment of the Friulian clergy,
emerged in the months immediately following the close of World War
I. The movement delineated an oppositional framework that challenged
the domination of the large landowners in Friuli. The political struggle
that ensued was aimed at a redefinition of rural social relations through
a reworking of the tenurial instruments. As advocates of the interests of
the countryfolk, leaders of the movement attempted to introduce new
ethical principles and evaluative procedures into the contractual system.

The theoretical significance of this discussion rests on the primacy of
cultural forces in shaping social and political struggles within peasant-
worker society. Political conflict and social strife in Friuli were predi-
cated on the clash between traditional sensibilities and rational urgencies. The performance of the clergy who were caught up in the agrarian
reform movement is particularly relevant in this regard.[1] What appeared
as a vigorous public assertion of the moral and political authority of the
church masked a deeper and more remarkable process. The clergy in
Friuli found themselves grappling with a sweeping redefinition of religious and secular ideals. Yet the effort to translate Catholic dogma and
practice into a modern idiom revealed the dissonant loyalties in which
the church was mired. The cultural ambiguities that preoccupied the
clergy were not mere parochial matters; rather, they went to the heart of
Friulian ethnic identity and folk consciousness.

The Social Church

The church enjoyed an unusual position in the rural society of the Venetian provinces. From the last phase of Austrian rule through unification,
the clergy operated with striking autonomy. The Austro-Hungarian administration permitted the clergy wide areas of responsibility with regard to local administrative matters. The Venetian church was also able
to respond aggressively after unification both to the secularizing influence of the liberal state and to the progressive philosophies of nascent

socialist movements (Stern 1975: 226–32). The activist role adopted by the "social church" in Friuli enormously strengthened Catholic religious and political legitimacy. This contrasts with the conservative, Vatican-dominated church of central and southern Italy, with its opposition to the Italian state, and its alienation of rural workers. The most prominent expression of this social activism was the creation of rural cooperative enterprises and mutual-aid societies to assist small farmers and tenants. The Friulian movement was inspired by clerical activity in Lombardy, where the first church-sponsored organizations (*casse rurali*) were founded largely in response to the growing power of the Socialist leagues in the countryside (see D. Bell 1986: 54–56; De Rosa 1970). The casse rurali in the rural districts of Friuli took a variety of forms, including banks, dairies, cooperatives owning farm machinery, and even a small paper mill. The enterprises were generally organized within local parishes and depended heavily on the clergy for leadership and organizational skills. These parish-based operations spread rapidly across the rural districts of the northeast during the last quarter of the nineteenth century, combining with Catholic workers' organizations [*società operaie*] to form the *Movimento cattolico*. The social policies of the Friulian church gained further impetus after the publication of Leo XIII's encyclical, *Rerum novarum* (1891), which set out the church's position on workers' rights.

From the outset, the Catholic Movement in Friuli turned its attention to reform of the contractual system. The movement addressed its program to the Agrarian Association, which historically had represented the interests of the landed gentry in the region. The Friulian Agrarian Association in its periodic meetings drafted basic standards for wages and rents, and other contractual conditions that would apply within the agrarian domains of its members. In this forum, the representatives of the Catholic Movement argued their agenda. Four general aims were articulated: (1) the limitation of fixed cash obligations; (2) the elimination of the gratuitous "gifts"; (3) the restriction of the amount of unpaid labor that could be extracted from tenants; and (4) the curtailment of potential abuses of tenant contracts by landlords and their agents. The goal of contractual reform, as well as of the casse rurali, was to provide some measure of economic protection, particularly from indebtedness, for tenants and small farmers. On a more fundamental level, the movement attempted to forge a moral and institutional counterweight to the hegemonic control by the gentry.

This early reform program did little to instill a political consciousness in the rural populace or, for that matter, to improve its overall material circumstances. The large owners continued to exercise control vis-à-vis the Agrarian Association, and through it, to dictate the basic terms of agrarian livelihood in the region with only modest concessions to the church. Yet this systematic criticism on the part of the Catholic Movement represented the first case of the contractual arrangements assuming a "political" reality, one that had clear overtones of agrarian class rifts. Clerical activism imposed a moral evaluation on the abstract terms and provisions of the land tenure system, creating an oppositional framework for understanding and interpreting fundamental issues of rural life and livelihood. These modest achievements laid the groundwork for a subsequent and far more aggressive assault on the institutional pillars of rural society that was to come at the close of World War I.

World War I and Its Aftermath

On the outskirts of Cividale, the pivotal battle of the Italian front was fought at Caporetto. Friuli, more than any other region in Italy, suffered from the direct effects of the conflict and invasion: 15,000 residents were killed, 85 percent of the industrial base in Udine was destroyed, and 135,000 inhabitants, 22 percent of the region's population, were resettled in other parts of northern Italy. As many as half of the farms in Friuli suffered some damage. Livestock, equipment, and other property were confiscated, damaged, or destroyed by the military. The conflagration struck directly at the human and material condition of the countryfolk.

Apart from the direct effects of the combat, there were governmental initiatives taken during the war that were to have important implications for the political atmosphere during the immediate postwar period. After the initial devastating defeats on the Friulian front, the government found it increasingly difficult to maintain the loyalty of the "war-weary peasant soldier." In response, politicians in Rome found it expedient to join the call for "land to the peasants." Prime Minister Salandra put the promise of land reform in the following exalted terms: "After the victorious end of the War, Italy will perform a great deed of social justice. Italy will give land and everything that goes with it to the peasants, so that every hero who fought bravely in the trenches can become economically independent. That will be the Fatherland's reward to its brave sons" (quoted in Schmidt 1938: 27). These promises were not forgotten by the rural folk and their clerical spokesmen.

The war and invasion also produced important, though short-lived, changes on the latifondi in Moimacco and Bottenicco. Acute shortages of labor in the area led to a modification and significant loosening of the rules governing the operation of these estates. Most prominent was the pooling of the labor of tenant families to perform much of the work on individual estates. New techniques for working the land were also tried, which apparently led to improved yields and a more efficient deployment of resources. Furthermore, the "great social distance" that separated tenants from owners was narrowed. Padroni, in the face of the emergency, assumed a more direct role in the management of their estates. These initiatives left a lasting impression on tenants, both toward the noblemen and toward the organization of production under leasehold agreements.

The Crisis of Authority

Confusion reigned in the aftermath of the Armistice. In the face of this chaos, an effective challenge was mounted against the Friulian latifondisti. The grievances that galvanized the militant challenge were the claims by the landlords on rents and debts accrued for the 1917–1919 period. The rural challenge was, once again, organized through the Catholic Movement, this time in the form of the White Alliance (*Leghe bianche*), which drew together the Catholic Labor Union and the Federation of Tenant-Farmers and Sharecroppers, though the Leghe bianche employed far more militant tactics. With a colorful leadership composed of radical clerics, tenant representatives, and a sprinkling of left-leaning aristocrats, the newly formed alliance challenged the power of the Agrarian Association and the landed gentry who controlled it. Even more important than the organizational and leadership changes in the Catholic alliance were the changes in the attitude and outlook of the countryfolk themselves. The military experience had given many younger members of rural families their first exposure to social conditions outside their country districts. These returning war veterans were often unwilling to reassume the economic burdens and dependent status concomitant with tenant life. They were also far less timid about expressing their desires and, when necessary, directly opposing their overseers. Moreover, many were able and willing to resort to violent tactics in expressing their disaffection with the status quo. Between June 1919 and March 1920, 175 Leghe bianche were formed in Friuli, using parish churches and other religious organizations as the focus of recruitment.[2] The White League was founded in Cividale in January 1920. Through late 1919 and early 1920, the alliance organized numerous rallies and strikes—sporadic protests by small groups of angry contadini spread through the countryside. Many of these spontaneous outbursts were distinctly violent in tone, and the protests and strikes left the latifondisti seriously shaken.

The Reform Program

In the face of mounting rural unrest, provincial authorities agreed to the formation of arbitration committees to negotiate the settlement of the rancorous claims and counterclaims stemming from the 1917–1919 agricultural years. Local magistrates were empowered to appoint committees composed of landowners and tenant representatives (who were not necessarily tenants themselves) to mediate specific disputes in their districts. This concession was an important victory for the countryfolk, inasmuch as it removed the litigation of tenant claims from the civil courts.

The Federation of Tenant-Farmers and Sharecroppers had tried to intercede in local disputes and negotiate settlements before the formation of the arbitration committees. After these committees were formed, the federation continued to press for equitable resolution of conflicts. It petitioned magistrates and other officials, suggesting standard criteria for the settlement of claims based on its own experience in mediating these explosive disputes. The federation also sought to secure the right to nominate tenant representatives directly to the panels. Another related and extremely inflammatory issue aroused alarm in the countryside. In a letter to the provincial magistrates dated April 1920, the president and secretary of the federation outlined the new problem.

> It has come to the attention of this Federation that the termination of contracts is increasing at an unusual rate in our land. We understand that some of these [evictions] could be motivated by sale [of property], others have no [legitimate] motive at all and disguise a struggle against the farming class, either to make worse the conditions of the lease or as retaliation. This situation has already aroused sharp alarm and resentment in the rural populace, not for the mere spirit of protest, but for the difficulty or impossibility of finding other farms to lease. (Quoted in Tessitori 1972: 301–2)

The federation urged that the arbitration committees invoke a decree that had been passed in January 1920 which permitted the postponement of terminations until the following year.

Simultaneously, representatives of the federation entered into direct negotiations with representatives of the Friulian Agrarian Association over a fundamental reworking of the entire tenurial system. A senior official of the Ministry of Agriculture was also involved in the negotiations, and appears to have played an important role in achieving a settlement. The inclusion of these three constituencies—tenants, landowners, and the state—in these proceedings marked a watershed in the social and political life of the region. The mere presence of the federation as a party to the negotiations with a state official as overseer provided the first inkling of the curtailment of the landowners' domination.

The broad thrust of the White Alliance's reform agenda was the eradication of the institutional inequalities and paternalistic idioms embedded in rural society, and the substitution of moral principles establishing the rights of labor. The translation of Catholic moral imperatives into bureaucratic principles gave new impetus to the rationalization of the tenant-landlord relationship.

There is, perhaps, no better measure of the intensity of rural unrest than the speed and lopsidedness with which the tenant and sharecropper federation won its claims. By early July 1920, the federation effusively announced to its members triumph in their struggle:

Victory has come! Your organization is recognized, accepted are your essential demands for the new farming system. You [members of the federation] will have in your hands the new agreement and you will think about it and insist upon its enforcement. The choice of contractual provisions is not left anymore to the owner's will only, but it is entrusted to the study of a committee in which your representatives are in equal number. The homage and the gratuitous or semi-gratuitous services are abolished forever. The improvements [of the farmstead] will be paid for year by year. The farmhouses (how many were like hovels up to now!) will have to be in accordance with the standards of hygiene and habitability. . . . In the case of sale of property, the tenant-farmer will have precedence in its purchase. Every controversy between tenant-farmer and proprietor will be settled by Arbitration Committees constituted by the two organizations [the Federation of Tenant-Farmers and Sharecroppers and the Friulian Agrarian Association]. Termination of contracts of this year and next year will also be controlled by the Arbitration Committees; and, if there are no serious reasons [for eviction], they will not take effect. Each debt for the year 1918 is abolished, except for damage compensation. Payments already made will be refunded to tenant-farmers. (Quoted in Tessitori 1972: 303–4)

The settlement between the agrarian association and the federation outlined with remarkable clarity new standards for managing agrarian production. To begin with, it set a three-year limit on the overall agreement, during which time a special "Technical Board" composed of three representatives of the federation and three of the agrarian association was to study the status of agriculture in the region. This analysis was to assess farming methods from district to district, land use patterns, demographics, and the relationship between labor and capital as defined by the leasehold contracts. From these deliberations were to come recommendations for wide-ranging improvements and modernization of Friulian agriculture. Procedures were also specified for renegotiation and revision of the agreement at the close of its three-year life, presumably to incorporate the recommendations of the Technical Board. Once the work of the Technical Board was completed, its members were to assume the duties of a "Joint Arbitration Committee" charged with resolving controversies arising from the implementation of various provisions of the settlement. Finally, provisions were made to utilize three-member arbitration committees at the district level to settle local disputes. These committees were to be composed of one representative of the tenants and one of the landowners, plus one chosen mutually or, failing that, by the district magistrate. Procedures were also spelled out for appeals of local decisions to a regional arbitration committee in Udine.

The specifics of the settlement significantly modified conditions of tenancy, and established explicit criteria for a vast array of operating procedures. These included such major issues as the abolition of certain types of rents and gratuities, rules for the division of the harvest, procedures by which expenses were to be allocated, conditions under which credit would be extended to the tenant, and guidelines for the payment of wages. The agreement also reached down to such detailed concerns as the tenant's right to stall a horse; the disposition of tree trunks, pruned timber, roots, and branches; even the division of government-sponsored production prizes between tenant and landlord. Although the concessions gained by the federation fundamentally altered rural social relations by establishing explicit tenant rights, the major thrust of the agreement was directed at strict accountancy and enforcement, rather than at a redefinition of the tenant-proprietor relationship. Foremost in the minds of the countryfolk and their representatives was the need to restrain the abusive practices that permeated the tenurial system. To uphold the rights of the countryfolk, the federation strove to define with great precision the tenant-landlord contract, establish procedures by which these relations could be measured, and create forums to regulate and enforce them. These imperatives became embodied in the standard leasehold agreements that followed in the wake of the settlement. The contracts, born out of the moral insights and political action of the Catholic Movement, yielded the most highly rationalized and bureaucratized form of the tenurial relationship that we find in the long institutional history of these social instruments.

The Reform Contract

The next contract to be examined comes from the Moimacco latifondo, for a farmstead that ran along the border separating Moimacco and Rubignacco. In fact, part of the land leased under the contract extended into Rubignacco. The document is titled "Mixed Farm Lease and Sharecropping Contract" (*Contratto di Affittanza Mista e Mezzadria*), and is dated November 19, 1925. The agreement conforms to the basic standards laid out in the 1920 agrarian settlement. By far the most striking aspect of this document is the precise mathematical rendering of central elements of the contract—most notably, land, rents, and wages.

A critical reform reflected in this document, one that depicts the extent to which labor had come to be rationally evaluated, is the careful documentation of wages. Under the heading "Rates for Cartage and Rendering of Labor between Agreed Parties" (*Tariffa dei compensi dovuti per carreggi e prestazioni di mano d'opera fra le parti pattuita*) comes a detailed specification of tasks and corresponding wages. In this particular contract there are *seventeen* separate terms dealing solely with wage compensation. Wage rates vary according to the type of work, the sex of the worker, the time of year, and the amount of equipment and number of animals contributed by the tenant. Women in each instance received half the wages of men. Higher wage rates applied during the busier agricultural periods between April and November. The daily rate for plowing with four animals was twice the rate for plowing with only two animals. There was even a meal allowance specified for the tenant-worker transporting goods for distances in excess of ten kilometers.

The properties leased under the agreement are described with similar precision. Each parcel is identified and categorized by its traditional name (*denominazione del fondo*), its number on an official survey map (*n. mappale*), its size (*perticata*), its use (*qualità*), and its class (*classe*). The total size of the leased properties was figured using two different measures: perticati (132.83) and *Campi Friulani* (38.27). The perticati were used in the official survey and are equal to the English "perch" or "rod." The Campi Friulani are the traditional units of measure equalling roughly one-third of a hectare. The entire podere included 13.283 hectares. As the listing of the land makes quite clear, the podere was fragmented, consisting of twenty-six separate parcels ranging in size from slightly more than a tenth of a hectare to just over one and one-half hectares. As mentioned earlier, the prevalence of these dwarf parcels was a result of forfeitures of property by prior generations of debt-ridden tenants.

Tariffa dei compensi dovuti per carreggi
e prestazioni di mano d'opera fra le parti pattuita

Opere di uomo dal 1.° Novembre al 1.° Aprile	6	—
" " " dal 1.° Aprile al 1.° Novembre	8	—
Opere di donna dal 1.° Novembre al 1.° Aprile	3	—
" " " dal 1.° Aprile al 1.° Novembre	4	—
Aratura con 4 animali al giorno	30	—
" " 2 animali "	16	—
Erpicatura con 2 animali	15	—
Sarchiatura con 2 animali	30	—
Rincalzatura con 4 animali	15	—
Carreggi per trasporti vari per conto del Padrone con 2 animali (per la sola andata) per Km.	1	—
		—·75
Per suddetti servizi che sorpassano i Km. 10 verso territorio		
compreso L.6 per notte e L.40 alle compre		
Carreggi sabbia, ghiaia, ceppi, materiali, calce e		
legname per costruzioni e riparazioni		
case coloniche e domenicali		
Ghiaia, sabbia, terra, ed. pietrame e torre al m.²	10	—
Trasporti servizi (culture, fieno e fieno) " " "	5	—
mattoni, ceppi e calce per ogni carreta		
con 2 carreta	15	—
" 1 carreta	10	—
Ove ricorre a lavori straordinari per Padrone		
ad limiti, ed ostetica de oblii i resta		
che somministra vitto, vino e L. —·50		
su onerose eccezioni i lavori di vie		
costruite e accuccata		

PROVINCIA DEL FRIULI DISTRETTO DI CIVIDALE

COMUNE DI MOIMACCO

CONTRATTO di AFFITTANZA MISTA e MEZZADRIA
DI BENI RUSTICI

L'anno millenovecento _____ addì _____ stabilitasi _____
del mese di _____ in Moimacco _____

Tra i Sigg. F.lli _____ co. de _____ fu _____
possidenti domiciliati Moimacco _____
Pietro fu Pietro
Co _____
domiciliato a Moimacco

viene concordemente conchiuso e stipulato il seguente

Top table (upper portion)

	Frumento	Granoturco	Contanti
Aratorio I Classe Campi N.ro	5.44	5 60	
" II "	0.38	9 90	3
" III "	10.52		
" IV "	4.38	1 50	255 —
Prato I "	41.72		295 —
" II "			
" III "	1.64		
Boschette o pascoli			100 —
TOTALE		37.94	28 — 3 — 818 —

AMMINISTRAZIONE

S. F.llo CO.ti de
BONMAGGIO (Udine).

Lower table

Comune censuario	Denominazione del fondo	N. Mappale	Periziato	Qualità	Classe	Campi Friulani
		107-107-168	2.03	Orto	1ª	
		106	3.47	aratorio		
		1388	13.52	"	2ª	
		8.11	11.—	"		
		1632	6.75	"		
		13355	2.80	"		
		591	1.95	"		
		598	1.75	"	3ª	
		1817	2.06	"		
		1987	3.82	"		
		1980	4.30	"		
		1945	65.98	"		
		1945	1.82	"		
		1941	1.12	"		
		2034	10.81	"	4ª	
		1053-1054	2.02	"		
		2044	3.48	"		
		2043	5.02	"		
		2116	2.50	Prato	1ª	
		1245	2.50	"		
					2ª	
		2247	14.61	"		
		998	1.91	"		
		8826	3.91	aratorio	4ª	
		3910	1.20	"	4	
		1638		aratorio	2ª	
						37 95
						— 32
						38 27

Fig. 11. The count's villa in Moimacco.

Computation of rents is figured on the final page of the contract. These calculations are derived from a series of mathematical formulas that require a system for classifying various types of productive land and the determination of a corresponding rental rate for each class of property. The rents are itemized by the use of land: plowland (*aratorio*), meadows (*prato*), and groves (*boschette*), and by its quality (classe 1–4). The fixed in-kind rents for plowland are calculated by multiplying the amount of land in Campi Friulani by a constant set for each class of land. This resulted in the quantity of wheat (*frumento*) and maize (*granoturco*) to be paid in rent. Using a similar formula, the cash rents (*costanti*) for meadows and woodlands were computed by multiplying the amount of land by a constant set for each class. The resulting rent was figured in lire.

Though the title of the contract refers to "mezzadria," there is little in the document itself to indicate a sharecropping system. The only reference to mezzadria concerns two and one-quarter campi of special vineyard (*vigneto specializzato*) for which no fixed rent is listed. Presumably, the vineyard was cultivated under a sharecropping arrangement.

The provisions absent from this document are perhaps as important as those included. Missing from this reform contract are the customary obligations that formed the regalia (or onoranza), as are the cash rents for the farmhouse, though productive land immediately surrounding the *casa* was leased. Spared these onerous terms, the tenant family gained a measure of security while losing some of the more offensive symbolic burdens of dependent status.

The End of the Reform Contract

Even though this contract reflects the impact of the 1919–1920 reforms, its content was obsolete from the moment the agreement was drawn. By November 19, 1925, when the document was signed, the regime of Benito Mussolini had been in power for three years. The Fascists had already begun to dismantle the statutory protections that tenants had won earlier in the decade.

The rural protests that began sporadically during the late nineteenth century rose to a crescendo in the immediate aftermath of World War I, and led to a carefully designed program of agrarian reform. The centuries of tenant-worker disaffection were framed and articulated through the parish-based Catholic Movement, the main target of which was the contractual system. The immediate result of the reform movement was the creation of the most rationalized form of agrarian contract to emerge during the seven hundred or eight hundred years of the tenurial system. Yet these agreements were peculiarly retrospective, echoing past abuses rather than remaking the relations of agrarian production. The reforms operated in the realm of legalistic "phantom objectivity," perversely furthering the bureaucratic premises of the contracts. The political action that grew out of the postwar "crisis of authority" attacked the *apparatus* of hegemony—the contracts—rather than underlying power relations. Ironically, the expression of power represented by the reform movement laid the groundwork for a recrudescence of the large landowners' power under Fascism.

The Onset of Fascism

In September 1920, all of Italy seemed on the verge of revolution. The year before, in the first postwar elections, the Socialists won a third of the national vote and captured between 40 and 60 percent of the electors in Emilia, Piedmont, Umbria, Lombardy, and Tuscany. The Catholic-backed *Partito popolare* (successor to the White Alliance) won a majority of the vote in Friuli and claimed a fifth of the nationwide vote. Spurred on by their electoral achievements and their success in organizing industrial and agrarian labor, the Socialists intensified their drive to take control of the nation's economy. This effort culminated with the spread of well-organized industrial and agrarian strikes—*biennio rosso*.

By September 1920, as many as 500,000 industrial workers were occupying factories in the North, while agricultural workers refused to work the harvest through much of the *regno*. These militant nationwide labor protests orchestrated by the Socialists formed the backdrop for the political struggle in Friuli, strengthening the power of the Catholic Movement in securing the agrarian concessions described above. The industrial struggle was, however, vastly more complex than the agrarian uprisings, and the difficulties of resolving and controlling the former had devastating consequences for the latter.

At the moment when revolution seemed imminent, the leadership of the Socialist party slipped into paralysis. Unable to decide on a unified course of political action, the Socialists lost control of the movement and bogged down in internal bickering. As a result, in the early fall of 1920 the organizations representing industrial workers entered into a vague and disabling compromise with the government. In exchange for promises of greater worker participation and control in industrial matters, the Socialists called off the strikes and sit-ins. The settlement left the participants in the protests disillusioned and vulnerable to reprisals. Fascist *squadristi* torched socialist organizations and brutally attacked party leaders. The party was in internal disarray. The Communists broke with the Psi in January 1921, and the Socialists suffered substantial electoral losses in May of the same year. The speed with which worker organizations dissolved, and the political strength of the Left dissipated, was startling. "The membership of Federterra [the Socialist workers' organization] is said to have fallen from 889,000 in 1920 to 294,000 at the end of 1921—a loss of nearly 600,000—and it shrunk to only 15,000 in 1924" (D. Bell 1986: 107–52; Schmidt 1938: 36–37).

The Counter-Reforms

After his triumphal "March on Rome" in 1922, Benito Mussolini and the Fascists wrested control of the government.[3] One of the first priorities of the new administration was to reestablish control over the countryside. The instruments proposed for this political end were the agrarian contracts. Mussolini's minister of agriculture, Giacomo Acerbo, portrayed the general problems posed by rural labor in essentially functionalist terms: "detachment from the land . . . had endangered the equilibrium and harmony of social forces" (quoted in Innocenti 1978: 35). The answer put forward by the Fascists was "class collaboration" and "ruralization," which were supposed to fit the larger scheme of the "corporate state." "By reestablishing 'attachment to the soil,' Fascism hoped to restore order in the countryside'' (Innocenti 1978: 36). Agrarian contracts became the centerpiece of the ''new'' rural policy and the principal bureaucratic mechanism for the mediation of ''class collaboration'' throughout the nation. In other words, the contracts became instruments in the service of the wider bureaucratic imperatives of national political integration.

Obviously, the tenant-landlord relationship that the Fascists envisioned could not be reconciled with the reform contracts of the early 1920s. Rather, the Fascists were interested in resurrecting a far more conservative arrangement to achieve their social and political ends. The government defined the basic principles governing labor in the ''corporate state'' in a document entitled *Carta del lavoro*, published in 1927. Using this document as a guide, regional agrarian associations ''studied'' and redefined tenancy relations to conform to local traditions. The deliberations of the Florentine Geographic Academy were particularly important, shaping not only the definition of contractual relations in Tuscany, but also influencing the drafting in 1933 of the *Carta della mézzadria*, which became the definitive fascist statement on the organization of agrarian production. The academy's research determined that the agrarian contracts could serve important social Darwinist ends. The tenant agreement was seen as ''an instrument capable of singling out the best elements of the rural masses, who could rise in the social scale'' (Innocenti 1978: 50–51). Thus, the thinking behind these deliberations was to institute tenure agreements that were not merely regulators of economic obligations between tenant and owner, but also decisive instruments of social control, ones that administratively defined class divisions in the countryside.

State and Contract

The adoption of the ''Charter of Tenancy'' in 1933 formalized what had already become practice throughout Friuli and the rest of Italy. The charter restored ''classical'' forms of tenancy, which reestablished many servile aspects of tenant status and thus the authority of the gentry.

> The details of the [Charter] . . . could not have been more favorable to the proprietary class. The Fascist desire for uniformity prevailed; a rigid interpretation of this institution, along traditional lines, became a matter of law. In fact, the principles of the Charter had a great influence on the legal definition of [the tenancy] . . .

Contratto di Locazione

Provincia dei Friuli - Distretto di Cividale - Comune di Manzano

fra il Sigg. ℔℔ .... Co. da

da una parte, ed i Sigg. .... Passiniente Alluisota dall'altra

e Mario .... domiciliato in Manzano .... Co. da

1. Il Sigg. ℔℔ .... Co. da

suddetto concede a titolo di affitto misto - mezzadria ai sopracitati

Passiniente Passiniente, Alluiboto e Mario

che in solido per sé ed eredi accettano, lo appresso descritto rea-

lità: Casa colonica al civico N. 32 terreno part. Cens. 122.83

pari a campi Friulani 37/94 in corrispettivo dei quali i con-

duttori si obbligano di pagare annualmente al Locatore, al suo

domicilio, a titolo di fitto, nelle epoche di consuetudine, i se-

guenti generi sani, netti e stagionati :

Frumento (consegna agosto)	Q.li 22.=
Granoturco (consegna gennaio)	" 2.=
Avena	

più, a fine giugno, in contanti L. 540 per la casa e L. 218.=
per il prato.

2. Il vino, le vinacce, i bozzoli e le frutta saranno divisi
per metà, come pure le spese per il seme buchi e la foglia di
gelso che si dovesse acquistare.

3. Qualora i Conduttori prestassero la loro opera per lavori
attinenti alla conduzione dello stabile sia col carro ed animali

sia con la persona, accetteranno i compensi fissati d'accordo,
come da apposita tariffa ; i lavori inerenti all'allestimento della
cantina e tinaia padronale ed alla conservazione degli attrezzi
e dei vasi vinari non daranno diritto ad alcun compenso.

4. Qualsiasi lavoro di innovazione o di miglioria dei terreni
dovrà essere eseguito dai Conduttori a richiesta del Locatore nel
luogo e nel modo da questi indicato. Le fossalazioni saranno
della larghezza di m. 2 e della profondità di m. 0,70 ; le buche
dei gelsi dovranno essere di mq. 4 e della profondità di m. 0,70.

Per questi lavori sarà corrisposto un compenso di L. 0,50
al mq. compenso che verrà pagato od accreditato per intero al
colono a fine lavoro, a tacitazione di qualsiasi diritto che in av-
venire potesse accampare pel medesimo.

5. Le piantine per i nuovi impianti verranno fornite dal
Locatore.

6. Prima di procedere alla vendemmia o al raccolto di qualsiasi prodotto divisibile, i Conduttori dovranno attendere le disposizioni del Locatore ; essi non potranno inoltre fare alcuna
innovazione nella casa o nei fondi senza il di Lui consenso.

7. I Conduttori non potranno seminare cereali se non alla
distanza di m. 1 dalle piante di viti o gelsi, e le erbe da fo-
raggio se non alla distanza di m. 3.

8. È proibito ai Conduttori subaffittare qualsiasi parte del
terreno loro affittato e prenderne in affitto da altri. Il concime
prodotto dovrà essere per intero utilizzato nella colonia.

9. Tutte le piante, vive o morte, sono di proprietà del
Locatore, e quelle che per ordine di Lui venissero estirpate
dovranno essere rese al domicilio del Locatore ; i Conduttori
avranno diritto alle ramate e alle radici ; allo spirare della locazione dovranno lasciare i vimini a beneficio del nuovo affittuale.

L'importo delle sementi foraggere sparse nell'ultimo anno verrà loro rimborsato.

10. I Conduttori dovranno allevare con la massima cura e diligenza quella quantità di bachi che dal Locatore verrà loro destinata. Il diritto di vendita del prodotto bozzoli è riservata per intero al Locatore il quale potrà trattenersi in tutto o in parte l'importo della metà spettante ai Conduttori a deconto del fitto del prato e della casa. La foglia che eventualmente sopravvanzasse potrà essere ceduta ad altri coloni o venduta, a parere del Locatore, il quale accrediterà ai Conduttori la metà del relativo importo netto.

11. I Conduttori dovranno lavorare con la massima diligenza i terreni loro affidati; i filari di gelsi e di viti dovranno venir vangati due volte all'anno e concimati con letame almeno ogni due anni; qualunque danno o peggioramento alle piantagioni e fabbricati di entità rilevabili alla fine della presente locazione verrà addebitato all'affittuale cessante.

12. Non potrà il Conduttore permettere nessuna nuova servitù passiva sopra i beni avuti in affitto e dovrà custodire con ogni diligenza tutte le ragioni e i possessi, dando prontamente avviso al Locatore in caso di novità; e ciò sotto sua responsabilità per i danni o spese che derivassero in caso di ritardata notizia.

13. La presente locazione avrà principio dal giorno 11 novembre 192 quanto alla casa e dal 15 ottobre 192 quanto alle terre, ed avrà termine alle stesse epoche dell'anno successivo.

Essa si intenderà però tacitamente rinnovata di anno in anno alle stesse condizioni, a meno che una delle parti non abbia dato legale e regolare disdetta entro i termini consuetudinari.

14. Tutte le piante a Bosco ceduo fino all'età di anni 3 formano parte integrale della colonia ed all'affittuale che eventualmente per qualsiasi motivo si allontanasse dalla Colonia gli verrà accreditato l'affitto già pagato per gli anni dovuti ed in ragione della superficie boschiva.

15. Il terreno coltivato a viti in filari a distanza non superiore a m. 8, sarà considerato vigneto specializzato ed il colono pagherà solo 1/3 del fitto in ragione di classifica.

16. I Conduttori si obbligano di osservare integralmente e lealmente gli impegni assunti col presente contratto e quanto non fosse indicato nel contratto le parti si rimettono alle disposizioni del Codice Civile.

17. Il conduttore si obbliga per tutta la durata dell loro locazione, di non fittare in convivenza terreni di affittuale e di fabbricare, sua proprietà, sia di non concedere in uso locazione a terzi e di non concedere ad altre persone, in con gli strumenti, né admicati nella edilita dei terreni suindicati.

Letta, approvata e sottoscritta, si accetta alli,

Moimacco, 11 Novembre 1930 IX°

AMMINISTRAZIONE
f.lli CO.ti de
MOIMACCO (Udine)

contract, as eventually stipulated in the Civil Code of 1942, which continued to be operative even after the Second World War. (Innocenti 1978: 55)

A number of points need to be stressed concerning the restoration of the "classical" tenant contract. Tenancy envisioned by the Fascist regime did indeed echo ancient contractual principles, but it also represented something new. The reappearance of provisions that favored proprietors certainly gave the contracts an internal character reminiscent of the eighteenth- and nineteenth-century tenurial agreements discussed earlier. However, the degree to which the tenurial relationships were defined and enforced by the state represented an important new departure. Although provisions governing tenancy were included in the Civil Code of 1865, the extent of state participation under fascism marked a fundamental change. The state essentially became the third party to the agreements and, as suggested above, the government used the contracts to further specific social and political policies. The promotion of "class collaboration" through the tenant contracts gave state sanction to "traditional" inequalities mediated by patronal relations. The outcome of the fascist policies was an intensification of hegemonic class rule in the countryside.

Tenancy Under Fascism

The changes envisioned by the Fascists are clearly evident in a contract dated November 11, 1930. The agreement covers the same podere of 37.94 Campi Friulani just described. The contract is also between essentially the same parties. The document is entitled "Tenancy Agreement" (Contratto di Locazione), after which the place and the parties to the agreement are specified. The contratto consists of seventeen provisions governing rents, wages, expenses, managerial responsibilities, accounting procedures, the duration of the agreement, and the grounds for termination.

With the first of these provisions, the specific form of tenancy is more closely defined. Like the earlier contract, this is a "mixed farm lease and sharecropping agreement" (titolo di affitto misto–mezzadria) binding the landowning counts and the three tenant brothers. The agreement also specifies that the brothers "jointly and severally and for their heirs" (che in solido per sé ed eredi accettano) accept the property that is subsequently described. Thus, the contract is not merely binding on three individuals, but on an entire family and its offspring. The brothers as representatives of the contracting entity—the tenant family—bind its members to the agreement.

Included in the first provision of the agreement are the fixed in-kind and cash rents. The fixed in-kind assessments are identical to the rents specified for the podere five years earlier, as are the cash rents for the meadowland. However, the addition of the rather substantial charge of 350 lire for the farmhouse marks a change. This charge represents a reinstatement of one of the "oppressive pacts" which had been the focus of earlier reforms. The second term sets out the mezzadria arrangement. The farm's production of wine, grape dregs (vinacce), and silk cocoons, along with the expenses for silkworm eggs and mulberry leaves, were to be divided on a fifty-fifty basis. In the same fashion, the costs for fungicides, for the purchase and repair of spray pumps, for compulsory insurance, and for fees involved in registering the contract were also to be borne on a fifty-fifty basis.

The third and fourth provisions cover the arrangements for wage labor. Term 3 appears as follows:

> For any work performed by the tenants pertinent to the running of the property, be it with cart animals or manually, the tenants shall accept the compensations established by agreement, as a proper [apposita] rate; work involving the owner's cellar and vat-room and the maintenance of wine barrels and wine-making equipment shall not be subject to any compensation.

This vague dictum diverges dramatically from the specificity of wage rates and tasks set out in the 1925 contract. The fourth term is more detailed, though by no means more favorable to the tenant. It specifies how ditches were to be dug and sets a compensation rate of 0.05 lira for a given quantity of earth moved. Many of the remaining clauses delineate how the tenant should manage the farm and its resources. For example, terms 6, 11, and 15 deal with the scheduling of the grape harvest and the care of grapevines and mulberry trees. Terms 8 and 11 deal with the proper uses of manure. Term 7 addresses how and where grain must be sown.

Throughout the agreement, the tenant's responsibilities and liabilities are carefully set forth, as in the contract from 1896 discussed earlier. There are two good examples of this: first, in term 11, "Any significant damage or deterioration of the plants, trees, and buildings shown at the close of the present lease shall be debited to the tenant," and then, in term 12, "Any damage or expense deriving from delayed news [of any damage] shall be the liability of the tenant." At the same time the tenant's share of the harvest was reexposed to elusive accounting procedures, as in term 10. "The right of sale of the cocoon product is entirely reserved to the lessor who may withhold all or part of the amount of the half-share due the tenant and credit it toward the rent for the house and meadow.''

Provisions 16 and 17 have the most important implications in terms of defining the social contours of this agrarian world. Provision 16 reads, "The tenants agree to fully and faithfully observe the commitments assumed with the present contract as well as to submit to the provisions of the Civil Code for that which is not indicated in the contract." Again, this provision renders the state a party to the agreement. Indeed, the terms of the contract are linked directly to the relevant, though unspecified, provisions of the Civil Code, thereby framing the mutual rights and obligations of the respective parties in terms of state prerogatives. The civil bureaucracy of the state was joined with the petty bureaucracy of the agrarian estate to form an imposing power arrangement that represented a distinguishing characteristic of fascist political economy in the countryside.[4]

Provision 17 of the contract is a handwritten addition to the standard agreement. It specifies that the tenants must lease any land they owned to third parties and not contribute any labor or draft animals for its cultivation. This provision stands in an important complementary relationship to term 8, which forbids the subleasing of land covered by the contract. Both terms strive for the same critical end, an attempt to achieve exclusive authority over tenant family labor and resources—a fundamental premise of "class collaboration." The effect of these two provisions was to isolate the tenant family by preventing the formation of cooperative relations with other tenant families through subleases, exchanges of labor, or the mere lending of draft animals. The family was also, through the prohibition on separate leasing agreements, prevented from establishing relations with other landowners. A contract drawn during the same period on the estate in Bottenicco makes these demands even more emphatically.

> Lastly, to better assure production and to better conserve the leased land, the Lessees undertake, for the full year of the lease, not to lease or sublease, in any manner, land belonging to other owners or to other lessees, not only, but likewise they bind themselves to not work their own land, presently owned or owned in future, but to lease it to third parties and not to cooperate with labor, with animals, or otherwise in the cultivation of their land, finally they pledge to devote all their activity to the cultivation of the land

leased under this contract and renounce now and forever all to the contrary.

With great precision, the contracts defined specific social relations, each of which had a fundamental bearing on rural class makeup. In this manner, the basic dynamics of *inter*–class collaboration and its complement, *intra*–class fragmentation, were bureaucratically instituted and enforced.

ALTHOUGH a largely unvoiced hostility to the rural status quo existed for centuries in Friuli, it was not until the clerical representatives of the countryfolk formulated an oppositional framework that the meaning and significance of rural society became a publicly "contested reality" (Habermas 1974). By the early twentieth century, three diverse sets of interests clashed over the definition of the tenurial system. The agenda of the Catholic Movement proceeded from a moral commitment to the rights of rural workers; the agenda of the Friulian Agrarian Association was rooted in the perpetuation of the hegemony of the large landowners; the agenda of the Fascists, though in many respects sympathetic to the gentry, was oriented to a separate set of bureaucratic urgencies, namely national integration. Though the three political programs were derived from radically different premises, the way these programs were to be instituted required the invocation of the same cultural demiurges. Each political clique strove to concretize its view of reality using similar reifying procedures, enmeshing clerics, gentry and fascists in a common "rational-bureaucratic" engagement.

Rhetoric and Political Identity

The efforts of the Catholic Movement in Friuli at social and political reform induced a fundamental cultural shift. Clerical leaders and tenant representatives took the largely concealed cultural experience of the countryfolk and interpreted it in terms of an abiding moral commitment to the rights of workers. By endowing this interpretation of social conditions with a systematic meaning, to which they gave public articulation, these agents were able to wrest new forms of popular political power. The induction and manipulation of a nascent form of "public opinion" permitted new types of social action and understanding to emerge among segments of the rural populace. An important question, however, remains unanswered—to what degree were the countryfolk actually "politicized" by the engagement that ensued in the wake of World War I? Or, alternatively, to what degree was the engagement framed by the traditional religious motives and sensibilities of the Friulani? These questions reveal the inherently equivocal nature of contemporary Catholic orthodoxy and practice. The church's traditional role as earthly guardian and protector of the countryfolk, and the White Alliance's efforts to transform the rural populace into a modern political constituency, created irresolvable contradictions (see A. Gramsci's late works—post–1926; Davidson 1984: 139–54). In the heroic passages in which the White Alliance announced victory to its members in the summer of 1920 we can discern these competing impulses.

> Tenants!
> Let's look back with legitimate satisfaction! Yesterday you were still scattered and forgotten, people abandoned to the competition game, to the domination of the stronger. An idea bound you together: organization! From a dispersed populace you became a powerful force which influences [the creation of a new social order], thanks to the faith in a renewed Italy! What value had the boasted indifference [of the opposition], the contempt? What value their threats or deceitful smiles? When you asked to discuss [the reform agenda] there were those who scorned you; you waited calmly; and the negotiations came. In the face of your legitimate demands they [representatives of the gentry] showed opposition; you found greater resolve, you engaged in the struggle, briskly and totally the resistance fell and victory arose. The babblers of the red flag tried to ambush you employing means without honor . . . you did not deem them worthy not even of a glance. [You] went on, united, victorious. With the same feeling you can now look upon those who claim the honors of a triumph that is only yours! (Quoted in Tessitori 1972: 293)

Couched in this rhetoric is a distillation of interests aimed at galvanizing tenants in a political struggle—the fundamental prerequisite of a politicized populace. The daily dilemmas, the sense of injustice and abuse that had for countless generations been experienced by Friulian tenants, were articulated by the leaders of the White Alliance in ways that not only focused outrage but also infused the experience with political significance. Moreover, as the passage suggests, there were alternative and competing ways of endowing tenant experience with meaning. On one hand was the paternalistic framework of the agrarian association; on the other was the competing, and from the point of view of the White Alliance, the dishonorable framework of the Socialists, "babblers of the red flag."

The tasks for the White Alliance and its successor, the Partito popolare, were formidable. In order to transform the countryfolk with their traditional sensibilities into an active citizenry in a modern state, a new cultural identity had to be crafted. The Catholic Movement had to "educate" the rural populace to reflect and to weigh rationally their personal interests, and then rebind them to a political agenda that represented those interests. What made this a particularly intriguing challenge was that the Catholic-backed movement attempted to fashion a modern political identity for its constituents using the sacred authority of the church. We can see, at the close of the document cited above, evidence of this dual orientation.

Tenants!

The battle is over; but the organization work is not finished: from today it revives its energy, untiring! The organization will be on watch so that the agreements will be enforced; the organization will be studying further reforms which experience will prove to be necessary; the organization has to think, above all, of a great new task: to prepare you to manage the land independently, by yourselves; your education therefore, your association in institutions of cooperative and mutual help to make your work more productive. A vast field of action in which all your strengths concordant and useful have to be displayed. United by a single ideal and by brotherly agreement with the small proprietors, with other rural workers, tenants, forward!

Neither hate nor the spirit of oppression guides you. After the struggle, set free by the new system [law] for working the fields, you can, with dignity, stretch out your hand even to the landowner, so that he might know the needs of the new epoch and might recognize the Christian justice of work. Neither grim envy or the spirit of destruction stirs you, nor the insatiable desire for pleasure; honest field workers, frugal, laborious, join to the purpose of a better, more just economic order the tutelage of a sacred patrimony of faith and morality that bestows on your spirit what cannot come to you by mere material betterment.

Fieldworkers!

In these ideals is your radiant future!

Forward! (Quoted in Tessitori 1972: 294–95)

In the vibrant language of these last few passages, the traditional moral authority of the Friulian church was fused with an emergent political agenda to yield a new vision of rural society. However, this bold ideological synthesis proved surprisingly fragile and self-limiting, as the collapse of the reform movement suggests. While political leaders were preoccupied with bureaucratic matters, the countryfolk continued to adhere to their ancient and largely unquestioning identification with the church. For the majority of the rural people, political participation was framed not in the "phantom objectivity" of contractual reforms or political interests, but rather in the idiom of their Catholic faith. Clerical practice, ethnic sensibilities, sacred beliefs, rural fatalism and truculence contoured the cultural terrain on which political consciousness and Friulian identity collided.

Church and Identity

Friulian priests challenged the injustice that circumscribed the lives of the countryfolk and labored to protect the vulnerable rural populace. Yet as the individual priest tenaciously struggled to serve his congregation, he often found his moral commitments and practice subverted by the institutional entanglements of the church. In his daily rounds, the priest engaged the objective conditions of his parishioners through the layers of ancient ecclesiastical sensibility and dogma. In the baroque intricacies of the clerical role lay vestigial imperatives that often submerged the priest and his church in the rural status quo.

The clerical view of the rural populace was generally sympathetic. One priest portrayed the spiritual status of the countryfolk:

> Rural families are more open to the life of the church because they have greater ties with nature. They are less subject to [religious] crisis, and to modern cultural distraction. In other [urban] areas individuals are subject to physical and moral pollution. Those in the fields are closer to the natural world. [People in] the countryside have always been more sensitive to spiritual matters. Rural people are not contaminated.

This general view of their parishioners as childlike and innocent served as a forceful rationale for the paternalistic stance of the clergy. (It is interesting to contrast this contemporary clerical view of the spiritual purity of the Friulani with the earlier inquisitorial insistence that countryfolk were vulnerable to demonic power and influence [see Ginzburg 1966].) Because the priests were largely recruited from the rural districts of the region, they were acutely aware of the social problems facing their parishioners. "They had the smell of the fields in their blood. They felt the problems of the rural poor because they had lived through those [same] misfortunes with their own families." In the face of intense poverty and atomistic social relations, the Friulian clergy over the past two centuries developed a pastoral strategy designed to foster community integration, social welfare, and cultural integrity. In other words, the church was committed to shoring up the weaknesses and filling the voids that crosscut peasant-worker society. In the words of an elderly Communist party offical,

> There was nothing sociable and [virtually] no reciprocal [assistance] among tenant families. Only if a major problem occurred, like a cow died, they would give something, or if the house caught fire, they would help get the possessions out. They helped each other only under unusual circumstances, but not as a rule. Everyone minded his own business.

An old priest made a similar comment:

> The life of these people was asocial. . . . Everyone cared for his own family. Everyone worked hard and succumbed. A man did not care about his neighbor or anyone else. It was not a communal thing, because each [tenant] had a separate contract signed by the lord.

The chronic uncertainties and impotence of the Friulani were socially expressed in the hostility, distrust, and weak community integration that infused intraclass relations. The reified agrarian system that pitted tenant against tenant also defined a social arena in which the priests plied their trade. Another priest summarized the role of the Friulian church as follows:

> The church united the countryfolk. They prayed and listened to the sermon together. The church was a place of unity. The priest was the peacemaker in conflicts among contadini. They [the countryfolk] were very combative. Two disgraced men in poverty, instead of uniting, fought.

The Friulian church tempered the inequalities between rich and poor through various redistributive arrangements. These efforts provided a modest amelioration of the desperate material circumstances of the poor. The priest continued:

> Charity has always existed everywhere. Monsignor Liva [a famous local cleric] did not only provide spiritual comfort, but also material support. Now the state has taken over, [and] things are different. The parish was the center of everything. Festivals, lotteries for charity, when the state was not there everything came from the church. The church provided a primitive form of social security. There was no insurance for retirement or unemployment. . . . It

was a disaster! The church had a positive attitude toward these problems. . . . When the Church saw emptiness it felt the necessity to intervene.

The social pragmatism and discipline of the Friulian clergy has, since the end of Hapsburg rule, served as the central pillar of the church's authority and legitimacy in the rural districts of the region. This is complemented by unostentatious and flexible rituals that stress the familiar, as opposed to awe-inspiring, spiritual bond between the countryfolk and their church. Its most distinctive symbolic themes coalesce around the trustworthiness of the parish priest (Stern 1975: 234). Through clerical devotion to the indigenous language and fundamental elements of traditional cultural life, the church assumed the role of de facto guardian of Friulian ethnic identity. In the daily engagements of the parish priest—the celebration of mass, the orchestration of the Catholic ritual cycle, the sponsorship of festivals, the routines of confession, marriage, baptisms, and funerals—these commitments were affirmed and sanctified. The roles of educator, counselor, champion of regional dialect and ethnicity, broker of parish-based charity and mutual assistance and, above all, arbiter of local morality and social conduct, though hardly unique in the Catholic world, were cherished emphases of and sources of pride for the Friulian clergy.

Thus, the modern historical development of the Friulian church involved the assumption of specific roles and spheres of authority that supported its benevolent hegemony over rural society. Many of these were familiar roles and areas of religious responsibility, while others were unusual by Italian standards. Yet these domains of authority and parochial and secular power were not autonomous—they were, rather, the outcome of an invidious social system that created various acute human needs. As one priest noted: "When the church saw emptiness it felt the necessity to intervene." Yet the emptiness and human suffering against which the priests often courageously struggled, were reproduced through the workings of a rural society to which the clergy were wed. The operation of this rapacious system, controlled by powerful landowners, paradoxically underwrote the church's legitimacy. As practitioners of good, the priests were dependent on purveyors of evil. The direct financial dependence of the parish priest on local gentry contributed to clerical paralysis in the face of obvious and at times outrageous abuse. Again, to quote a priest:

On the social question regarding the relationship between proprietors and their workers the church was gagged [*imbavagliata*]. When the owners stumbled, the priest was pleased. The padrone had an infelicitous [*infelice*] influence. When ownership was fragmented there was more freedom, when it was concentrated there was less. This [latter] situation was very difficult for the priest. He whistled to himself [resisted passively]. . . . You cannot demand anything of don Abbondio [the weak priest in Manzoni]. With injustice not everyone is a fra' Cristoforo [the strong monk].

One modest case symbolized for local priests how the authority of the church was subservient to powerful landowners. Because of a long delay in the arrival of the count, a parish congregation and priest were forced to wait before commencing mass. The priest became increasingly enraged by the delay and finally rang the small bell that initiated the service. This apparently minor gesture was viewed as a significant act of protest, and was actively discussed among local clergy. A priest commented on the rules under the old rural order with the simple axiom, "He who pays commands."

Without question, the church-sponsored reform movement constituted a bold effort to break out of this malignant interdependence. Yet even as clerical elites struggled to redefine and politicize social conditions in the region, their coworkers in rural hamlets continued to frame their practices along ancient theological principles. On a number of occasions informants described how they sought help and counsel from their parish priests in dealing with specific cases of egregious mistreatment. Their despair was usually rejoined by their confessors with a stern insistence that it was not for the worker or tenant to protest God's plan, but to endure without question the conditions of their existence. It should be added that when priests became aware of misconduct by owners or overseers, they often instigated private remedies to relieve the abusive conditions or secure assistance for the victims. Nevertheless, the posture of the clergy on the parochial level was to demand from their parishioners unerring respect for both sacred and secular authority while holding out hope for transcendental redress of their miseries. For many parishioners, this theological stance provided an acceptable and meaningful response to their anguish.

Many of the fundamental premises of Catholic theology and Friulian clerical practice ran counter to the goals of the White Alliance, specifically to the emergence of a politicized populace. The legitimacy of the church has for centuries rested on the highly paternalistic and largely benevolent exercise of its social and ideological power. The formation of a fully politicized populace capable of independent distillation of common rights and interests, the framing of social and moral agendas, and the delineations of systematic programs of reform, directly undercut

the supreme clerical role, that of unchallenged interpreters and mediators of the earthly and supernatural realms. The political agitation,
much of which was orchestrated by the clergy, revealed precisely the
deep and abiding dependence of the church on the status quo from
which its authority curiously came. The politicizing of social conditions
in the region by diverse groups threatened to superannuate the clergy's
most prominent roles, spheres of responsibility, and sources of power.
In subsequent decades, particularly in the post–World War II era, with
the democratization of the judicial and political systems, the development of the welfare state, and the emergence of new arbiters of moral
and ethical values, the priestly roles were dramatically attenuated, and
their authority waned. Elderly priests look back ruefully on the vigorous
church which recruited and trained them. They proudly describe the
wide responsibilities they assumed and the skill and subtlety with which
they served their congregations. There are few figures in contemporary
Friulian society more intimately aware of the disenchantments of their
world.

Aftermath

Domenico F. (1876–1962), a tenant on the estate in Bottenicco, became
one of the most prominent leaders of the Tenant-Farmer and Sharecroppers' Federation in Friuli and was ultimately elected to the Provincial
Council as the representative of Cividale. Domenico was an arch rationalist in economic and political matters. Yet like the clergy with whom
he aligned himself, he was ensnared in traditionalist ties which frustrated the achievement of the ideals he publicly articulated so ardently.
I was introduced to Domenico through documents that I came across
accidently in the archives in Bottenicco. Specifically, a long letter from
Domenico to the count caught my attention. It alluded to the politics of
the early 1920s and portrayed social rifts within the estate. In the summer of 1985, I was able to locate a number of Domenico's close rela-
tives and interview them. This chapter concludes with a brief discussion
of Domenico F. in terms of the crosscurrents that buffeted his public
life, and his relations to his lord and his family during and immediately
after the reform struggle of 1919–1920.

Domenico was raised on the latifondo in Bottenicco, and much of his
political outlook and activism were derived from his experience as a
tenant. His son, now in his sixties, described his father's temperament
and political aspirations as follows:

> Domenico was a fanatic in three areas: religion, music, and poli-
> tics. So much so that he had to change residences from Bottenicco

to Moimacco and finally to Palmanova. Other tenants tried to make things difficult for him. Domenico had a strong feeling for justice. He made many speeches before the Provincial Council. He had a way of cutting into injustice. Because of his work the tenants on the estate [in Bottenicco] did not have to pay rents for the war years. The count had respect for him. Domenico was a fighter. He would go from door-to-door with the membership list [*tessera*] signing up members for the Partito popolare. He was very intelligent. He was a strong union leader. . . . . He was a fanatic about politics.

The son added an offhand comment on his father's vanity and poverty. ''At the first meeting of the Provincial Council [to which he was elected in 1922], Domenico was ashamed because he did not have the money to buy a necktie.''

Domenico, at a very early age, came under the tutelage of his count. The count recognized that Domenico had unusual potential and made a special effort to see to it that the young boy was taught to read and write. The count also tutored him in agricultural methods and encouraged Domenico to experiment with new farming techniques. Because of Domenico's warm patronal bond to his count, his relationships with other tenants and even with members of his own family were often frayed.

Domenico had three brothers—Giusto, Cesare, and Luigi. Luigi was the gastaldo of the estate. Domenico, Giusto, and Cesare cooperatively operated one of the large poderi. The domestic relations among these brothers and their wives were intricate. On the level of politics and economics, Domenico and Luigi were progressive, while Giusto and Cesare were conservative. Domenico's political activity was in fact deeply resented by Giusto and Cesare, who viewed it as detracting from his contribution to the work on their farmstead. With the collapse of the reform movement and the rise of fascism, their ridicule of Domenico's political involvements became increasingly bitter. Domenico also was the focus of political reprisals. He was once assaulted by small band of fascist thugs who roughed him up and forced him to swallow copious amounts of olive oil. The thugs claimed they had attacked Domenico only because they had failed to find the local priest. (Fascists generally drew their support from professionals, medium-sized landowners, government employees, the police, and the military in Cividale.)

The lengthy letter mentioned earlier from Domenico to the count detailed the domestic conflicts among the brothers and reflected on the turmoil that had followed the collapse of the reform movement. The handwritten letter, dated March 11, 1923, was ostensibly an apology for a misunderstanding that occurred between Domenico's wife and the count. It opens, "Most Illustrious Count. . . . First of all I would like to apologize if my wife was not able to explain to me clearly what you had told her the other night when you invited the three brothers to your palace." Domenico's wife had apparently represented him at a meeting with the count and Domenico's two siblings. For some unexplained reason, the wife misconstrued what had transpired at the meeting. The resulting misunderstanding was the pretext for the written apology. Domenico's absence was significant, in that we know that serious tensions existed between him and his brothers. Indeed, the meeting itself seems to have been called by the count to resolve the conflicts among them.

Domenico continues in the letter to make a broad apology as well as an oblique justification for his past political activity. "In my opinion, the cause of controversy in the Nation, as in families, must be blamed on the war and, for us Venetians on the invasion above all. . . . I admit my faults which were to have concerned myself too much with public matters; but my actions should not be totally ignored, if we think of 1920 . . . in those days spirits were still irritated." In this passage, Domenico recalls his activism and acknowledges that conflicts among the brothers stem, at least in part, from the postwar crisis. The letter becomes more specific, indicating that family tensions centered on efforts to rationalize the management of the tenant farm. As noted earlier, the war permitted a loosening of the rules that regulated agricultural operations on many of the large estates. The situation allowed for experimentation, particularly in terms of stimulating tenant cooperation and introducing new farming techniques in response to the acute labor shortages brought on by the war. The letter makes a number of direct references to conflicts over implementation of new agricultural techniques among the brothers. "If the brothers [Giusto and Cesare] would have been more grateful for my work during the war and, moreover, if they would have listened to me and used the experience which I had obtained during the war to advance agriculture, surely I would not have participated so much in public life."

The letter then goes into considerable detail regarding the problems caused for Domenico and his wife as a result of the cooperative relationship among the brothers.

The new regime in the family: Since 1919 the brothers have adopted a system whereby they divided the profits from tenant farming among themselves and all three worked outside the farm in order to provide for their individual [family] needs. As long as our parents lived, the provisioning of the household was the responsibility of our mother. She relied on the revenue from the sale of milk, vegetables, etc. [for household income]. After the passing of our parents, we sold the milk and crops wholesale. In this manner credits and debits were recorded revealing the economy of the household. But the brothers [Giusto and Cesare] thought the expenses were overstated, without thinking that the family had doubled in size and the profits from crops were reduced and vegetable marketing was disappearing. At that time my wife [who had taken over from Domenico's mother] did not know which way to turn to balance the budget. She was compelled to withdraw from the communal pantry. I wish to add that after ten years of oppressive misery [caused by the joint arrangement among the brothers] she is so exhausted that she cannot carry on anymore. She cannot even plan the provisioning of the household [from day to day or month to month].

Domenico stipulated his conditions for reentering a contractual relationship with his siblings.

I have no objection to reaching an agreement with the brothers, but the focal point of the agreement must be the intensification of agriculture through a rational method of working the land as it was done during the war and invasion, even if it means to join together many families. In those days the breaking up of grassland was done better than now, the manure was spread on top [to decompose] before plowing while nowadays we see the dung-heaps [standing like] mountains; the manure is carried to the fields even if wet.

Here Domenico becomes an unabashed advocate for modern techniques and the abandonment of traditional practices. Domenico arrogantly dismisses his brothers' conservatism: "It is sufficient to say that nobody wanted to listen to good [presumably rational] advice regarding business or work." He insists, as a stipulation for reentering the cooperative relationship, on a commitment from his brothers to adopt a scientific approach.

The missive ends graciously: "While thanking you for your concern, I send you my warmest thanks. Most faithfully, Domenico F." The tone of the entire letter reaffirms the strong affective bond between tenant and lord, one sustained by trust and loyalty. There is also a direct acknowledgment by the tenant of the lord's concern and interest regarding Domenico's family difficulties. One problem weighing on the mind of the count may have been the discipline of Giusto and Cesare, whose behavior had apparently become increasingly unruly. The attempt to recruit Domenico into a cooperative arrangement with his brothers was perhaps aimed at restoring stability among the tenants by inserting a trusted client of the count.

Within a few months, however, Domenico had decided to move his family to a new podere in Moimacco, indicating that an agreement among the brothers could not be worked out even with the intervention of the count. At about the same time, Luigi's wife became involved in a serious scandal. It was alleged that she had been pilfering the count's wine cellar and larder and selling the goods, in league with an army officer, to soldiers in Cividale. When the count discovered the theft, he ordered Luigi off the estate in twenty-four hours. Ironically, Giusto and Cesare were initially able to weather the departure of their two progressive siblings.

A final postscript to the episode appeared just over three years after Domenico's letter was drafted. It came in the form of a legal notice from the clerk of the pretura, evicting the two remaining siblings. The fates of Giusto and Cesare and their families were thus sealed. For reasons not made explicit in the archives, the brothers were evicted, ending a family tenure of more than four decades. The count was not directly involved in the legal proceedings; in fact, the legal papers show that he was not even in residence on the estate at the time of the termination. The eviction was requested and carried out by a lawyer in Cividale under a "power of attorney" granted by the nobleman. The eviction was impersonally handled through legal instruments and by professional middlemen. There is not a trace of any personal tie between tenants and lord. Indeed, in this finale, the roles of the lord and tenant are represented as mere legal abstractions, the "plaintiff" and the "defendants."

The contradictions in Domenico F.'s life were manifold, similar to those that beset his clerical counterparts. Here we have the political activist, a staunch advocate of workers' rights, who was at the same time bound to a highly developed patronal relationship with his count. Indeed, Domenico's literacy and rationalist sensibilities were imparted at the knee of his overlord. His public role and patronal tie further complicated Domenico's domestic relationships by inserting new bases of strife and conflict. He became profoundly alienated from his conservative brothers who were deeply suspicious of Domenico's outlook and aspirations. Ultimately, Domenico could not sustain the deep contradictions that assaulted his public and private identities. He removed himself from public life, severed his tie with his count, and retreated to another farmstead in an adjacent hamlet.

PEASANT-WORKER politics are rooted in a cultural terrain. In Friuli, it is an ancient terrain on which the countryfolk have drawn their livelihood, forged their social relations, and crafted their supernatural ideas and sacred practices for a millennium. The political experience of peasant-workers is difficult to abstract. It is expressed most frequently, to use Marc Bloch's phrase, in a "mentality attached to things tangible and local." The clergy, who have a long history of traversing this landscape and probing its dark intrigues, inspired a movement to redefine the assumptions underpinning rural society in the early decades of the twentieth century. Clerical activists and their allies formulated a robust political program that introduced new moral principles and accounting requirements into the regulation of rural social relations and agrarian production. The program was supremely rational. Armed with their disenchanted agenda, these political elites achieved a stunning mobilization of the countryfolk in the midst of an enveloping national crisis. Though they mobilized their constituents, they did not politicize them. The rational discourse that dominated the public sphere could not penetrate the strata upon strata of traditional sensibilities that preoccupied the rural populace. Many aspects of these traditional broodings were, ironically, ecclesiastical inventions nurtured for centuries by clerical practice.

Elements of Folk Consciousness

THE CHURCH of San Francesco is a formidable structure. Next to the Duomo, it is the largest religious edifice in Cividale. Its substantial thirteenth-century exterior walls and tower survey the deep abyss through which the cold waters of the Natisone run. The graceless facade of the church faces a vacant piazza just behind the communal post office, where scores of stray cats inhabit the ancient masonry and scavenge the plastic garbage bags of nearby residences. Four centuries ago, a fearsome clash of religious idioms began here, incited by local representatives of the Inquisition. In the course of more than eight hundred heretical inquiries, masterful inquisitors and forlorn peasants became involved in an extraordinary interchange that continues, albeit in a different form, to be played out in the Friulian countryside to this day.

This chapter opens with a short recapitulation of the history of the agrarian cults which the Inquisition in Friuli so vigorously suppressed.

Fig. 12. The church of San Francesco, site of the heretical inquiries in Cividale.

The well-known work of Carlo Ginzburg (1966, 1983), on which this introduction is based, depicts the intricate clash between Friulian folk beliefs and Catholic dogma (see Eliade 1976: 69–92).[1] The main focus of the chapter is, however, the contemporary supernatural beliefs of the Friulani, many of which appropriate the same metaphors as the agrarian cults of their ancestors, and the relationship of these beliefs to contemporary Catholic theology and practice. Though this discussion can stand alone, it also has significance for the portrayal of peasant-worker life. It is the tenacious hold of a folk consciousness—which continues to mediate the experience of the modern world—that is the essence of the peasant-worker's cultural stance. This chapter traces the development of an intriguing aspect of folk belief, the projection by the Friulani of their existential dilemmas and economic vulnerabilities onto the clash of good and evil spirits. It also lays the groundwork for related theoretical questions to be explored in chapter 7. These questions address how Friulian folk consciousness infused the life in the silk mill of Rubignacco.

I Benandanti

From the record of the early inquisitorial trials, the elements of a popular tradition that was pervasive in the rural districts around Cividale during the sixteenth century can be reconstructed. At the center of this tradition were beliefs in heroic battles, fought by countrymen—benandanti—armed with fennel, to protect their crops from harm by malevolent spirits armed with sorghum. Adult males who had been born with a caul set out at specified times of the agrarian calendar, the Ember Days, to fight off these witches and warlocks who threatened the harvest and thus the economic security of the countryfolk. The imaginative substance of this "agrarian cult" linked adherents in a shared representation of the supernatural world, one which the participants viewed as not incompatible with their Catholic faith. A fairly detailed, though not totally consistent, description of the enchanted pursuits of the benandanti emerged from the testimony of one of the first witnesses (Battista Moduco) brought before the inquisitors in Cividale:

> I am a benandante because I go with the others to fight four times a year, that is during the Ember Days, at night; I go invisibly in spirit and the body remains behind; we go forth in the service of Christ, and the witches of the devil; we fight each other, we with bundles of fennel and they with sorghum stalks. . . . And if we are the victors, that year there is abundance, but if we lose there is

famine. . . . In the fighting that we do, one time we fight over the wheat and all the other grains, another time over the livestock, and at other times over the vineyards. And so, on four occasions we fight over all the fruits of the earth and for those things won by the benandanti that year there is abundance. (Quoted in Ginzburg 1983: 6)

The cultural symbols and motifs at the core of this folk tradition permitted personal interpretation and embellishment. For example, one witness (Paolo Gasparutto) conjured an angelic captain who led the benandanti in battle. The plasticity of popular beliefs and the freedom allowed for spontaneous interpretation and reinterpretation at first confounded the inquisitorial court (see Le Roy Ladurie 1979: 288–99). With each witness there emerged a new and slightly reworked portrayal of the cult. Precisely because the cult's form and definition slipped so easily from the inquisitors' grasp, their prosecutorial logic suspected these beliefs were inherently diabolical. In the uninhibited religiosity of the early benandanti and the immediacy of their supernatural experiences, the priests saw heretical motives. Unwittingly, the countryfolk stumbled into perhaps the most central, and from the standpoint of the church, the most untenable, theological thrust of the Reformation. In their naive espousal of a direct relationship with the supernatural—unmediated by the church—the benandanti came dangerously close to the "errors" of Lutheranism.

Shamanistic practices were also widespread in sixteenth-century Friuli, and were loosely tied to the magical motifs of the benandanti. The shamanistic role was usually filled by women who sometimes referred to themselves as benandanti, and who specialized in divining the status and wishes of deceased loved ones and administering traditional cures to the ill. They also provided advice and counsel for those with problems revolving around family relations, romance, and money. For these more or less classic shamanistic services, these women received a modest fee ["five *soldi*, sometimes a mouthful of bread"]; sometimes they performed these rituals merely to gain some local notoriety among their neighbors and friends (Ginzburg 1983: 35). These women—like their male counterparts—took pride "in their role as defenders of the community against evil forces that threatened it; they were not witches, and it was not even conceivable that their good works would be persecuted by the inquisitors" (64). Nonetheless, it is not hard to see the ease with which the inquisitors were able to incorporate the shamanistic roles of these women into the broader diabolical picture they had developed of the benandanti, and thus prosecute these women on the same heretical premises (see Le Roy Ladurie 1979: 342–56).

Inquisitors managed to read demonic meaning into the testimony of hapless countryfolk by adapting the accounts of the benandanti to formal theological preconceptions: ''The meeting of the benandanti and of witches were nothing but the sabbat, and the 'company' of benandanti which falsely proclaimed that it enjoyed divine protection and fought under the guidance and aegis of an angel was diabolical'' (Ginzburg 1983: 11). In the bewildered testimony of the peasant can be discerned a loosely systematized world view—one infused with magical content (Ginzburg 1980; Schluchter 1979: 28; Weber 1951: 226). By contrast, in the priest's self-assured cross-examination one can discern a systematic and categorical metaphysic in which the supernatural realm has been dogmatized. Thus, disenchantment by the Inquisition did not entail an extirpation of magical content, but rather the imposition of an approved formula by which ritual and belief could be incorporated into Catholic natural and supernatural domains.

The clash between the refined and codified ecclesiastic dogma of the Inquisition and the symbolic vitality of the Friulian folk religion was distilled in the verdict against one early benandante, Paolo Gasparutto. Again, the court's decision revealed two divergent metaphysics, one ruled by an extreme—one might say remorseless—formalism, and one ruled, as Max Weber puts it, by a ''mystical but inwardly genuine plasticity'' (Weber 1946: 148). Gasparutto's case was brought to a close on Sunday, November 26, 1581, before a ''large multitude,'' as previously, in the ''venerable church of the convent of San Francesco in the city of Cividale by the altar of St. Anthony'' (Ginzburg 1983: 167).

> For ten continuous years you abided among witches, called by you benandanti, believed in your heart, and time and again confirmed with your mouth that this was one of God's works. Indeed, most execrable of all, you affirmed and firmly believed and said that whoever went against this sect acted against the will of God. Moreover, you confessed to us out of your own mouth that when you were twenty-eight, during the Ember Days in the month of December, in the night following Thursday at about the fourth hour, a devil appeared before you in the form of an angel who called you by your own name and said: ''Paolo, you must go to fight for and sustain the crops against the witches.'' You promised him to go and the angel promised to send you a man of Vicenza who would summon you and lead you. And he came precisely in the month of December, on a Thursday, at the fourth hour of the night, and

spoke to you, saying: "The captain calls you forth to battle." Thus, repeatedly, you went to these diabolical pastimes, led by the devil and by the captain from Verona, and gave yourself over to these works. And what is impious and most execrable, you committed idolatry every time you attended a spectacle of this kind and adored the aforesaid evil angel in the same way that our Lord Jesus Christ must and ought to be adored in churches and other places. (Quoted in Ginzburg 1983: 168)

The mysterious benandanti were formally translated by the court into witches. This simple legal transformation of members of the agrarian cult into diabolical figures permitted all of their activities to be scrutinized within the schema of demonological scholarship and the relevant canon law. The court forcefully rejected the syncretism at the heart of the benandanti's work. The claim that the profession of the benandanti was performed in the holy name of God was in itself a transparent heresy.

The sentence against the benedanti further reveals the church's strategy for eradicating any vestige of folk religion in the countryside. It also presents the formula for the reincorporation of the threatened heretical soul of Gasparutto into the protection and mercy of Holy Mother Church. Gasparutto was required publicly to "abjure, revoke, detest, and disown" all the heresies which the court had defined. Again, these included his ten-year membership in the benandanti, his participation in their spectacles, his recruitment of others into the cult, and his false belief that the benandanti were doing the work of God. The court required Gasparutto to confess that the adoration he paid the angelic leader of the benandanti was in error, as were his notions that souls could leave bodies. He was also compelled explicitly to equate benandanti with witches and swear that any new knowledge brought to his attention about these illicit matters would be reported immediately to the inquisitor.

The punishment phase of the sentence included five particulars: (1) six months in prison; (2) fasting and prayers of forgiveness every Friday of the Ember Days for the two following years; (3) confession and partaking of the Eucharist at the Resurrection, at the Assumption of the Blessed Virgin Mary, and at Nativity, for a five-year period; (4) sending his caul and the cauls of his children to the Holy Office of the Inquisition; and (5) "in the Rogation processions before the Ascension of our Lord, it will be prohibited to you and to your domestics to carry viburnum [fennel] branches, nor are you to keep said viburnum in any form in your home" (Ginzburg 1983: 170).

The sentence deprived the former benandante of the cauls and the fennel that were the basic paraphernalia of the cult. It also required Gasparutto to perform Catholic rituals at precisely the times that the benandanti were traditionally active. This penance was intended not only to secure forgiveness for past infractions, but also to restore the primacy of the church's ritual cycle in the countryside. The fifth part of the court's sentence is the most explicit on this score. If the primary function of the benandanti was the ritual protection of the harvest, then they were directly in competition with the church's fertility ritual of Rogation, at which time the priests blessed the fields and the coming harvest (Ginzburg 1983: 23). Thus, by compelling Gasparutto to participate in the Rogation processions without the fennel weapons of the benandanti, the church forced him to submit to its exclusive power over the supernatural realm.

These first encounters between the inquisitorial court and the benandanti of Cividale represented more than merely a trying personal experience for the defendants; they commenced a wider interaction between the popular folk consciousness of the countryside and the codified dogma and bureaucratic rigidities of the church, which was in the throes of a counterreformation preoccupied with fending off subversive ideas that might cross the Alps and threaten its dominion. The sentencing of the two benandanti was an important public event witnessed by a "great multitude," and the proceedings were widely discussed throughout the urban and rural districts of Cividale in sermons of parish priests and, no doubt, in informal gatherings on street corners, and in shops, peasant farmsteads, and middle-class villas. As the trials and inquiries proliferated over the next half-century, the cultural encounter gained a historical momentum and an intricate dialectical character. The result was the gradual disenchantment of popular beliefs and an increasing consciousness by the countryfolk of the abstract concept with which the church defined and regulated both sacred and diabolical ideas. Ginzburg's study brilliantly depicts this reformulation of rural consciousness through the testimony of the poor souls dragged before the ecclesiastical courts of Friuli. The case of a benandante from Moimacco marked a crucial turning point in this disenchantment and reformulation of folk beliefs, and the specifics of this case against Giovanni Sion will be briefly examined below.

Assimilation of the Diabolical

In April 1623, forty-seven years after the first inquiries into Paolo Gasparutto's peculiar activities, the case of Giovanni Sion was brought to the attention of the local inquisitor. This young peasant from Moimacco was working as a servant in the household of a noble family in Cividale and, to relieve himself of the guilt and remorse he was apparently experiencing, confessed his participation in the secret spectacles of the benandanti.

In Sion's initial interrogation on April 29, a surprising revision of the earlier picture of the benandanti and their practices emerged. Giovanni Sion testified that three years earlier on a Thursday during the Ember season of Christmas, he was visited by another servant from Moimacco, Gerolamo of Villalta, who offered to take him to a place where he would be given money and jewelry and "see and enjoy many beautiful things" (Ginzburg 1983: 108). Giovanni quickly agreed to go. Gerolamo stripped and anointed himself with an ointment, and to Giovanni's astonishment "a lion appeared and Gerolamo mounted it." Giovanni also clambered aboard the beast and "in a wink of an eye" they found themselves at a place called Picenale in the midst of an orgy. "There we saw many people come together, who were dancing and sporting about, gorging themselves with food and drink, and who threw themselves on beds and publicly committed many dishonorable acts" (quoted in Ginzburg 1983: 108). Sion insisted that he refused intimacy with the witches and declined to accept their dazzling gifts of gold and silver: "I always stayed apart with six in my company called benandanti" (108). He also claimed that these were "real" celebrations, and not dreams or illusions as other benandanti had portrayed their nocturnal "profession" (109–10).

Subsequent interrogations of Sion in August of the same year further revealed "a popular equivalent to the image of the diabolical sabbat which for decades inquisitors had tried in vain to impose" (107–8). The following account, presented at the inquisitorial court in Cividale by the would-be benandante, indicates the degree to which the assimilation of formal "diabolical" elements into traditional folk religion had taken place.

> I arrived at a beautiful palace and was led to a hall by the above-named Gerolamo. At the head of this room sat the devil, dressed as a captain with a black hat and red plume, a black shock of hair and a black forked beard shaped like twin horns; on his head were two horns similar to a goat's and his feet were the hooves of an ass, and he held a fork in his hand. I was immediately instructed by Gerolamo that I should reverence him, as I did, by moving only my feet, as we do for the Most Holy Sacrament. (Quoted in Ginzburg 1983: 111)

Earlier, Giovanni Sion had briefly been held in custody at a convent, during which time he was carefully examined by don Pietro Martire da Verona, the priest who had originally heard Giovanni's unusual confession. The priest noted in a letter to a colleague:

> We tested him quite thoroughly here in the monastery the last few days . . . and during this time he made many willing efforts; and it amazes me more and more how the things which he says occurred resemble what is in the books. He does not omit anything, and what he tells once he tells unchanged all the other times. (Quoted in Ginzburg 1983: 110)

Clerical specialists had finally achieved what they had long sought. The popular beliefs of the benandanti, as the case of Giovanni Sion and subsequent cases for the next quarter-century demonstrate, finally converged with the ecclesiastical codes which defined the borders of the sacred and diabolical universes. The supreme irony is that priestly efforts had instilled in the culture of the countryfolk precisely the symbols and motifs they had sought to eliminate from rural consciousness. The church's institutional formulation of witchcraft had made its way from the learned texts and treatises of demonological scholars, through the legal procedures of the inquisitional courts, into the cultural imagination of the peasantry. Simultaneously, the autonomous Friulian myth of the benandanti became deracinated from its organic context and distorted to the point that it lost virtually all its cultural integrity. The term "benandanti," which the inquisitors never seem fully to have understood, had by the mid-seventeenth century lost much of its hold on the countryfolk. The meaning of "benandanti" had become remote and elusive even to the heirs of the myth, who continued—though with declining frequency and urgency—to be harassed by the Holy Office. In the person of Giovanni Sion, the inquisitors had found their first rustic accomplice, if not ally, in disenchantment.

The strange work of the Inquisition in and around Cividale had nonetheless accomplished critical changes, both intended and inadvertent, in the lives of the countryfolk. The inquiries of the Holy Office marked the intrusion of a cultural logic that not only subdued the mysterious benandanti, but began a disenchantment of popular folk belief and tradition in general. The legal-bureaucratic procedures of the inquisitorial courts served as a medium to scrutinize and transform the magical world of the Friulani. At the core of this disenchantment was an assault on the unity of event and meaning which imposed a tension-ridden dualism in rural consciousness (Schluchter 1979: 28). The routines and experience of country life were divorced from an indigenous "natural philosophy" and cosmology. The intellectualized doctrines of the church, in Weber's words, eroded the "primeval immediacy of man's relation to the world." Yet the work of the Holy Office had not eliminated notions of witchcraft from the minds of the countryfolk; far from it. Rather, the work of the Inquisition fashioned an unlikely synthesis of folk beliefs and "superstitions" of the Friulani and formal Catholic dogma (see Ginzburg 1980; Ciceri 1983: 319–410; Le Roy Ladurie 1979: 296–99). Although the inquisitorial trials of the sixteenth and seventeenth centuries might form the most dramatic episodes of Friulian folk religion, of at least equal theoretical importance is the subsequent history of these cultural ideas and beliefs, a history that extends into this century.

Contemporary Folk Beliefs

Ginzburg implies—in references to the trial of Giovanni Sion—that by the seventeenth century, the traditional concept of the benandanti had been weakened, if not lost, and trial records certainly seem to support this conclusion. In the summer of 1985, I began to inquire in Cividale whether or not any vestigial notions of the benandanti still existed. What I found surprised me. I began with a local folklorist who remembered his "peasant" mother telling him stories of the "*benandans*" or "*belandans*"—Friulian equivalents of "benandanti." It is interesting to note that the second term, belandans, adds the idea of beautiful witches to the notion of good witches (see Ginzburg 1983: 100). The folklorist had read *I Benandanti*, and he assured me that the benandans and belandans that his mother had described fit Ginzburg's depiction closely. In a second interview—conducted, ironically, in the residence (*canonica*) of the Church of San Francesco, the seat of the Inquisition in Cividale four centuries earlier—an elderly monsignor confirmed that he had encountered widespread belief in the benandans among his Friulian-speaking parishioners years earlier. He further indicated that among the Slavic-speaking parishioners with whom he had worked more recently, the ideas of the benandans continued to exist, and that there was even a Slavic variant of the term, "*Kerstniki*" (Ginzburg 1983: 195). From these preliminary inquiries I went on to interview residents, often very elderly, of rural hamlets around Cividale concerning their folk beliefs. The remainder of this chapter is devoted to the nature of these folk beliefs and their peculiar relationship to contemporary Catholic doctrine and practice (see Ciceri 1983: 319–573).

There continues to be substantial reluctance to discuss folk beliefs, particularly regarding witches. For instance, one informant whom I have known for seven years, a woman in her mid-eighties, denied fif-

teen times during the first five minutes of a taped interview any knowledge of witchcraft. "No, no, never, never, we [Rubignacchesi] are not
stupid. It is ignorance that creates such ideas." Within thirty minutes
the same informant began to provide a rich portrait of folk beliefs in
witchcraft that existed in the hamlet. By the end of the interview she
offered to take me to meet an elderly male acquaintance of hers who
still harbors strong beliefs in the traditional supernatural world.

What emerged from the interviews in Rubignacco and other rural
hamlets was evidence of a pervasive—if not obsessive—fear of witchcraft that engulfed eastern Friuli prior to World War II. "There are still
people who believe in witches, not many. Forty years ago almost everyone, especially women, believed in them," said one informant. The
basic elements of this folklore embraced witches, magicians, the evil
eye (*malvoli*), supernatural beasts and the like (see Ciceri 1983: 255–
317). Arrayed against these malevolent elements were benandans or
good witches ("*stregoni buoni*"), the power of the Church to bless and
protect individuals, and a wide variety of folk practices for identifying
witches and warding off curses. All these elements were incorporated
in tales and fables that were regularly recounted in gatherings of adults
and children, to entertain the former and frighten the latter (see Ostermann 1940). Yet there is no doubt that the day-to-day significance of
these beliefs was not in the realm of entertainment or mere diversion,
but as expressions of deep-seated anguish and despair that gripped the
poorest strata of Friulian society.

Virtually every productive and reproductive activity in the countryside was seen as vulnerable to the foul play of witchcraft. As they had
in the Middle Ages, countryfolk believed witches capable of threatening
the harvest, domestic animals, love, marriage, and the health of family
members (see Facchin 1985: 95–103). The unexplained death of a cock
or calf, a destructive hailstorm (particularly one that laid waste one
peasant's field while leaving adjacent fields untouched), the sudden illness or death of a child, a young wife's infertility—all were blamed on
the activities of local witches (see Evans-Pritchard 1976: 18–32). Witch
accusations were typically, though not exclusively, made against
women who were in some way eccentric or physically unattractive.
Usually these women were old, were unmarried or widowed, and lived
alone. Their curses were thought to be transmitted by way of the evil
eye or through mysterious poisons or spells. Suspicions of witchcraft
were by no means limited to these classic victims, women living on the
fringes of the community. What is perhaps most disturbing about the
character of witchcraft around Cividale was the sheer number of witch
accusations among neighbors, friends, and acquaintances, both male

and female. Very routine occurrences ranging from the death of a piglet to a minor domestic squabble could be blamed on a neighbor who happened to visit on the same day or on a friend who cast an oblique glance as she passed a family member in the street (see Dionisopoulos-Mass 1976; Garrison and Arensberg 1976; Gilmore 1987; Herzfield 1981; Maloney 1976; Moss and Cappannari 1976).

Fear, suspicion, jealousy, guilt, and envy found substance and form in the realm of witchcraft. The following case demonstrates how supernatural explanations were woven through the details of a family tragedy. A ninety-year-old woman provided an explanation of her mother's death in 1899 using this folk nexus. The story involves a curse or spell cast on the mother, who was at the time in her early thirties, and the family's attempt to enlist the help of a shaman, referred to by the informant as a ''doctor,'' to save the dying woman.

> My mother died at the age of thirty-three. She was beautiful and gracious. Everyone wanted to marry her. She could have chosen among a throng of men who wanted to marry her. One day she went to the the Church of the Madonna delle Gracia in Udine for mass and on the steps of the church she met her former suitors. They told her that even after four children she was as beautiful as ever. The men claimed she had broken their hearts by not marrying them. They insisted that she and a [female] friend go with them and have a drink. She answered ''No, I have to go to mass.'' She refused five or six times before relenting and going with the men to the bar and having a drink. After taking some wine she thanked the men and returned home. That evening she ate her meal and began to vomit. From that time onwards she could not eat without having serious problems. Seven or eight months later she died. They [the suitors] had put something in the wine to curse her and so she died. I cannot forget how my father told me about it. My mother was incredibly beautiful. My father did everything. He brought her to all the [medical] doctors. Finally he took her to a ''doctor'' up in the mountains. He had a reputation as a good doctor. He said that my mother's blood was poisoned and that she should have been brought [to him] sooner. Shortly thereafter she died. Two or three days before her passing family members heard an owl shout ''death to her, death to her'' [''Crep, Crep'']. The owl brings death.

The message of the vignette is simple. The beautiful mother is lured by jilted suitors away from mass and the protective power of the church. She is cursed by a poisoned drink of wine from which neither medical doctors nor the belated intervention of a shaman can save her. Her doom is finally sounded by an owl's doleful cry. In this manner, the premature death of the beautiful mother is shrouded in a supernatural explanation that provides meaning for her loved ones, a meaning that transcends the inexplicable existential reality.

Various procedures were employed to identify witches. Most were quite simple, though each permitted great latitude for interpretation. "If some animal dies in my house and you happen to be there I would start to have suspicions. I would ask in the village if anyone had heard of similar things. If they had heard such things, that is how a witch was born." "Witches could be recognized because they let some word slip. Like she would take a child in her arms and say, 'Let us hope that he will grow well,' and if something happened to the child, she was obviously a witch." Suspicions also could be aroused by those who pried into other people's business or, in the case of women, by merely wandering outside unattended after the Ave Maria had tolled. More elaborate divinations were also performed.

> When a person was sick we would carefully remove their pillow. We would open the pillow and examine the feathers. If we found the feathers in small bundles in the shape of a crown or in the shape of a coffin, the sick person had been cursed by a witch. We would go to the priest and ask for a benediction and then burn the feathers at a cross-road. . . . I heard once about a guy who was sick. They took his pillow and some woman suggested that they burn the feathers in a different way. The woman said that the feathers should be put in a pot without water and heated from below. They did this and suddenly a woman knocked at the door crying "Please stop it, please stop it, I cannot bear it anymore, I am burning." She lifted her skirt and showed them that her lower legs were burned—she was certainly a witch.

To protect oneself from witchcraft, one carefully shunned the suspected witch—"people did not meet them happily"—and quickly had the priest bless any animal, person, or thing that came in contact with or even within sight of the witch. The classic gesture of inserting the thumb between the index and middle fingers was used to ward off curses and the evil eye. Crossed brooms hung on a door or against the side of a house were also used to scare away witches. One informant described a more direct method. "When you realized that a witch had done something evil to you, you would go to her house with wood sticks and threaten to beat her up unless she removed the curse."

Shamans were also employed to ward off witchery and misfortune in a way that is reminiscent of the benandanti described by Ginzburg. In one instance, a family with a herd of cows and a mill consulted a "good witch" (*stregone buono*) when their cattle became ill. The shaman carefully inspected the stalls where the cattle were kept. He informed the family that the large spikes to which the cows were tethered had been cursed and must be removed. The spikes were removed, and the cattle were cured. Shamans also filled the role of traditional healers, using charms and herbal treatments that are very similar—if not identical—to those prescribed by Gasparutto and his contemporaries. In Slavic-speaking areas there were women known as *zahovarja tohude*, "she who scares away evil." These women from time to time received limited acceptance from the local Catholic clergy, who viewed them as exceptionally religious ("charismatic") parishioners. One of the most important rituals performed by the zahovarja tohude was to pray intensely while barefoot in the open fields just before the commencement of the harvest. Their prayers were directed at preventing snakebites to which field hands are extremely vulnerable. In addition, in the event of a snakebite these women prayed over the wound and were said, even by a priest who observed one of these procedures, to reduce the swelling and neutralize the effects of the poison.

Thus, many of the roles filled by the benandanti were, until quite recently, extant in the areas around Cividale, even though a unified view of the ancient agrarian cult and its "night battles" appears to have been extinguished. Specifically, the notion of "good witches" persisted despite the fact that the terms benandans and belandans were, at best, poorly understood. The most perplexing change came not in the definition or practice of the benandanti, but in the relationship of the Church to the enduring folk beliefs.

The Parasitic Equation

The church, in the period after the Inquisition, had managed to insert its specialists in the roles once filled by the benandanti. A middle-aged man gave a brief account which closely approximated the folklore of the benandanti as an organized agrarian cult. "There was talk about a fellow who during thunderstorms saw the benandans ascending into the sky and fighting with warlocks [to protect the crops]." A more common reworking of the tale was related to me by an elderly woman. In this account, a peasant actually chastises the priest and orders him to assume the role of the benandans.

I remember a peasant man who met the old parish priest after a storm and said to him, "Signor priest, where were you during the thunderstorm? Isn't it your duty to prevent storms?'' and he answered [incredulously], ''I should prevent them?'' During the thunderstorms the witches would unchain themselves. Two rose from under the bridge in Premariacco, two from under the bridge in Orsaria, and four from under the Devil's Bridge in Cividale. And the peasant responded to the priest, ''It is your duty to prevent this!'' The old priest thus began the custom, every time a thunderstorm threatened, of opening his window and lighting a candle on the sill and praying with breviary in his hand, and the storms would immediately vanish.

In yet another case, an old woman made the substitution even more directly. ''No, we had no figures like the benandans. We went to the priest. We brought our shirts to be blessed. The grain we fed the chickens was blessed. The livestock and all the crops we had blessed.''

The assumption by the clergy of the role once filled by the benandans—the role of protector of the countryfolk from misfortunes and malevolent influences—rather than eradicating the folk beliefs, thrust the church into a parasitic relationship with the traditional Friulian view of the supernatural world. By assuming the role of the ''good witches'' the clergy became ensnared, albeit inadvertently, in precisely those traditional beliefs about good and evil that had sustained the benandans. This ongoing interplay between orthodox Catholicism and Friulian folk beliefs was not merely a matter of subtle ideological deviance or quirkiness; on the contrary, it had very real and disturbing consequences in the daily lives of the countryfolk.

Catholic theology embraces various representations of evil. In the words of a priest who specialized in local folk beliefs:

It [superstition] is a product of man's mentality. It is a natural instinct to believe in the supernatural. Since the supernatural is a part of the Christian Revelation, that is what Christ revealed and what God revealed in the Bible. [The church] says that God exists, that bad spirits exist, and good spirits exist. From this the simple people draw their ideas. We have in the gospel that there are evil spirits who occupy the body of some person or these bad spirits bring illness. . . . Religion says that there is one God, that God has angels and, unfortunately, one group of those angels rebelled and became evil. These devils are real beings who with the permission of God continue to harm the human species. They harm humanity in two ways, a spiritual way, because they teach men to do morally corrupt things, they [also] hurt men physically. This is the truth, this is the truth. It is true that there exist bad spiritual beings that we call devils.

The spiritual conflict of the Friulian countryfolk resulted from the church's rejection of the folk representations of evil. These beliefs are, in Catholic orthodoxy, no longer relegated to the realm of heresy, but merely to the realm of "superstition." For understandable reasons, the countryfolk did not make a fine distinction between orthodox and folk representations of malevolence. The outcome of these divergent cultural interpretations is an intriguing ideological interdependence in which the countryfolk and clergy inadvertently support each other's religious ideas.

Jeanne Favret-Saada (1980) has recently characterized the contemporary priestly dilemmas vis-à-vis witchcraft in the French Bocage. Her insights are applicable to the equivocal position of the Friulian clergy:

> Faced with a bewitched, one can imagine that the priest is in a more awkward situation than the doctor (psychiatrist), for evil, misfortune and the supernatural mean something to him. But what they mean has become singularly blurred by many centuries of theological brooding. The dividing line between the ranges of the natural and supernatural has been fixed by Catholic orthodoxy; but the reasons given have scarcely been assimilated, especially since each late pronouncement does not categorically cancel former ones. (1980: 6)

A local Friulian priest was asked how the Church eradicates superstition, and his answer reveals the interweaving of the two belief systems from the Catholic viewpoint.

> It is still a difficult task because the human being exaggerates and these exaggerations originated in the fact that the supernatural does exist. If the supernatural did not exist, that is to say, if the church said we are only human beings and nothing happens after death, we would not have any superstitions. Superstition is a collateral of faith. Superstition is an exaggeration of faith.

As a practical matter, the clergy have a very difficult time dealing unambiguously with witchcraft and other folk beliefs. In response to the hypothetical question, "What would you do if a parishioner brought a child to be blessed against witchcraft?" the priest answered as follows:

> I would answer, "Do not believe in witches!" But let's be clear, there exist people who can harm us with the help of the devil. Like the devil himself can harm us. Actually, actually, we have to say that what we call witches could exist and sorcerers [*maghi*] could also exist, that is men who do bad things. . . . That evil spirits do

exist and that they use men and women to do bad things is a truth that cannot be denied.

This theological equivocality was most prominent in the arena of church ritual. When asked what the church blesses, the priest answered, "People, animals, objects, clothes, land, seeds, harvests, woodlands, fields, everything, everything" (see Favret-Saada 1980: 7). "During Rogation, God is invoked so that he keeps storms away and protects the crops." It is not surprising that the countryfolk interpreted these rituals as protection not from abstract malevolent forces, but from what they believed to be real living and breathing personifications of evil— witches. Though they found it difficult to admit openly, there is little doubt that the clergy knew exactly how the rural folk viewed the benedictions they sought from the church, as revealed by the following rather comical incident that occurred in the early 1970s. A young priest newly arrived in the diocese was asked by a peasant to bless his rabbits. When the priest accidentally discovered that the purpose of the blessing was to protect the animals from witches, the young cleric expressed his outrage before a group of surprised parishioners. To quell the uproar, an elderly priest was quickly brought on the scene to bless the rabbits as the young priest was led away, doubtless to be familiarized with the local theological ropes. A more typical clerical response to these conflicting interpretations was revealed in a brief interchange between a priest and a particularly audacious informant. The informant asked if there really were witches and if the benedictions provided any protection. The priest answered her with a refined circularity: "Were it not for the persecution of evil spirits, there would not be blessings."

The perverse elements of this local clerical ritual industry, based on a tacit cultural misunderstanding, breathed life into folk fears of witches. Virtually every valued animate or inanimate object vulnerable to calamity or misfortune of any sort was brought by the Friulani to their church for its repeated and ambiguous benedictions. The same Holy Mother Church that had chastised Gasparutto four centuries earlier for having his caul blessed nine times, continued to offer, usually for a small fee, ritual protection for maize, silkworms, grapevines, chestnut trees, cows, chickens, picks, plows, cattle stalls, dwellings, linen, sick children, sore backs, and perhaps even a caul or two against ill-defined forms of evil that threatened humanity. Since the Inquisition, the tables had turned. The inquisitors believed they knew, if nothing else, what evil was and how it operated in people's lives. The countryfolk in the sixteenth century had a more supple and enchanted view of good and evil. In the modern world, the church lost its rigid bureaucratic grip on evil, while the Friulani narrowed and personified their concept of it. The countryfolk identified the sources of the malevolence that continually encroached on their lives in the quirks, idiosyncrasies, and jealousies of their friends, neighbors, and acquaintances. Evil in this disenchanted world came to be manifested in the banalities of intractable poverty and misfortune that defined the social existence of the hapless countryfolk.

In their reflections on the persistence of traditional representations of the supernatural, a number of informants identified the economic circumstances prevailing in the pre–World War II period as the foundation of these beliefs. One middle-aged woman from Rubignacco stated unambiguously, ''The bad luck [brought by witches] was really poverty.'' Another elderly female informant, commenting on those people inclined to strong apprehensions about witches, said ''They were very hungry poor people,'' and her daughter added with emphasis, ''They were hungry!'' Yet another informant living in a different settlement put it this way: ''They [those who believed in witches] were very weak because they did not eat much, they had hallucinations, they had dark houses, that's why they saw spirits.'' It is no wonder that when these interpretations were brought to the attention of a local priest, he dismissed them out of hand. What the priest was willing to concede, however, was that the fear of witches and accusations of witchcraft caused severe anguish among many parishioners, most of whom were otherwise ''good Christians.'' Mired in their theological broodings, the clergy were ineffectual at thwarting the morose obsessions of their parishioners and the antisocial consequences of these fears. Priestly equivocation, if anything, inspired greater distress.

The prevalent anxieties and apprehensions of the countryfolk revolved around imminent economic ruin and destitution. These fears were enmeshed in the very real vulnerabilities implicit in the institutional arrangements that regulated rural labor and thus the fate of the countryfolk. The chronic uncertainties and powerlessness of the Friulani were culturally transmuted and expressed in the idiom of witchery. This grim preoccupation was draped over the intimacies of rural community life, and infused the consciousness of the rural poor. It was on this cultural terrain that the rationalization of the socioeconomic realm and the disenchantments of the supernatural realm collided. As the beliefs in witches (and benandans) lost indigenous cultural meaning, they gained a sterile psychological utility. The abstract formulas that ruled the social life of the countryfolk and determined their economic fate were projected onto the play of supernatural forces. Using the deformed vestiges of traditional folk beliefs, the Friulani affixed their anxieties on what were perceived to be menacing characteristics of the weak and socially estranged among themselves (see Taussig 1980: 109–11).

THE FOUNDATIONS of Friulian folk consciousness have been explored in this and the previous two chapters, as have the contemporary religious, political, and economic imperatives that have recast the sensibilities and experiences of the countryfolk. Chapter 7 represents the finale of this discussion and analysis. In the intense personal struggles of the women at the silk mill to interpret the industrial system using their variously modified folk beliefs and Catholic morality, we have the basis of peasant-worker awareness. The efforts of these women to make sense of the alien calibration of human energies that pervaded the silk mill did not yield a uniform consciousness. Rather, they gave rise to a loose and often shifting peasant-worker awareness that adapted elements of folk outlooks and convictions to the novel social predicaments of the factory.

The Industrial Realm

THE FACTORIES that encircle Rubignacco brought with them new forms of order and of anarchy to the lives of the countryfolk. The silk mill (filanda) operated in Rubignacco from the late nineteenth century until it closed in the early 1950s. The manifold challenges of wresting an industrial system from a rural world were played out within its walls in the daily routines of production. This drama, staged at the industrial core of peasant-worker society, will be investigated through factory records and the reminiscences of former mill employees, all of whom are women. Their haunting descriptions cover the last phase of the factory's operation, from about 1920 to 1950. A disconcerting combination of bitterness and nostalgia pervades the accounts of these women; residual anger about working conditions and outright mistreatment at the hands of their overseers is tinged with a sad fondness for the time and place where their childhoods and youth were spent.

Fig. 13. Portrait of silk workers, 1926, with the "saintly" padrone at right.

Silk production spanned the agrarian and industrial realms in Friuli (see Merli 1972: 81–83, 432–36; Poni 1976: 444–97). Historically, the intensive labor of tending cocoons was performed on virtually every farmstead and large estate around Cividale. The mulberry trees that lined country lanes provided food for the developing chrysalises. The local silk cocoons (bozzoli) were dried at municipal facilities near the railway station and sent to the filanda in Rubignacco a few blocks away.

Textiles in general, and silk production in particular, were central to the first phases of Friulian industrial development. As early as 1805, 572,000 kilograms of cocoons and 42,000 kilograms of spun silk were being produced in the region. By midcentury, more than 100,000 kilograms of silk thread was being spun annually (Parmeggiani 1966: 22). Textile mills were the largest industrial employers in Friuli through the late nineteenth century and into the first decades of the twentieth century, with silk processing accounting for the majority of jobs. In 1890, there were 13,242 textile workers; by 1914 the number had increased to 15,665. In both surveys the textile employment constituted 58 percent of the region's industrial work force. However, during this period the silk industry had begun a slow decline, from 30 percent to 27 percent of overall industrial employment. Textile employment peaked at 16,664 in absolute terms during 1937–1939, after which it declined precipitously to only 6,967—or approximately 9 percent of the industrial work force—in 1961 (Parmeggiani 1966: 149–53). Records from the filanda in Rubignacco show that in the early 1940s it employed approximately 150 women and produced between 1,200 and 1,500 kilograms of spun silk per month.

Efforts of the former silk workers to interpret their industrial experience reveal a social awareness rooted in Friulian cultural sensibilities. This awareness is relativized by Catholic morality, folk belief, ethnic identity, and familial values. Peasant-worker awareness is contrasted in the following pages with the emerging consciousness of residents of le baracche di Rubignacco, where new ideas—increasingly divorced from rural traditions and outlooks—were adopted. The changing circumstances of the cossans altered their social position and provided a new framework of meaning and basis for identity. The material permits us to trace in preliminary fashion the transition from peasant-worker awareness to working-class consciousness.

Many of the conventions that guided factory production in the countryside were drawn from principles originally laid down within the latifondi. This was most pronounced with regard to authority relationships, which were organized along bureaucratic lines and conceptualized along patronal lines in the two domains. The concept identified in the sociohistorical literature as "industrial paternalism" was, in Rubignacco, closely tied to the patronal or clientelist ideology that framed agrarian social relations (Guiotto 1979; Hareven 1982; Joyce 1980; Perrot 1979; Reid 1985). Specifically, the conduct of the padrone of the silk mill conformed in many respects to the conventions of ownership and supervision described in chapters 4 and 5 in reference to nearby agrarian operations. These conventions were inherently ambiguous, fusing traditional symbols of guardianship with bureaucratic power, and thus creating relationships that commingled benevolent control with outright coercion (Hareven 1982: 38–68). The managerial relationships at the silk mill will be described in terms of "patronage" as opposed to "paternalism," to convey the continuity between the social history of the latifondo and that of the small-scale rural factory in Friuli (Le Play 1982; Thompson 1978).

Most, if not all, of the women who labored in the silk mill resided in the rural hinterland surrounding Rubignacco. Local Friulian surnames predominate in factory records. Former employees estimate that during the pre–World War II period, about 80 percent of the laborers lived in the countryside. The industrial labor of these women was integrated with the agrarian routines of modest family farmsteads (Scott and Tilly 1975), and the women brought to the silk mill a homogeneous cultural background, a common language, mutual ties of kinship and friendship, and shared social predicaments. The integrity of their ties to the countryside defined them as peasant-workers. The experience of silk workers in Rubignacco can thus be contrasted with that of other textile workers who curtailed their relationships with rural society by seeking employment and taking up permanent residence in industrial centers at some distance from their ancestral villages (Dublin 1979; Hareven 1982; Messenger 1975).

The Walk to the Filanda

The workday's troubles began with the trek to the mill. The young girls and women woke well before sunrise to prepare for the day's labors. Children were fed, livestock tended, and a packet of polenta and perhaps some figs or grapes were hurriedly collected for the silk workers' midday meal. Down the hillsides and along the muddy roads, workers set out for the filanda from rural hamlets including Purgessimo, Prestento, Torreano, Moimacco, Orzano, Bottenicco, Feadis, and Rualis—even from the more distant Slavic-speaking settlements of San Pietro, a full ten kilometers away.

We walked; some had bicycles. When it snowed everyone walked. We wore only clogs. I never owned shoes or boots. We woke up very early. Yes, every day. It was a heavy thing to do. Mothers had to neglect [*dovevano trascurare*] their children and everything else.

In my time I was little. I was a child [11 years old]. I was slim. I walked 5 kilometers to get to work. In the morning and at night [I walked] through the wind and rain or whatever else that came.

In the winter we did not have overcoats. I made one out of a military blanket. Others wore shawls. [When we got to the filanda] our knees were like ice. A friend lost a clog in a fast-moving stream. She had to go barefoot for the entire winter.

Those living on the southern bank of the Natisone River faced added difficulties as they passed through the center of Cividale on their way to Rubignacco. As workers approached the outskirts of Cividale their numbers grew, creating small clusters of five to ten women. These groups crossed the narrow Ponte del Diavolo and made their way past the Duomo and through the center of the comune to reach the filanda. This part of the journey—both to and from the mill—served as a painful confirmation of the poverty and social position of the silk workers.

We had the name *bigatarie*. We would walk barefoot from Purgessimo to the outskirts of Cividale and there put on our clogs. We were embarrassed to be seen barefoot in Cividale.

Another woman carried a pair of cloth shoes that she discreetly put on for the passage through the urban center. She felt acutely ashamed when the Cividalesi stared at the noisy clogged feet of her coworkers, and for this part of the trek she separated from them and walked alone.

Their poverty, their youth, and their tattered appearance identified them as silk workers. "As soon as we went to work we were baptized bigatarie . . . because as soon as we came out of the factory people would smell our stink." Although bigatarie literally means "silk worker," the term also has strong sexual connotations. The Friulian root *bigat* refers to silk cocoons, but *biga* also translates as "vagina." Hence, bigatarie not only described the work roles and socioeconomic status of these women; it further implied sexual debasement. "When we came out of the factory we always had to confront 'le bigatarie, le bigatarie, le bigatarie.' " Scuffles occasionally broke out in Cividale between silk workers and catcalling urban residents. "For us it was an offense to be called bigatarie."

After pressing through the center of Cividale, crossing the railroad track, and walking under the looming furnaces of the cement works, the workers arrived at the perimeter of a large estate. Entering through its tall iron gates, the women proceeded along a beautiful drive overgrown with chestnut trees and surrounded by manicured gardens. The drive ended before a palatial eighteenth-century villa, crowned by an ornate clock. Here they would make a left turn and enter a courtyard surrounded by a three-story structure attached on one side to the factory owner's villa. The cocoons were stored and processed and the silk was spun in various sections of the building that surrounded the courtyard. Most of the women passed through arched doorways on their way to their workstations. After climbing two flights of stairs, the workers arrived at a large L-shaped room with high, peaked ceilings supported by decoratively carved wooden beams. Light streamed through the tall windows that lined the walls of the main spinning room. The rows of tightly packed workstations wedged the women against each other and their equipment. The room was filled with the sound and motion of fast-turning machines that relentlessly spun the silk. Steam billowed from vats of boiling water, permanently fogging the sealed windows and making it difficult to see from one end of the spinning floor to the other. Accompanying this strange, vapor-shrouded scene was the overwhelming stench of the mashed and decaying carcasses of countless silkworms which glazed every piece of machinery and seeped into each crevice and pore of the structure.

> The water was boiling, dirty and stinking. Oh, the water smelled terrible. Our faces were the color of the bozzoli because our faces were in the steam all day long. Oh, did we stink!

> When we left the factory . . . we would leave some perfume as we passed.

> It was terrible on Monday when you had to go back to work because of that stink.

The workers' complexions were so discolored by the steam that people believed they were all tubercular. One woman, who had worked at the filanda for more than thirty years, admitted that she had never learned to tolerate the smell. Each night she had to wash her clothes because she repeatedly vomited on them while confined to her workstation.

Fig. 14. The villa of the former owner of the
silk mill in Rubignacco. Note the clock.

The Industrial Process

The dried bozzoli arrived at the ground floor of the mill, where they were sorted by quality into two grades. This operation was performed by four or five sorters, the *cernitrici*. These workers also weighed the daily quota of bozzoli for each workstation in the spinning room. Adjacent to the sorting area on the ground floor were the coal-fired boilers that provided steam to run the spinning machines and heat to boil the water used to process the raw silk. The cernitrici distributed the bozzoli to novices known as *scopine*. Scopine were the least skilled and lowest-paid employees; most were mere children of only eleven or twelve years. The scopine delivered the day's quota of bozzoli to one of the fifty-four workstations on the third floor or twenty on the second floor

169

Fig. 15. The abandoned silk mill in Rubignacco.

of the factory. At each station sat a *maestra*—a spinner—for whom the scopine worked as assistants.

Bozzoli were dumped into vats of scalding water where they were mechanically stirred to soften them so that they could be easily unraveled. Care had to be taken not to over- or under- "cook" the cocoons, for either could foul the spinning equipment or adversely affect the quality of the silk. The scopine's main task was to pull bozzoli out of the water when they reached the proper consistency, and pass them on to the maestra. The only way to judge if the cocoons were ready was through touch; hence the scopine were forced constantly to immerse their hands in the boiling cauldrons.

The maestra had to be given a steady supply of bozzoli. With fantastic skill, the spinner removed a filament from each cocoon and fed the tiny fiber through a spindle and onto the spinning equipment. This delicate task had to be accomplished continuously with great speed and acuity. The thread was formed out of three to seven spun filaments that were wrapped onto a spool of finished silk. Each maestra operated four or five spinning machines at once. Behind the maestra stood workers known as the *nodine*. There were approximately twenty nodine who were poised to intervene in the spinning process in the event a thread severed. If a thread broke, the maestra immediately stopped the machine and the nodine quickly knotted the loose filaments. Finished spools of silk were collected, weighed, tested for quality, and stored by two or three women who worked in the silk room (*stanza seta*). The other silk workers generally referred to these women as *le preferite*, the preferred or privileged ones. This designation came from the "clean" nature of their work and the peculiar relationships between these women and the proprietor.

The workforce of 150 or so employees was overseen by the padrone and salaried female managers, the *direttrici*. The direttrici were responsible for maintaining discipline and order on the factory floor. They were recruited from the ranks of the maestre and used their knowledge of the spinning process to ensure that the speed and quality of the work were maintained. However, it was the presence of the padrone, who regularly paced the spinning room floor, that most forcefully set the tone and tempo of the factory routine. He was an engineer by training and the workers referred to him as *l'ingegnere*. He did most of the hiring and firing of workers, determined salaries, imposed fines and suspensions, and kept some of the factory records. His son, trained as an accountant, helped with the bookkeeping and drove the company truck to and from Milan to deliver and sell the finished spools of silk. The only other male workers at the filanda were two or three men who stoked the boilers and repaired and maintained the machinery.

Factory Records

Still cluttering a corner of one storage area were ledgers that provide a fragmentary record of the last decade of the mill's operation. In the pages of these books are the familiar columns of figures and accounting formulas that sustained the petty bureaucracy. A somewhat different picture of the organization of the mill emerges from these records than from the memories of former employees. The hierarchy of skills and the calculation of wages are far more refined in the ledgers than in the workers' recollections. A more precise nomenclature for job categories is also used. The base period for this statistical summary is February 1942 to February 1943, a time period used because it coincides roughly with the time frame most prominent in informants' memories. It is also the period for which the most complete factory records are available. Table 7.1 lists the various job classifications within the mill, the number of employees in each classification, and their respective regular and overtime wage rates. Table 7.2 depicts the average number of hours worked per month, deductions, and monthly take-home pay for the various classifications. The equivalent terms used by informants for job categories

TABLE 7.1
SILK MILL JOB CLASSIFICATIONS AND DAILY WAGE RATES IN LIRE, FEBRUARY 1942–FEBRUARY 1943

	Number of Employees		*Regular/Overtime Wage Rates*	
	2/42	2/43	2/42	2/43
Filatrici provette (Experienced silk spinners)	35	33	11.26/12.93	12.40/14.25
Filatrici semplici (Silk spinners)	3	8	10.42/11.98	11.45/13.15
Annodatrici fisse (Silk knotters)	7	7	9.66/11.10	10.95/12.25
Mezzanti di 2ᵃ (Part-time workers)	15	5	9.32/10.71	10.25/11.80
Mezzanti di 1ᵃ ed annodatrici (Part-time workers and knotters)	8	9	9.11/10.46	10.00/11.50
Mezzanti di 1ᵃ (Part-time workers)	16	0	8.42/9.67	NA
Scopinatrici di 2ᵃ (Brushers)	15	7	7.30/8.49	8.50/9.77
Scopinatrici di 1ᵃ (Brushers)	12	17	7.05/8.09	8.15/9.35
Apprendiste (Apprentices)	10	0	6.57/7.64	NA
Assistenti (Assistant managers)	2	2	16.23/18.65	17.85/20.50
Stanza seta (Silk room workers)	9	8	9.50–12.00/ 10.90–13.80	12.45–13.26/ 14.30–15.20
Cernita-varie (Sorters and variously skilled)	8	7	8.70–10.50/ 10.00–10.71	9.55–10.25/ 11.00–11.80
Uomini (Men)	3	2	18.70–28.80/ NA	20.90–31.70/ 24.80–36.45
Nuove assunte nel mese & ritornate (New and returning workers)	18	12	6.57–8.00/ 7.64–12.93	7.25–11.45/ 9.20–10.35
Total Workforce	161	117		

172

are also listed. Table 7.3 tracks the movements of individual workers between job categories, showing promotions, demotions, and turnover.

The statistics are largely self-explanatory. The work force decreased by 27 percent during the year. Most of the attrition occurred in the part-time, apprentice, new, and return worker classifications. However, the number of spinners (*filatrici provette* and *filatrici semplici*) actually increased slightly from thirty-eight to forty-one, and total silk output was stable. A differential of 15 percent above the regular wage rate was paid for overtime. Overtime was accrued for work in excess of eight hours per day. The two managers received significantly higher wages than any other female workers; however, the most glaring discrepancies existed for the two or three male workers, who made more than twice the wages of even the most highly skilled women. By and large, wage rates were fixed by classification. There were, however, many cases of individual adjustments that raised the daily compensation for a particular worker above that of others in the same classification. This is understandable in categories where skills and tenure vary significantly, particularly among the *nuove assunte & ritornate*, *cernita-varie* and those employed in the stanza seta. These factors also might explain the less frequent and less dramatic wage adjustments within the other job categories. Everyone at the mill received a raise during the year. For spinners, knotters, and managers the increase was in the 10 percent range, while for the scopine the increase was approximately 15 percent (see D. Bell 1986: 36–38).

The records for April 1942 show employees working nine hours per day for six days a week. It was quite common for the workday to be extended to ten hours during the year. The mill also experienced intermittent closings of a few days to a week roughly every two or three months, though not in April 1942. The gross pay of the workers, summarized in table 7.2, included their regular and overtime payments, a 10 percent increment for each hour worked. Deductions were substantial, amounting to approximately a third of gross pay. They included small fines for misconduct or poor workmanship, union dues, withholding for social security, and health and family benefits. The computations for these deductions are complicated and difficult to follow. The entries are, however, occasionally stamped with an official seal, which suggests some form of outside auditing. Fines were widespread during the month, involving 89 of the 155 workers. They were most common among the spinners, of whom 76 percent had wages docked. The assessments varied from under a quarter to well over half a day's wages per month (see D. Bell 1986: 29).

Table 7.3 details movement by workers among job categories. It was derived by tracing the assignments of each employee from February

TABLE 7.2
REGULAR AND OVERTIME HOURS PER WORKER, AND GROSS AND
NET MONTHLY PAY, APRIL 1942

	Regular Hours	Overtime Hours	Gross Pay*	Net Pay*
Filatrici provette (Maestre)	180	21	310	214
Filatrici semplici (Maestre)	182	26	255	168
Annodatrici fisse (Nodine)	206	24	285	201
Mezzanti di 2ª	158	18	207	140
Mezzanti di 1ª ed annodatrici	155	17	201	134
Mezzanti di 1ª	127	15	154	94
Scopinatrici di 2ª (Scopine)	80	9	87	57
Scopinatrici di 1ª (Scopine)	157	18	160	111
Apprendiste	122	14	129	86
Assistenti (Direttrice)	206	24	480	342
Stanza seta (Preferite)	185	24	293	198
Cernita-varie (Cernitrice)	192	23	252	171
Uomini	198	11	663	494
Nuove & ritornate	55	7	98	76

* Monthly pay computed in Lire.

1942 to February 1943. The only exception is the filatrici semplici, who were followed from April 1942 to May 1943 because of the unusually small number in the category in February 1942. During the year 27 percent of the workers remained in their classifications, 30 percent were promoted, less than 1 percent were demoted, 4 percent left temporarily, returning later in the twelve-month period, and 39 percent left and did not return. The *assistenti* were the most stable group, followed by the women in the cernita-varie, stanza seta, and filatrici provette classifications. Workers in the three *mezzanti* classifications were the most likely to be promoted, followed by the women in the filatrici semplici group. The two *scopinatrici* categories had the highest percentage of workers leaving employment at the filanda during the base period. The data on male employee turnover are perhaps overstated because of the

TABLE 7.3
PROMOTIONS, DEMOTIONS, AND TURNOVER,*
FEBRUARY 1942–FEBRUARY 1943

Filatrici provette

23	66%	Appeared in every pay period
3	8%	Left and returned during the year
9	26%	Left during the year

Filatrici semplici (4/1942–5/1943)

2	20%	Appeared in every pay period
6	60%	Promoted to Filatrici provette
2	20%	Left during the year

Annodatrici fisse

| 4 | 57% | Appeared in every pay period |
| 3 | 43% | Left during the year |

Mezzanti di 2ª

12	80%	Promoted to Filatrici semplici
1	7%	Promoted to Annodatrici fisse
1	7%	Appeared in every pay period
1	7%	Left during the year

Mezzanti di 1ª annodatrici

6	75%	Promoted to Mezzanti di 2ª
1	13%	Left and returned during the year
1	13%	Left during the year

Mezzanti di 1ª

4	25%	Promoted to Mezzanti di 2ª
6	38%	Promoted to Mezzanti di 1ª ed annodatrici
1	6%	Demoted to Scopinatrici
5	31%	Left during the year

Scopinatrici di 2ª

6	40%	Promoted to Mezzanti di 1ª annodatrici
1	7%	Appeared in every pay period
8	53%	Left during the year

Scopinatrici di 1ª

| 4 | 33% | Appeared in every pay period |
| 8 | 67% | Left during the year |

Apprendiste

1	10%	Promoted to Mezzanti di 1ª ed annodatrici
1	10%	Promoted to Scopinatrici di 2ª
1	10%	Promoted to Scopinatrici di 1ª
2	20%	Left and returned during the year
5	50%	Left during the year

Assistenti

2	100%	Appeared in every pay period

Stanza seta

6	67%	Appeared in every pay period
3	32%	Left during the year

Cernita-varie

1	13%	Promoted to Filatrici semplici
6	75%	Appeared in every pay period
1	13%	Left during the year

Uomini

1	33%	Appeared in every pay period
2	66%	Left during the year

Nuove assunte nel mese & ritornate

1	6%	Promoted to Scopinatrici di 2ª
3	17%	Promoted to Scopinatrici di 1ª
14	78%	Left during the year

* Percentages rounded to nearest number; hence totals do not add up to 100 percent for each category.

small number in the sample. When this group was followed over a longer period, it appears much more stable. Overall, these data suggest a dichotomy between relatively stable and unstable segments of the work force differentiated by sex, skill, income, and tenure.

The statistical data from the filanda provide a picture of an orderly bureaucratic domain. The neat columns of figures and bookkeeping computations convey a rational matter-of-factness that contradicts the managerial rifts and personal struggles spoken of in the accounts of former employees. Nevertheless, a few statistical records do give an inkling of tumult. The most interesting example is an intermittently kept cost accounting calculation figured in the margins of the ledgers. At the end of seven monthly entries, the bookkeeper computed the cost of labor per finished kilogram of silk. The figures are provocative: February

1942, 42.00 lire; April 1942, 43.92 lire; June 1942, 35.07 lire; October 1942, 30.90 lire; December 1942, 23.45 lire; February 1943, 41.15 lire; March 1943, 35.00 lire. As shown above, wages increased during the period covered by these entries only between 10 percent and 15 percent. The enormous swings in the average cost of labor—a 30 percent decline from April to October, a further 25 percent decline from October to December, followed by a 75 percent increase between December and February, and finally a 15 percent decline from February to March— hint at a lack of administrative control. Unfortunately these entries abruptly come to an end in the spring of 1943, when a new handwriting style appears in the ledgers.

The reflections of the former silk workers, as will be seen below, penetrate the bureaucratic artifice of the mill and expose a far richer and more challenging social and cultural milieu. Indeed, these accounts suggest a significantly less rationalized organization than the one conveyed by the fastidious bookkeeping entries; more important, they demonstrate the persistence of traditional patterns of interaction, outlook, and identity.

Working Conditions

The harsh working conditions in the filanda were inseparable from the "black poverty" (*miseria nera*) that circumscribed rural society. A chronic lack of employment was the central defining feature of industrial life. The problem was particularly bleak for women, since the filanda was the only major employer of female labor. Even so, workers were not eager to seek employment at the mill—far from it. For most women, employment at the filanda was loathsome, undertaken out of grim necessity or pressing misfortune.

> Our father died, so how could we survive? We had to go [to work at the filanda].

> My husband was unemployed and I had a daughter!

> There were many girls. . .we didn't have many chances to work. So we went to work to survive. The poverty was great.

The padrone regularly found ways to circumvent government regulations that forbade the hiring of children under thirteen years of age.

> Sure, he [the padrone] took me. I was eleven. To tell the truth he did not want to hire me because he was controlled [by the author-

177

ities]. He had his doubts, but he took me anyway, because my
father went there in tears begging him to take me. He [the padrone]
took pity on us and hired me.

Securing employment was a trying and often humiliating experience
forced onto mere children in face of the calamitous circumstances that
assailed rural families. The problems for these workers, however, only
began with getting the job. As one former silk worker put it: "Yes, it
was difficult [to get employed], but it was even more difficult to hold
onto it. The work was disgusting."

By far the most punishing aspect of the work process involved the
simple task of removing the bozzoli from the vats of boiling water.

It was boiling water. There was a small basin of cold water where
we would dunk our hands. We would put our hand in the boiling
water, pull out the cocoons and then thrust our hands into the cool
water. We went through a lot of pain. All our hands were rotten
[*marcie*].

It seemed like my hands would never heal. They were so burned
and eaten that the skin would peel away. I had raw flesh exposed.
It was excruciating to put the injured hand back into the water the
next day.

My hands at night were covered with large blisters. The flesh was
all eaten. They changed the water only once a week. It was rotten.
Let's not even talk about the smell!

In many cases, the blistering was so severe that fingernails would fall
out, leaving the women's hands lacerated and disfigured. Also common
were chronic eczema over their hands and arms, loss of sensation in the
fingers, and arthritic joints. These medical conditions often persisted for
years after the silk worker left the filanda. Adding to these miseries was
the knowledge that these physical distresses publicly stigmatized them
as silk workers. "People looked at our hands and said, 'Here are the
bigatariis!' "

These working conditions made for an extremely stressful appren-
ticeship for the young girls who labored as scopine.

Q. Were the young scopine depressed?
A. Eh, they were, they were, they were. We took pity on them.
They cried, poor [little girls], all the time. They came down-
stairs to eat and did not even feel like eating. "Why are you

crying?'' we asked. ''[The maestra] threw boiling water at me
. . . she pulled my hair.''

The maestra would beat up the young girls. The maestra had to
demonstrate to the padrone that she was harsh to them.

Work conditions at the filanda had a particularly gruesome impact on
the daily existence of pregnant women and new mothers. A former
worker recounted her experience after the birth of her first child in the
mid-1940s:

My husband was unemployed. I had to return to work eight days
after the birth of my child. Eight days after childbirth! If you didn't
go back that was it.
Q. How did you nurse the child?
A. I didn't nurse him. . . . I went to the lavatory to force out the
milk. I developed an infection on my breasts from wringing out
the milk. My hands were filthy from the water and the bozzoli.
It was not only me . . . many others contracted the same infection. I don't know how I survived the illness. I weaned my son
on cow's milk and barley. The doctor at the hospital said that I
had enough milk for two children. He said, ''You would do well
to serve as a wet nurse.'' But I had to milk myself, to pull the
milk out in the lavatory. I made an agreement with the direttrice
so that I could slip away unseen, when I couldn't stand the pain.
She [the direttrice] had a little conscience. . . . So when the padrone was not there, I would slip out, four or five times a day,
maybe more. But the direttrice said, ''Be careful that the padrone doesn't see.'' We had to run!

The woman ended her account bitterly: ''About the lives of the women
at the filanda there is a book to be written, if they [the silk workers] are
willing to tell the truth. The padrone was a beast, a beast!''

On those questions concerning the technical operation of the factory
there is a monotonous consensus among former employees. Basic steps
in processing raw silk and spinning filaments, the temperature of the
water, the stench of the bozzoli, the operation of machinery, even the
division of tasks and responsibilities appear to be clearcut in the minds
of informants. By contrast, on matters concerning social rifts and antagonisms within the factory, there is confounding disagreement. Interpretations of the social interplay among workers, managers, and owner are
contentious, rooted in a shifting set of perspectives on the industrial
drama performed in the filanda. The interpretive stances taken by various actors are tinged with outrage, deception, self-interest, bewilder-

ment, and lingering fears. The social reality is elusive. It is accessible only through the conflicting recollections of former participants.[1]

L'Ingegnere

The principal player was the engineer, whose character deeply influenced the social routines of the filanda. Like the proprietors of the large agrarian operations, he acted as sovereign in his domain, conceding little if any authority to outside individuals or agencies. This prerogative of ownership permitted the padrone great latitude in dictating the basic terms and conditions of employment, the division of labor, and the allocation of managerial responsibilities. During the era before World War II, when union power and government regulation were poorly developed, workers had few means to resist the actions of the padrone. Workers nevertheless attempted to restrain and subvert the behavior of the engineer by several important informal methods. Some of the patterns of resistance were drawn from agrarian traditions and superimposed on industrial relationships. In particular, certain social ties that developed in the filanda mimicked the clientelist relationships that prevailed in the agrarian realm. There also originated in the filanda and other industrial settings altogether new types of relationships different from any that existed on the latifondi. The emergence of skilled workers—like the maestre in the filanda—who were able to gain a limited influence over their work conditions and their terms of employment represented an important social departure. Above all, however, it was the haphazard collisions and the active manipulations of old and new cultural assumptions that gave these early factory operations their distinctive social texture.

Beast and Saint

Individual character and moral attributes loomed large in the early industrial environment, where labor-management relationships were imperfectly rationalized. Eccentricities of owners and managers had a profound impact on workers' perceptions of conditions at the mill. Employees were inclined to interpret their experiences primarily in relation to the moral character of their overseers. This accounts for the shifting perceptions of work life within a given factory when overseers were replaced or ownership changed hands, even though the nature of the work itself was unaltered.

The owner of the filanda, l'ingegnere, was widely acknowledged, though with some important exceptions, as being an absolute "beast."

Yet the prior owner, who is well-remembered directly or by way of reputation, was esteemed as a "saint." A woman drew the contrast between the two proprietors as follows:

Q. Did l'ingegnere abuse you?
A. Not only that, he was filthy, filthy, filthy. I tell you the truth. . . . The *prior* padrone would do nothing [immoral] to a woman, not even in a dream.

Another woman commented on the moral stature of the earlier owner of the mill. "With him [the saintly padrone] we worked in a godly fashion." The transfer of ownership did not change the gruesome physical demands of spinning silk; it did, however, transform employees' perceptions of the quality of their work lives. Abuse and mistreatment were experienced through a moral idiom that gave their travails a highly charged personal meaning rather than a wider social significance. For many at the filanda this interpretive stance contributed to their sense of profound helplessness and resignation.

Disenchantments of the Factory

Time and accounting for time are central for instilling the "rational matter-of-factness" of factory routine and the creation of consensus around its "second nature." The engineer actively manipulated time, albeit somewhat crudely, in his efforts to impose his will on the running of the mill and the lives of his employees. However, unlike the machines that could be tuned and regulated to serve unquestioningly the padrone's will, the workers dissented from the engineer's calibrations of time and work.

The bad thing was that the direttrice said we should begin work at 7 A.M. but at 6:30 A.M. we all had to be working. If we got there at 6:35 A.M. they would take half or even a full hour off our pay, even if it was twenty-five minutes before the appointed starting time.

We hadn't swallowed our polenta and the bell was ringing again saying that we had to go upstairs [to our work places], twenty minutes before the meal period was over. . . . He [the engineer] took advantage of us.

This deception was disconcerting to the women, adding further hardship to their work lives. Yet the deception itself failed. The workers generally knew exactly what time it was. After all, the grand clock mounted on the padrone's villa was in clear view of many of the mill workers.

Directly linked to the issue of time was the calculation of the amounts and quality of work, which also became a point of contention. Evaluating each worker's performance was central to factory discipline, which came to be enforced through fines, suspensions, firings, and various forms of threat and intimidation.

> At night they would remove the silk. It took eight to ten hours to produce a spool. If you didn't produce the padrone would have bad words for you. He might even take it off your pay. . . . Every maestra had seven or eight kilograms of bozzoli that had to be processed each day. If you wasted silk they would know by weighing the spool and they would come and say, "Look, you have not given all you could give." They would fine you. . . . [However], if you produced more [than your quota], nothing!

> We had to shut up and cry because there was miseria nera. I knelt, because he [the padrone] had suspended me for three days, asking for mercy, saying that I would never make a mistake again. . . . He had his little work table. Sometimes he would just sit there and watch or walk back and forth behind us.

> "Look here, look there, look up, look down, see how much waste there is!" These are the words of the padrone. They would fire workers for nothing. If the direttrice did not like the worker she put her feet on the worker's head. "She doesn't belong, that one must be eliminated."

The mistreatment, abuse, and insecurities that workers endured seemed from their perspective to be enmeshed in the very nature of industrial production. Many of the silk workers who denounced the padrone as a "beast" believed the fines, suspensions, and verbal threats were a necessary part of factory discipline nevertheless (see D. Bell 1986: 29; Merli 1972: 160–62).

It was on the issue of wages, however, that the workers most unequivocally drew the moral distinction between the beastly and the saintly padrone.

> We counted the hours and minutes worked so that he [the padrone] would not cheat us. We prayed to God that we would get the [pay] envelope each month.

We didn't know anything. They made the pay envelopes. We didn't know what the hourly wage was. They would turn us like a wheel [that is, cheat them]. I worked for eight years and only got pension credit for four years. I had to go back to work to earn credits for a pension.

There was a padrone [at the silk mill] who was enough of a bastard alive, and may he be at the depths [of hell] with the devil dead. . . . He would take advantage of us in recording our work and paying us our wages.

When the engineer brought in his young son to take over the bookkeeping, the situation changed. The son's careful accounting of wages, coupled with his evenhanded treatment of workers, elevated him in the eyes of the women to the position of saintly foil to his corrupt father.

Through feats of legerdemain, bombast, and outright coercion, the engineer strove to control the operation of the factory and impose his stern view of social reality on its work force. Workers were compelled to submit to the brutal and, at times, ludicrous means wielded by the owner to manage the mill. Nonetheless, the women developed techniques for resistance, either through complicity or subterfuge, that challenged the engineer's outlook and increasingly eroded his authority.

Opposition, Collaboration, and Resignation

In the pre–World War II filanda, class-based interests and concerns were only faint stirrings in the imaginations of a distinct minority of the workers. Social antagonisms on the vapor-shrouded floor of the factory were enacted in a loosely choreographed guerrilla warfare. Rather than coalescing around working-class notions, the silk workers' outlook was submerged in peasant-worker broodings. These preoccupations formed around an amalgam of folk beliefs and suspicions, clientelist deceits, Catholic morality, sexual politics, and nascent proletarian insights. After she described for me in detail the manipulations of time and wages, I asked a former silk worker if she or any of her coworkers ever considered getting together to protest. She answered:

We thought about it many times. We would say, "Let's not go upstairs [to our workstations] until the *right* time." There was always one who had a clock. "Let's not go upstairs until 1 P.M., okay? Everyone agrees?" Quarter of one the bell would ring; we were not united, we were not together. Those who went up were well treated and we who went up at the right time were sent home

Fig. 16. The main spinning room floor of the abandoned silk mill.

for two or three days. It wasn't a union, so we couldn't do things together. First, the women would say "yes" [agreeing to the protest plan] and then what would happen would happen. We had to shut up because there was poverty and we couldn't open our mouths.

Aborted protests often led to conflicts among workers and eventually to a sense of resignation about their condition.

We became mad at each other. There was much discord [*Era tutta una zizzania*]. "Why would you say that you would stay downstairs and then go up?" To tell the truth we had bitter arguments. We would say things of all colors to each other [that is, curse one another]. But it was a hard time and that was the way it was. There were those who wanted the padrone to regard them well . . . and there were those who were punished. Even if we didn't make mistakes he would accuse us of making mistakes. Downstairs [in the silk room] there were those he [the padrone] liked, and they tested the spun silk. Those women in the silk room would say to the engineer, "This maestra has made a mistake," but she may not have made an error.

Q. Did the padrone reward those workers he liked?

A. He didn't want to be seen by us rewarding those women. He was a coward with us workers, a coward, very cowardly [*vigliacco, vigliacchissimo*]. If it [the engineer's behavior] was done today—Madonna!—I don't know what they would do to him . . . but at that time we had to shut up because there were no jobs.

Immediately after World War II, workers—particularly the skilled maestre—became more bold in their dealings with the owner.

> I and five or six other maestre with good tongues had an argument with the engineer because he gave us second-rate bozzoli and pretended to sell first-rate silk. He called us subversives. He was drunk. He called the carabinieri. The carabinieri came with their machine guns [to subdue the uprising]. [When the maestre saw the carabinieri] we threatened to quit. The padrone apologized for calling the police and the carabinieri departed laughing.

In a similar way, the following incident depicts the growing assertiveness of the skilled maestre as they began to recognize the acute dependence of the mill and its proprietor on their special talents. It is also noteworthy that a sexual idiom was invoked in the account to express the conflict between owner and workers.

> In the afternoon he [the padrone] drank and he started to say all kinds of things and mistreat us. One day ten or twelve maestre were called into his office. He told us things of all colors. We went back to work. The conversation upset us. It was winter and very cold. We were working in boiling water but our backs were freezing [from drafts that blew through the mill]. Suddenly, the engineer stormed out of his office and began to open all the windows in the spinning room. He yelled, "Air from the mountains because the cows [*vacche*] are here" [*vacca, vacche* (pl.), is commonly used to mean prostitute]. Of course we did not keep quiet. I started to yell from the other end of the factory floor, "Yes, we are cows and you are a big bull, but we will never give it to you." He immediately called twelve or so maestre downstairs and kicked us out, saying, "Never come back again. If you return I will throw you out the window."

In the absence of these maestre, the factory almost immediately began to have serious problems with the quality of the silk produced. One hundred *quintali* of substandard spools were actually returned from Milan. Less than a week after the incident, the padrone sent his clerk to the homes of the fired maestre, asking them to return to their jobs. I asked the former maestra, who described the firing incident, why the engineer called her back. She answered:

> Because I was an expert, more than anything else. . . . Threats were part of every day's business . . . workers were fired. But like I said, those who were better workers were braver and had good tongues; we knew we did our job well. So we got upset if we were mistreated.

Skill served as an effective counterweight to the power of the owner. The division of labor that developed in the filanda conferred on certain workers valued skills that gave them a voice in regulating production. It also gave them power to oppose the arbitrary demands of the owner. By the time the silk mill closed, the maestre were receiving wages that approached those of skilled workers in other local industries. The mercurial behavior of the engineer, in reaction to the unfolding self-awareness of the maestre, reveals both the new limitations on his power and his helplessness to stem the significant shift of control within the factory. His actions in the post–World War II period seem a parody of the earlier tyranny he exercised to rule the lives of his employees.

Le Preferite: Sexual Politics

Misdeeds and indiscretions are often hinted at when people in rural districts around Rubignacco discuss the old filanda. The goings-on within the mill were the subject of intense interest among outsiders, as "there were all those young women," and this created a situation ripe for crude speculation and innuendo. Over and above the anomaly of the female work force and male overseer, rumors worked their way out of the mill and lent substance to peoples' suspicions. Sexual undercurrents were evident in the narrations of former silk workers regarding their dealings with the engineer, coworkers, and outsiders. Some of the sexual abuse was blatant. "This I can say, he [the engineer] had the vice of touching us. He would take some slaps, strong slaps, and then he would go away." Other forms of sexual abuse were far more subtle and insidious, intruding on the social underpinnings of the factory. Authority relations, working conditions, job security, and ties among coworkers were vulnerable to the veiled interplay of sexual politics.

> We were jealous because some of the women were put in the silk room; it was a clean job. They came to work better dressed and more painted.

There were those three or four who were well-treated. They did what they wanted because they made agreements with the padrone [*si mettevano d'accordo col padrone*]. We didn't see anything that could be said. But we knew that when we finished, the preferite would remain longer and have their pleasures with the old man. . . . They [the preferite] came late [to work]. They stayed home half the day.

One day one of the preferite said, "Look, I have to go dancing tonight but I don't have shoes. I know how to get them." The others said, "How can you get them?" She answered, "Easy." At noon she put herself together and went to the office of the engineer and in the evening she returned with the money for the shoes. Later we checked her pay envelope to see if she had asked for an advance . . . but there was no sign of it. That's why I say . . . yes, there were those who did what they wanted. The beautiful ones [*le belle*] . . . they were his privileged ones and he would not have fired them if they had broken the filanda apart.

Thus, hidden in the shadow of the petty bureaucracy of the factory, was an arena in which a clientelist idiom was used to reshape the terms of employment and modify the status of a select few, the preferite. As was the case on the latifondi, the formal authority of factory officials over the lives of the work force empowered them to fashion illicit relations through which their illegal or immoral wants could be satisfied. Conversely, by way of these agreements, the preferite achieved dramatically improved working conditions and enhanced job security, which sharply distinguished them from the other silk workers. As with all clientelist ties, a question arises regarding the degree to which they are "voluntary." The basic social context in which these agreements were fashioned was one of profound inequality between the parties. Yet the padrone appears to have avoided open coercion in favor of plain treachery to initiate the collaborations.

Q. Would he [the engineer] have fired women who resisted his sexual advances?
A. No, no, he was cunning [*era furbo*]. He was shrewd at his deceptions and the women were ignorant.
Q. Did he lead these women to think they would be favored?
A. Yes, instead of putting them at the basin working in the hot water, he put them at cleaning silk.
Q. Did he blackmail the women, did he explicitly ask for favors?

A. I don't know. . . . They made agreements.
Q. Were the women afraid of him?
A. Yes.

Whereas the maestre were increasingly willing to challenge openly the practices of the padrone to protect their interests, the preferite made collaborative "understandings." Although the agreements served their immediate ends, so that the preferite improved their lot at the filanda, these clientelist understandings also affected their relationships with coworkers and could potentially have compromised their moral standing in the wider community. Thus, the preferite tried to keep these relationships concealed, or at least vague. "The preferite would only talk to those they knew they could trust. What they did was something hidden. It was not public."

The preferite and the padrone were not alone in their attempts to conceal these clientelist activities. The majority of the workers at the filanda who were in no way directly involved in the illicit collaborations were also committed to guarding the secrets. For them, it was vital to cover up these activities for two reasons: first, revealing this kind of practice was a dangerous affront to the padrone which could undermine their own security at the mill; second, the collaborations made by a small minority implicated all the silk workers in the unsavory behavior. Gossip was not very precise, and it tended to generalize and stereotype the behavior of all the women at the mill. For these reasons, coworkers covered for the actions of the preferite, however distasteful they felt those actions to be, to protect their own standing and security.

Sensitivity concerning the behavior of the preferite endures among former silk workers to this day. Women who discussed with great frankness the abuses and mistreatment they experienced at the filanda, even cases with sexual overtones, avoided the issue of the preferite with a common defense of reticence or outright denial.

He [the engineer] had sympathy for them. They were very pretty. I don't know what kind of sympathy. I don't know what he did with them. . . . We didn't see anything, but they were privileged.

I don't know [about the preferite]. I cannot say. I never heard anything. Nothing ever happened to me.

She [a preferita] must have had. . . . She must have been, what do I know?

More than thirty years after the closing of the filanda and the death of the engineer, fears linger and embarrassments persist among the women. After reflecting on her denial of knowledge of the activities of the preferite, a former silk worker murmured, "We heard something about that, didn't we? Yes, maybe things happened. Yes, in the silk room [they] would have pleasure down there at that place."

One woman, described venomously by a coworker as "the ripe finger of the padrone" and identified by others as one of the preferite, was interviewed. She is a handsome woman in her early sixties, living in a comfortable apartment in a working-class neighborhood not far from the closed filanda. Over a series of interviews, she displayed an unwavering determination to portray the nobility of the engineer and the benign conditions at the mill. Unlike the other preferite, she had significant responsibility in managing various aspects of the day-to-day running of the factory. Not surprisingly, she refused to concede any knowledge of foul play. Her description of working conditions was so glowing that it gave the mill the air of an exclusive club. With characteristic understatement she acknowledged the problems faced by workers at the mill:

> They [the silk workers] would wake up early. What they were interested in was getting home early [in the evening] because they had chores to perform. They did not like walking at night; they were very young. Walking ten kilometers before and after work was fatiguing.

She dismissed the workers' sporadic protests with an effortless condescension.

> Some people protested working conditions, but most were content. Their claims were very stupid. . . . If they didn't like it they could just walk [quit]. It happened more than once.

The flaunted privileges enjoyed by these women were not lost on the other workers. The discrepancies in treatment were a source of jealousy and resentment. The position of the preferite represented a standard against which other workers could measure their own degraded lot. A maestra with unusual nerve and a "good tongue" recounted how she articulated her anger directly to the engineer.

> "Look, signore, you give us a half-hour fine because we got here late [due to a raging storm]. Some [preferite] come here at 8:30, some 9, some even at 11. You smile, everything is okay." You

know this is what I told him because he had those women at his service.

The treatment of the preferite was thus capable of provoking, among some workers, particularly the maestre, an awareness of the injustices that pervaded the operation of the mill. Yet the mere intimation of these judgments was dangerous, because it threatened the padrone's control and implicated all the silk workers in the immoral conduct of a few. For the majority of the work force, this double bind led them to deny or repress any critical understanding of the complex world in which they lived. Again, the maestre, because of their skill and modest job security, were willing to break out of this bind, at least episodically, and voice their protests.

Authority relations within the filanda mimicked those prevailing on large Friulian agrarian operations. In both settings, managerial practice fused bureaucratic principle with patronal ideology. For the women who worked at the silk mill, power relations were (and continue to be) evaluated primarily in a moral idiom that bound their fate to the character of the old padrone. Deference to his power was instilled by practical fears of job loss, suspensions and fines, as well as religious anxieties disciplined by the church. An amelioration of conditions in the workplace and insecurities of tenure could be negotiated through collaborative understandings for a select few. These clientelist "agreements" bound a very small minority of the workers to the owner and wove sexual politics into the social fabric of the workplace. Though few in number, the bonds between preferite and padrone altered the overall texture of social relations among the women, exacerbating jealousy, strife, and fear. Most of the workers found these social complexities and moral dilemmas overwhelming, leading them to seek refuge in their religious faith and peasant fatalism. Although the terms of employment for the preferite and other workers at the filanda were different, the outcome was the same—they acquiesced to the authority of owner and overseer. Patrick Joyce described these forms of patronal submission in the context of the nineteenth-century textile industry in Lancashire and West Riding. "Deference is to be construed as a continuum of feeling in which the affective and the coerced are never strangers, and the inward and outward never distinct" (Joyce 1980: 95). The broadly shared assumptions of the silk workers and their padrone regarding the prerogatives of ownership, rights and obligations of workers, and norms of supervision reverberate with the cultural conventions that have for centuries guided social practice in the agrarian operations of the Friulian countryside. It is precisely this cultural convergence that ties the social history of the latifondo to that of the small rural factory in Friuli.

Many aspects of the silk workers' experience parallel those of textile workers in a diverse range of historical settings. The recurrent themes, particularly for female workers, are of competing demands of wage work and domestic responsibilities; pregnancy, child rearing and marriage; ties of friendship and kinship; long hours and appalling working conditions; worker protest and submission to authority; enduring religious outlooks and folk beliefs; and the blending of nostalgia, resignation, and despair in their reminiscences (Dublin 1979; Hareven 1982; Joyce 1980; Messenger 1975; Reid 1985; Scott and Tilly 1975). There is, however, a powerful underlying consistency to the silk workers' experience in Rubignacco that distinguishes it from the experience of textile workers residing in more urbanized industrial settings. The location of the mill in the countryside and the residence of the work force in rural districts created a distinctive industrial environment. The enduring social and economic commitments of the silk workers to their rural households, along with the persistent hold of Friulian ethnicity and identity, conferred on these women a peasant-worker awareness which coincided with that of the sojourners described in chapter 3. It is this peasant-worker awareness that bound members of these diverse segments of rural society together in a shared cultural experience.

Peasant-Worker Perspectives on
the Industrial Experience

A unified working-class outlook had not developed among the silk workers, particularly in the pre–World War II period. A number of characteristic peasant-worker sensibilities were, however, brought to bear by the silk workers on the social life of the filanda to make sense of their industrial experience. Three major interpretive perspectives can be loosely differentiated from the silk workers' accounts. The first peasant-worker perspective was more or less coterminous with the outlook of the engineer and shared most notably by the preferite. This view held that the workers were unworthy, undisciplined social inferiors who deserved their lot in the factory. The padrone was viewed in this paternalistic scheme as a benevolent figure providing discipline, order, and livelihood for his work force. The second perspective appears to have developed late in the filanda's history. It held that the silk workers were the mistreated victims of a corrupt padrone who cheated the women by unfairly manipulating the rules. The audacious outbursts of the maestre were the most public expressions of this perspective. This was, however, not a systematic view of the factory system; it was focused on personal conflicts and evaluations. Furthermore, this perspective allowed that the inequalities of the factory were a natural part of the social order. The third, and most widespread, peasant-worker perspective was born out of a collision between powerful religious dogma and the helplessness experienced by the women in the filth and grime on the spinning room floor. Impressed on these women was a view of social reality that convinced them to abandon any critical evaluation of their work lives. This vision was rooted in the grim Catholicism espoused by the Friulian clergy that conveyed a supernatural justification for the silk workers' debasement and held out the promise of redemption in the afterlife. Although permitting the women a compelling means to endure their trying circumstances, the Catholic interpretation insisted on an unquestioning faith and discipline that precluded even the most modest objective insights.

None of these prevailing viewpoints alone appears to have been entirely satisfactory to the silk workers. One can detect in their reminiscences subtle shifts among the three interpretative frameworks. The first two perspectives have been explored above; what follows are the portrayals that resonate with the third conceptual perspective, which was by far the most dominant, as well as the one most deeply embedded in a Friulian ethnic outlook and identity.

> We were all sad and exhausted by the work and by the hunger. The dampness gets to you. Sometimes we couldn't breathe. . . . The machines had to run all the time and never stop . . . we had to shut up and cry and that was it. Oh God, oh Mary, what kind of life it was!

> The priest repeatedly told us to work hard, be good, and thank God that we had jobs. The priest was very severe with us.

> I had to thank God every day and night that I had a good character to endure the work.

> We were poor and this was combined with ignorance. The idea of objecting to the padrone was unthinkable. We were raised simply and we were shy. . . . We did not have those instincts [to protest].

The empirical problem with this conceptual stance is that, although the spiritual interpretation was widespread, it tended by its very nature to be unvoiced. When articulated at all, it was most often framed in an idiom of religious devotion and transcendence. However, even on the metaphysical plane, fearful social pressures circumscribed this outlook. For those few women who grappled with the injustices of the factory, as well as for the vast majority who simply despaired of their fate, the priests were often unsympathetic figures. Priestly indoctrination, which terrified many of them, demanded a total obedience to church and secular authority. This pastoral insistence was based on the theological premise that the countryfolk could not question the status quo, which was, after all, God's design, or trespass on the clergy's interpretive hegemony. Perversely, this dogmatic position gave a quasi-religious endorsement to the control and behavior of the engineer and his ilk.

Complementing rural Catholicism was an agrarian conservatism that weighed on peasant-worker perceptions in this early industrial setting. One woman drew a direct analogy between her understanding of the factory and her family's running of a small peasant farmstead. She expressed perplexity at the mechanical repetition by which her family planted, tilled, and harvested, year in and year out, without regard to changing family needs and wants. She believed that the same unquestioning Friulian outlook shaped her behavior at the filanda. She aired her unresolved frustration, now verging on blasphemous despair, as follows:

> But God, now I say to myself many times—Pig God [a very strong obscenity]—okay, we were poor, but we were really poor and ignorant, because we did not know, we got to that point [of questioning our circumstances] and stopped there. We did not try to react, to think, to do something different. It was that way and that was it.

Another informant echoed this viewpoint:

> Q. Did you think the engineer exploited you?
> A. Who thought, who would have thought, we were just thankful for the money. We hadn't gotten to the point where we could say, "Look, he is buying a new house and we cannot make ends meet." It was all personal. At that time it was natural that he had a car and I had to walk. It was normal.

Most of the women experienced their work lives within an intractable and uncritical vision of the filanda. The daily drudgery, grueling working conditions, and low wages were seen as part of the natural, if not supernatural, order. From their resignation the silk workers took refuge in a form of alienation buttressed by religious dogma and rural fatalism that detached them from the industrial experience. These fears, frustrations, and despairs were expressed in the idiom of folk belief. In the collusion of witches, demons, and spirits, these chronic anxieties were symbolically enacted and psychologically deformed.

New and Old Outlooks

In the summer of 1983, many former silk workers were still struggling with their experiences at the filanda. Intimated in many of their reminiscences were the signs of a reassessment of the past in terms of new, post–World War II standards. These attempts at reinterpretation have, in most cases, brought forth long-suppressed anger and bitterness.

> To tell the truth, it makes me very angry [to think about my treatment at the filanda], but I try not to think about it. Maybe it is because I have not worked there for a long time. But when I talk to women who stayed there for many, many years, like my sister, they still have the rage.

An arresting discordance has developed out of the efforts of some former workers to rethink their work lives, while others steadfastly maintain their uncritical stance. Two maestre, each of whom had worked at the filanda for more than 25 years, were independently asked essentially the same absurdly simple question. Their responses elegantly reveal the divergence between the new and the old interpretative frameworks.

Maestra #1
Q. Was the engineer rich?
A. Yes, of course, indeed so. When he came, his pants had holes in them. Then he became a billionaire [in lire]—but with our sweat. He made himself a lord on our sweat. . . . He got fat and made a lord of himself on our sweat.

Maestra #2
Q. Was the factory owner rich?
A. I don't know. I don't think he was as poor as we were [spoken without a trace of irony].

Both maestre were intelligent and articulate informants. The first maestra saw an unequivocal relationship binding her labor to the padrone's wealth. Her view is consistent with the post–World War II understanding of the industrial world that has developed among many of her cohorts and in the wider working-class society. The second maestra responded with a disarming innocence that reduced the question of the engineer's wealth to an irrelevance. Her view was consistent with a devout Catholicism that continues to define her experience of the filanda. The strict Catholic viewpoint did not allow the industrial experience to have a discrete meaning independent of a religious vision. The details of her life and relationships at the filanda lacked meaning in their own right. For this woman, the unfathomable burdens of work were instead to be endured, not questioned. The complexities of the industrial regime were mystifying, and hence the specifics of factory operation, social inequalities, and human debasement were in and of themselves meaningless.

A sad and disconcerting final thread runs through the accounts of these women. The silk workers' reinterpretations of their work experiences are linked in a new, critical light with their nostalgia for childhood, adolescence, and early adulthood. In discussing her experience, one former employee recounted in graphic detail the distress that she and her coworkers endured at the filanda. Then in poignant counterpoint she interjected, "There was harmony among the scopine. We laughed a lot. We were beautiful." In a similar fashion, another silk worker ended a long reminiscence of the strains of her career at the filanda with the unsettling coda: "We were happy, but very poor. We talked. We laughed. We danced. Things have changed too much." Thus, amid the sweeping social crosscurrents of the filanda, the girls and women forged friendships and intimacies that transcended the harrowing routines of their day-to-day lives. They found beauty and humor even within the squalor of the mill. Nostalgia for those times and those relationships continues; they represent for many of the women the most compelling involvements of their youth and adult lives.

The convergence of experience among the former silk workers and other segments of peasant-worker society, particularly the sojourner described in chapter 3, is unmistakable. This shared cultural stance rests on a number of overlapping characteristics that contour a distinctive peasant-worker awareness, and distinguish it from working-class consciousness. The elements of this cultural orientation include a juxtaposition of outlooks which, from the standpoint of an outside observer, might seem incompatible or illogical; patterns of disengagement by which individuals refrain from or renounce active questioning of their social circumstances; a tendency to personalize rather than politicize the conditions that define their work lives; a manipulation of clientelist relations to buffer, when possible, the insecurities of wage employment; a commitment to the livelihood and social integrity of a rural household; and, perhaps most important, an enduring fidelity to Friulian religious and ethnic sensibilities. Yet percolating in this peasant-worker milieu were transitional potentials that could provoke proletarianization. The emerging self-awareness of the maestre certainly suggests this potential among the workers at the filanda. In addition, a series of historical events intruded on the lives of the silk workers, stimulating among many a reassessment of the loose consensus that sustained order and discipline in the factory.

Vengeance

One exceptional incident during the Italian Resistance (1943–1945) initiated widespread questioning of the old order at the filanda. The event, which has taken on a mythic quality for many of the former silk workers, involves the fate of the young padrone—the engineer's son—at the hands of the partigiani. The action of the partigiani was drawn out of the old norms of honor and vengeance to strike at the misdeeds and immorality of the engineer. Yet at the same time, the incident was critical in reframing the past and prefiguring a class awareness, if not consciousness, for many of the silk workers.

In terms of appearance, character, and behavior, the young padrone, at least in the hearts and minds of the silk workers, was a complete inversion of his father.

The son understood us. Of course he reprimanded us sometimes. He was, after all, a padrone.

Many of the workers were madly in love with the son of the engineer. But he never looked at them. They were pretty, very pretty girls. But the son would reprimand them like everyone else. He looked at the work, he didn't care if one was pretty or ugly.

The young padrone would go to Milan [during the war] to buy pasta for the employees when food was scarce. His car would return to Rubignacco riddled with bullets.

What follows is a typical reminiscence of the encounter between the engineer and the partigiani as recounted by a former silk worker. The account reveals the depth of feeling that the incident still evokes among the women.

He [the engineer's son] . . . I would have given—look at the cross—I would have given my life for him. They [the partigiani] killed him and it was all his father's fault. The partigiani had been tipped off that the silk was leaving the factory, [but] the padrone had not supported the partigiani. Five quintali of silk were about to leave. The father said, "Go, son, go." He went and never came

back. The partigiani attacked the truck driven by the son. Had I
been there when they caught him . . . I would have given my life.
I would have given my life. I would have defended him. . . . The
first thing I would have told them was "Look, if you kill this man,
you kill an innocent. He is not guilty of anything. It is his father.
The guilt is his father's. If you kill, you must kill the father."

The consensus among the silk workers was that the partigiani publicly
offered to release the son in exchange for the old padrone, indicating
that the partigiani were fully aware of who was responsible for the conditions at the filanda. The padrone would not accept the offer, and the
son was executed. The only dissenting view came from one of the preferite, who rewove the story in an interesting way. She claimed that the
engineer told her that *he* had offered himself to the partigiani in exchange for his son. In her reconstruction it was the partigiani who refused the exchange, leading to the execution of the son.

The murder of the much-loved padrone is an important historical
event, not just for the silk workers but for the wider community. It
constitutes one of the most significant actions in the area during the
Resistance. Even in this wider context, the incident is understood as an
action taken to redress personal wrongs and reassert community morality as much as to achieve the broader political ends of the partigiani.
Although the engineer did not contribute to the partisan cause, neither
does it appear that he was an important supporter of the fascists. His
treachery and avarice seem to have been merely apolitical. Nevertheless, the resistance movement succeeded in endowing this conduct with
a political valence that wrapped around the traditional act of vengeance.
It was the reframing of traditional notions of justice and morality in a
new political idiom that was crucial. For those silk workers who struggle to reassess their lives at the filanda in a new political light, the death
of the young padrone is their point of departure.

Le Baracche: Peasant-Worker Transitions

Drawing a contrast between peasant-worker and emerging proletarian
outlooks requires a return to the rural ghetto of Rubignacco, le baracche, and the fate of the cossans.[2] Within the barracks the power of
traditional practice and identity that had sustained country life for a millennium began to wane. The opportunistic scavenging that characterized cossan livelihood did not draw them into the enduring obligations
and responsibilities characteristic of small-scale, peasant-worker cultivators. Nor were they bound to the ancient aspirations of agrarian au-

tarchy and cultural traditionalism that preoccupied the worker peasantry. In the post–World War I era, the work lives of the cossans were increasingly oriented toward wage earning, though they were punctuated by long episodes of unemployment. The reliance of the cossans on public housing, charitable handouts, and petty theft put them in an unusual relationship to outside institutions and further distinguished them from other segments of rural society. Despite their dependence on these institutions, the cossans enjoyed a measure of immunity from government control and the moral authority of the church.

> When the owner realized that something [usually maize or potatoes] had been stolen, [he made a formal complaint]. . . . The comune sent an official to look over the fields or, if they knew the thief, they would make a charge before a judge. But it wasn't fair to complain about a poor devil who did not have anything. So nothing was ever done.

The church actively assisted residents of the barracks. Through the Congregation of Charity, meals, clothing, blankets, and small cash handouts were provided for each family. Rubignacchesi claim that these cash subsidies were often used by the cossans to attend the local cinema in Cividale. Despite this assistance, the clergy never attained the influence and authority they enjoyed in the rest of the parish. On the contrary, when the local fascists wanted to recruit thugs to rough up a priest, they went to le baracche.

The barracks consisted of eight crude rectangular structures, each about fifty meters in length and four meters in width. The buildings were little more than two parallel walls topped with asphalt roofing material which was supported by a series of poles running down the middle of the earthen-floored interior. Each building contained a latrine and a brick oven. One communal tub served the residents of all eight structures, and makeshift walls partitioned the barracks into family quarters. As the number of families grew, apartments were divided and redivided to accommodate new arrivals. It was not uncommon to find families of ten or twelve members inhabiting these quarters. Many families had little—if any—movable property, and at night members could be seen tightly packed together, asleep on the wood table provided with the apartment. One man who lived in the barracks intermittently from 1922 until his forced eviction in 1967 described the general conditions in the rural ghetto.

> There was a misery that cannot be understood today. Cattle live in much better circumstances. The comune threw people into the bar-

Fig. 17. A view of Rubignacco from the site of *le baracche*. The *campanile* of the
parish church of San Marco and the chimney of the brick factory
are visible in the distance.

racks. There was no other place to send them. . . . Living there
we received a legacy that we did not deserve. The generation before ours or perhaps the one before that had been taught to
beg. . . . It was normal to live like that. It was normal to be unemployed. It was normal to be hungry.

Again, the fact that the cossans could secure rudimentary shelter without entering into relationships that simultaneously bound their labor to
a landlord fundamentally modified the conditions of their status. By
assuming responsibility for housing destitute families, the municipal
government severed the invidious connection between shelter and livelihood that had been a central feature of cossan dependency. This status
realignment was echoed by one former resident who understandably ob-
jected to being called a "former cossan." While acknowledging that
"cossan" and "sotan" were terms commonly used to designate residents of the ghetto, he preferred to use "*sotto operai*" when referring
to himself and his former coresidents of the barracks. By the early twentieth century, members of the cossan group had, indeed, begun to assume many of the characteristics of a proletariat.

New types of relations that were explicitly political developed in the

199

barracks, based on bonds that were rooted in commonly perceived interests and concerns. A retired labor leader and Communist Party official described the motives and perceptions that induced these political ties. This informant lived in the barracks for virtually its entire history and was the last resident evicted by communal authorities before the demolition of the structures in 1967.

> Everyone in my family was unemployed. Because of the ignorance in which we lived we were disturbed. I went to school only until the fifth grade. So, I started to study French and a little bit of everything else in order to break the cycle of ignorance. We set up a communist cell and tried to teach the others [in the barracks] to read and write: to read Italian literature, to study foreign languages, to discuss the national and international situation. The cell began in 1933, [and] soon thereafter five or six of us were arrested. I was sent as a political prisoner to Perugia and I turned nineteen in prison.

Although most of the members of the group, including the informant, were released and never tried, the leader of the cell was sentenced to a six-year prison term. In the post–World War II period the former prisoner and leader of the cell in Rubignacco rose through the ranks of the Pci to a position as member of parliament.

The political texture of the barracks was bustling and raucous: "There was a mixture of every political type." Fascists and communists lived in close proximity, putting a premium on guile and secrecy. There were intimidations and acts of opportunism, but there were also lively debates that fostered political education and organization within the ghetto. Through these means the cossans uncovered ideas and sensibilities that allowed them to avoid the enigmatic brooding that preoccupied other segments of peasant-worker society. Above all, they *politicized* their experiences. They actively examined their social circumstances with concepts drawn from books, periodicals and pamphlets, group discussions, and personal reflections. These intoxicating discoveries induced new forms of self-awareness and consciousness that established for the cossans a shared proletarian identity. The communists were most active in adopting and tailoring an analytical framework that provided a panoramic grasp of the social reality for their adherents. As Sartre says, "Words wreak havoc . . . when they find a name for what had up to then been lived namelessly" (quoted in Bourdieu 1977: 170). In fact, it was more than mere words, it was an oppositional language—sometimes referred to pejoratively as *sinistrese*—that empowered the cossans to objectify and disenchant their world. This language not only gave "scientific" logic to the processes of wage work, it also revealed pragmatic strategies to oppose and ultimately transform those conditions (see D. Bell 1986: 65–66; Bourdieu 1979; Eley 1981: 447–55; Habermas 1974: 49–55; Kertzer 1982).

Although the interests of workers and those who operated and managed the small factories and workshops that ring Rubignacco fundamentally diverged, the logic that guided their understanding of the industrial system unfolded in tandem. The labor organizations and political parties that became the institutional expressions of new proletarian ideals in the post–World War II period developed a bureaucratic orientation drawing the workers into areas of uneasy consensus with the proprietors. Ongoing struggles and negotiations between labor and management further defined reified areas of agreement regarding such topics as wages, working conditions, work rules, grievance procedures, hirings and firings, and pension benefits, all in the idioms of law and accountancy. The rationalizing compulsion drew together these opposed groups in a precise delineation of the spheres of factory activity, enumeration of rights and duties that differentiated various work and managerial roles, and specification of rules by which the bureaucracy of the factory was regulated. Although the socioeconomic circumstances of peasant-workers were dramatically improved by the emergence of strong worker organizations, many continued to eye these developments with indifference or even distrust. Thus, a decisive contrast in outlook and cultural orientation can be drawn between proletarians, managers, and proprietors on the one hand, and various segments of the worker peasantry on the other. The former groups, though radically at odds in terms of identities and interests, were nonetheless inextricably tied to a common logic and discourse that yielded a consensus on the rational instrumentalities governing the industrial regime. The latter groups were aloof from these bureaucratic concerns and devoted to unvoiced sensibilities that were largely incapable of engaging the systems of factory production.

The demolition of le baracche in the late 1960s and the construction of new public housing completed the proletarianization of the cossans. As these tough and boisterous folk were moved, in some cases against their will, to the new urban working-class neighborhoods of Cividale, their lingering ties to the terrain of the worker peasantry were severed.[3]

Peasant-Worker Despair

Portrayed in the searing reminiscence concluding this chapter are the unsettling crosscurrents that have historically buffeted peasant-worker awareness. It is an exceptional account that should not necessarily be construed as "typical" of peasant-worker experience. In this narrative of an eighty-year-old peasant-worker, with parenthetical comments by his wife, two apparently unconnected stories are joined against the backdrop of World War II.

Q. Were there people [at the cement factory] asking for women before they hired you [during the 1920s and 1930s]?

A. Yes, yes, yes. . . . If the worker didn't have a pretty girlfriend or a pretty wife . . . nothing. If they did, they [the managers] would hire them. They would bring the women up to the cave [where cement and stone were quarried].

Q. Were the workers angry?

A. Of course, that is an understatement. But what was the alternative? [His wife adds: "We also had to bring food to the capo of the factory."] Those that had wealth could get jobs easily by bringing butter, vino, cheese, and salami. Those that had nothing stayed home.

Q. Did the capo actually take advantage of workers' wives?

A. Yes, yes, yes!

Q. Did they do this often?

A. Ostia! [The Eucharist!] There was a young guy there [at the factory] who is now dead. He lived there at the intersection of those two roads. Yes, it was there, where my daughter worked as a servant, you know and . . . and then . . . well . . . and . . . and she was willing to. . . . Oh God, [should we] die of starvation? Ostia! . . . and so the young guy said, "Well, I will talk to the chief of the carabinieri." And between the two of them they put things right. . . . I got the job down there . . . there at the factory, and if not, what would the alternative have been? We did not have anything to eat.

Q. But did the wives of the workers, their daughters, their sisters. . . .

A. Eh, young stuff, they did not do it as a job [they were not prostitutes].

Q. Did they go there [to the cave]?

A. They sent them there and . . . and. . . .

Q. Many times?

A. Eh, eh . . . [His wife interjects: "Great, great, great hunger."] Eh, bless you [spoken to his wife]. The things that I saw I wish to no beast. The anguish I felt, I hope not even an animal will go through. Now I am calm and all that but . . . but sometimes it gets to me, you know. [He raises his hands to his head and twists them slowly, then spreads his arms with a long sigh.] What I felt under the bombing . . . and with my own hands thousands of corpses all in pieces . . . take the little boxes and put them in there . . . eh, in Africa, in Germany, and also here [in Friuli]. Nobody here, not even in the province, went through what I went through. You know, I am not saying this out of vanity. But what I did . . . and they loved me. I was respected, because I had courage that was exceptional. Up there [in Germany] picking up the pieces. Hundreds of them under the bombs. I picked them out of the ruins. Some were just girls, pretty girls. I felt great pity. I would tell my comrades, "Lift that stone and I will pick them out." I took them and put them into boxes. Off we went with the truck full. Even at seven in the morning on Christmas day.

In the blackest form of clientelism imaginable, parents were forced to arrange the rape of their child. The profound insecurities and vulnerabilities of this peasant-worker family exposed them to unspeakable debasement. The power of petty officials of the cement works to extend or withdraw employment breathed life into these illicit clientelist ties. Far from preventing these acts, the police served as go-betweens in the extortion. This vile abuse was visited not on an individual, but on an entire family whose members experienced the act in terms of overwhelming rage and disgrace. The experience was framed in an intensely subjective idiom and *not* politicized. As the disquieting juxtaposition of the two stories suggests, the informant sought redemption from his dishonor in the macabre heroics of an undertaker scavenging the battlefields of foreign lands.

Conclusion

THIS WORK has been concerned with how the rationalizing imperatives of the modern world, particularly as expressed in industrial capitalism, recast rural society and culture. The people of Friuli, who have struggled to engage these powerful impulses through their indigenous traditions and outlooks, have been the subjects of this study. The premise of the project has been that viewing European development from the standpoint of its rural hinterlands evinces an unexpected picture, one that challenges basic assumptions regarding the nature of the modern world. A dual framework evolved during this research to draw together Friulian historical and ethnographic data. The concept of peasant-worker society, which is my own formulation, became the theoretical focus around which socioeconomic relations were investigated. The notion of "disenchantment of the world," which was drawn from the work of Max Weber, became the concept that guided the analysis of cultural issues. As the research progressed, however, it became evident that the struggles that animated the lives of Friulian peasant-workers pitted enchanted against disenchanted cultural perspectives. The two frameworks thus intersected in an unanticipated way to yield a relatively unified analytical orientation.

In writing the text I tried as much as possible to bind these theoretical concerns to the specifics of the Friulian case. My first obligation was to the ethnographic and historical realities of the Friulani. However, at every step in the development of these ideas, I recognized that the material provoked questions reaching well beyond the boundaries of the region. In this conclusion I summarize the findings of the study, both in terms of their relevance for the anthropology of Friuli and, more importantly, in terms of their broader comparative significance.

The peasant-worker phenomenon has been widely noted in the sociohistorical and anthropological literature of Latin America, Asia, Africa, and rural Europe, but has escaped serious theoretical scrutiny. This study's goal has been to create a general, albeit preliminary, framework for the analysis of peasant-worker livelihood, society, and culture. This required a systematic portrayal of the peasant-worker milieu of Friuli in terms of its enduring social and cultural dynamics, as well as its potential for change and reconfiguration. I have aimed to raise new theoretical questions and provide alternative perspectives on a number of classical questions pertaining to rural society. I am confident about the insights derived from Cividale and its surrounding rural districts, even eastern Friuli; I am less sure about the validity of these ideas in other parts of Europe, not to mention Asia, Africa, and the New World. Nevertheless, in summarizing this aspect of the study I have tried to present it in a form that can serve as a guide for future research to address these issues in other settings, and thereby to assess the comparative significance of the framework.

The first section reviews peasant-worker theory in terms of its potential for probing rural society and culture. This summary focuses on the following issues: (1) the structural preconditions for the peasant-worker adaptation; (2) the matrix of labor involvements that sustain this type of livelihood; (3) liminal, transitional, and phantom characteristics of worker peasantries; (4) the nature of peasant-worker identity, outlook, and awareness; and (5) working-class formation within the peasant-worker milieu.

Structural Preconditions

The concentration of capital, the presence of a significant land-poor as opposed to a landless population, and endemic under- and unemployment, form the preconditions for peasant-worker adaptation. These recurrent structural conditions, which have historically prevailed in Friuli as in much of the European hinterland, meant that dependence on a single source of income or subsistence would not provide a secure livelihood for a broad range of the rural populace. Peasant-worker strategies were a response to chronic vulnerabilities which have for centuries circumscribed rural livelihood and defined the lot of the rural poor. The evolution of the peasant-worker phenomenon represents an alternative course to proletarianization, which is generally viewed as the inevitable outcome of this type of structural circumstance.

Peasant-Worker Matrix

This study's fundamental insight is that wage labor can emerge and spread in the countryside without participants cutting ties to agrarian holdings or divorcing themselves from the indigenous culture. The behavior of the Friulian peasant-worker demonstrates that enduring commitments to wage earning—whether on the latifondo, in a rural factory, or in a distant urban center or frontier settlement—can exist without the creation of a working class. Peasant-worker livelihood, as was seen in chapter 3, has for generations been punctuated by a shifting and blending of labor involvements that connect small-scale peasant cultivation with the spectrum of wage-earning activities. This phenomenon is represented diagramatically in the Peasant-Worker Matrix. The important dynamics captured in this matrix are the intricacies of rural labor careers, the fluidity of labor identities, and the potential reversibility of the transition from one productive category to another. Rural labor is in a state of ongoing reconfiguration which contrasts with views that posit a permanent proletarianization—that is, a transition from subsistence agriculture or craft production to full dependence on agrarian or industrial wages.

However, another dimension exists that is difficult to diagram. Peasant-worker livelihood generally is not pursued solely by an individual, but typically is coordinated among members of a rural household committed to the preservation of a family-based agrarian holding. The motives that sustain peasant-worker life are embedded in familial commitments and obligations that can be abstracted from two points of view. From the "peasant" perspective, the wage economy offers solutions, however modest, to the social and financial predicaments of small-scale agrarian producers. From the "worker" standpoint, access to an agrarian holding provides subsistence security in the face of chronic uncertainties that circumscribe marginal wage employment. Obviously, these motives are complementary and rarely exist independently in peasant-worker calculations and outlooks. Unfortunately, these modest protections were not lost on employers, who discovered that they could lower wages without threatening the subsistence of peasant-workers.

The theory, as presented in this work, permits an assessment of the enormously varied labor involvements that have formed the center of the development of livelihood in rural Europe for centuries and yet defy

PEASANT-WORKER MATRIX

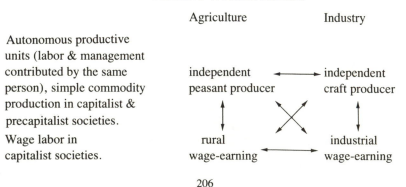

neat classification. The remarkable behavior of Friulian sojourners most boldly expresses the analytical challenges of these productive arrangements. Their labor careers traverse rural hamlets, urban industrial centers, and colonial outposts; their productive engagements span rural wage work, tenant farming, homesteading, industrial employment, mining, construction, military and domestic service, and innumerable scavenging pursuits. Chapter 3 examined how other segments of the worker peasantry in and around Rubignacco forged their livelihoods with similar disregard for the static occupational categories that limit our perceptions of country life. The distinctive productive activities of peasant-workers are, from a methodological standpoint, inaccessible using virtually all conventional labor statistics. They can be reconstructed only through the careful depiction of the life histories and labor careers of countryfolk.

Peasant-Worker Society and Culture

The concept of peasant-worker society and culture was developed to explore the unfolding of wage-based relations in country life. Again, the idea that wage labor, indeed industrial wage labor, can be adopted by countryfolk *without* the need to sever ties to small-scale cultivation or indigenous traditions, characterizes this social and cultural milieu. These basic circumstances, moreover, distinguish the realm of the peasant-worker from that of the worker or peasant with whom he constantly intermingles. This study developed two lines of investigation of these issues. The first attempted to distinguish the social groups that predominated in Rubignacco in terms of the nature and persistence of their peasant-worker involvements. The second attempted to portray the cultural sensibilities and outlook of sojourners and factory workers in the hamlet in terms of the clash between enchanted and disenchanted orientations to the world.

Three features differentiate the problems posed by peasant-worker society and its constituent groups. Liminal, transitional, and phantom characteristics, respectively, reflect the abiding social dynamics, the potential for change, and the methodological ambiguities that imbue this milieu. Liminality—the central feature of this type of society—expresses the potential of peasant-worker groups to reposition themselves in relation to various productive spheres over extended periods of time. The transitional feature of peasant-worker groups reflects a transformational potential whereby the shifting of labor involvements is curtailed, and working class formation or, less frequently, repeasantization, ensues. The phantom quality obscures empirical perception of peasant-worker groups. It derives from a mistaken inference, perpetuated by census and other forms of survey data, which equates occupational roles with discrete social categories, thus shrouding the liminal character of rural labor from observation. In Rubignacco, liminality was most pronounced among the sojourners, transitional potential was expressed in the proletarianization of the cossans, and the phantom nature was most pronounced in the composition of the braccianti.

Central to understanding peasant-worker society is a sense not only of the internal makeup of its constituent groups, but also of the shifting interactions among these groups and of their links to other types of rural and urban societies, whether within or at great distances from the homeland. This society is difficult to bound and is better conceptualized in terms of an enduring social flux than in terms of rigid structures and fixed conventions. Yet this social realm is, from the standpoint of the participants, endowed with coherent meaning drawn from the sensibilities and outlooks of rural culture. This framework of meaning persisted even in the midst of industrial settings like the silk mill. Examination of this framework offered a radically different perspective on the integrity of peasant-worker society. Accounts of sojourners suggested that powerful cultural motives defined peasant-worker life in ways that are *not* reducible to the interplay of socioeconomic variables. The commitment to Friulian ideals expressed in the language, religious practice, folk beliefs, rustic tastes and, above all, in the routines and intimacies of a modest farmstead, sustained enchanted bastions in which ethnic identity was actively reaffirmed. To preserve these enclaves required, however, that the sojourner set out on daunting forays into the wage economy, and risk entanglement with its dangers and allures.

The cultural orientation of peasant-workers entails a general aloofness from the complex social and political experiences that define wage labor in capitalist societies. Though these individuals participate in various forms of wage earning, often for extended periods of time, their identities are tied to a separate cultural framework, in this case one relativized by Friulian ethnicity. Peasant-workers therefore tend to interpret their experiences in wage-earning settings as intense personal struggles, instead of attaching wider social or political significance to their fate. The peasant-worker awareness articulated by silk workers in Rubignacco and described in chapter 7 constituted a specific expression of this cultural struggle. Three variations of this awareness were present at the filanda. Two were found among clearly identifiable segments of the work force. The third represented a viewpoint that in one way or another shaped the outlook of all the women. The preferite expressed an alignment with the padrone's perspective defined and perpetuated by clientelist relationships and sexual politics. Their orientation echoes notions of hierarchy and authority reminiscent of those prevailing in the realm of the latifondo. The maestre, by contrast, increasingly perceived the value of their labor and the modest power it conferred on them. These perceptions led the women to experiment with intermittent protests about working conditions. Their behavior and sentiments expressed incipient proletarian insights. The awareness most pervasive at the mill cut across all segments of the filanda's work force. It was an awareness embedded in Catholic morality, rural fatalism, and familial values, that forced the women to renounce any critical questioning of their social circumstances. This left the silk workers in highly personal struggles—largely unvoiced—with gruelling physical conditions, chronic economic vulnerabilities, pressing social concerns, and troubling moral dilemmas. Thus, the same ties to the countryside that maintained ancestral bonds to family and community, and sustained Friulian identity, also perpetuated traditional forms of domination, dependence, and renunciation.

Working Class Formation

The social awareness of the silk workers was contrasted with the emergence of working-class relationships and perceptions among the cossans of le baracche. The growing dependency on wage earning and the availability of public shelter provoked a realignment of cossan status. New transitional relationships developed, based on commonly perceived interests and concerns. Residents of the rural ghetto actively examined their social circumstances with concepts derived from books, pamphlets, and discussions. The ideas they uncovered allowed the cossans to bypass the concerns that dominated other segments of peasant-worker society, and embrace notions of change. Above all, they politicized their experiences. The communists were most active in channeling these new impulses. Through the actions of a communist cell, a framework for understanding human relations under capitalism and strategies to reform them were communicated to the cossans. Out of these experiences a working-class consciousness emerged in the barracks. The cossans uncoupled themselves from peasant-worker cultural preoccupations and adopted an outlook rooted in perceptions of class struggle. The razing of the rural ghetto in 1967 and the decampment of residents to the urban neighborhoods surrounding Cividale completed the transition from peasant-worker to working-class identity.

Comparative Research

The socioeconomic analysis will—and probably should—continually conflict with the cultural analysis of the peasant-worker phenomenon. This study has proposed that the central struggles in peasant-worker life are cultural in nature, opposing enchanted and disenchanted outlooks and sensibilities. The comparative analyses of these issues demand a precise ethnographic depiction of local indigenous traditions. Interpretation of these cultural clashes no doubt will reveal an enormously varied mixture of political, religious, and ethnic idioms. By contrast, the comparative investigation of socioeconomic aspects of the peasant-worker phenomenon will lend itself to abstraction and generalization. Issues such as the role of peasant-workers in provisioning rural households, underwriting social security, establishing sexual divisions of labor, managing the dislocations of industrialization, and promoting or retarding economic development, can be addressed from a social scientific perspective. Despite the obvious tensions between these two orientations, it is essential that they are not dissociated. I have taken pains to show that by fusing these two interpretive perspectives we can arrive at a new and challenging view of rural society. Conversely, fragmentary analyses of peasant-worker society have distorted or entirely obscured an understanding of this remarkable milieu. By maintaining a unified approach to the domains of the peasant-worker life, we may also be able to glean new insights into the nature of peasantries on the one hand and working classes on the other.

THE FOLLOWING SECTION summarizes issues that have more relevance for the anthropology of Friuli, Italy, and Europe: (1) the emergence of contractual relations; (2) the management of latifondo and factory; (3) bureaucratic organization and patronage relations; (4) Catholic dogma versus folk beliefs; and (5) clerical activism and political identity.

Contractual Instruments

Chapter 2 traced the decay of feudal societal ideals in the face of a new cultural dogma that used rational concepts to delineate organizational principles, productive formulas, and social inequalities. Agrarian contracts were the instruments by which feudal relations—expressed in highly personal, quasi-familial bonds—were translated into impersonal economic ties. Not only did the rational idiom define increasingly precise rules and procedures to regulate human conduct; it also created a new institutional framework for managing agrarian production. The most prominent features of these bureaucratic entities were: (1) legally binding contracts that defined productive relations, associated rights, and obligations and procedures by which responsibilities were executed and enforced; (2) rent formulas that replaced traditional notions of equity and reciprocity with accounting procedures for allocating productive and market risk between lord and peasant; and (3) managerial strata responsible for planning, overseeing, scheduling, and recording estate operations.

The reformulation of agrarian relations along rational bureaucratic lines represented a major step in the disenchantment of public life and the displacement of enchanted ideals and values to the private domains of the rural hamlet, agrarian household, and folk consciousness. Subsequent clashes between these two cultural idioms were fought along the threshold that divided the public from the private sphere.

Management of Latifondo and Factory

The same cultural demands that guided the development of agrarian contracts also defined the principles on which the latifondo and later the rural factory were organized. Once human relations were conceptualized as utilities, entirely new organizational possiblities were created. The bureaucratic capitalism that emerged in Friuli embraced four basic procedures to calibrate social relations and channel human energies: (1) the circumscription of discrete spheres of productive activity; (2) the assignment of roles, usually in hierarchical relationship to one another, with associated rights and duties; (3) the delineation of mathematical measurements to audit human performance; and (4) the specification of arrangements to enforce the rules that governed these operations and instilled discipline among their personnel. Both agrarian and industrial enterprises were ruled by the fluctuating value of the commodities they produced and the costs incurred in production. Profitability determined their success or failure.

Major organizational differences were, nevertheless, present. The operation of the latifondo continued to require that significant control be placed in the hands of tenant families. Hence, ongoing managerial needs were orchestrated vicariously in the media of contract and law. By the late nineteenth century the professional managers, the gastaldi, were increasingly involved in planning, control, and oversight. It was, however, in the rural factories like the filanda in Rubignacco that the shift to more direct means of management evolved. Individual performance came under precise measurement and control using the tech-

211

niques and nomenclature of accountancy. Industrial labor was evaluated through differentiation of skills, measurement of work time, establishment of wage rates and production quotas, and exaction of fines and penalties. Factory routine was guided and enforced by these social abstractions.

Thus, a rational-bureaucratic ethic developed within the Friulian latifondi by which large-scale agrarian production was instituted. Land, labor, and capital were joined to yield what can be described as bureaucratic capitalism. This institutional ethic was transferred to the rural factory, where it was refined to meet the demands of industrial production. The social histories of the latifondo and the rural factory were bound together by a managerial orientation that was rational in nature, and an institutional framework that was bureaucratic in structure.

Patronage and Bureaucracy

Although the latifondo and the rural factory were organized along bureaucratic lines, the Friulani continued to understand human relations through a patronal idiom. The ideology of patronage encompassed a traditional morality embedded in folk consciousness and articulated by the clergy. In this familial idiom, abstract power relationships were translated into a language accessible to the countryfolk. Moral vestiges of patronage—faith, trust, equity, and devotion—continued to be invoked well into the twentieth century, even though they had long since lost their authority as dominant public ethics. Classical forms of patron-client bonds persisted in the rural districts of Friuli in the form of godparentage between tenant family and padrone. These relationships did not, however, constitute a major integrative force in the countryside. More significant was the corruption of patronal ideals and the creation of black clientage.

Endemic unemployment, combined with an enormous land-poor and landless population, preempted the exercise of moral authority by tenants and workers to bargain an amelioration of their social and material circumstances. Patronage stripped of a sense of guardianship became an instrument for the powerful to wring submission from the powerless. Paralleling the formal bureaucratic world of the latifondo and factory was a shadowy realm in which illicit relationships, like the agreements made by the preferite, were forged. Officials, by virtue of their positions, could extort concessions, bribes, and favors from underlings and those dependent on their special administrative services. As the veneer of guardianship was stripped away, in its place was revealed a stark view that held that the countryfolk were inherently inferior, and that abusing them was not a serious moral problem.

Folk Consciousness and Catholic Dogma

Peasant-worker awareness is drawn from ancient folk beliefs and perceptions. A pivotal dimension of rural consciousness arose out of an interchange between indigenous supernatural motifs, like those expressed in the cult of the benandanti, and formal Catholic dogma. The eight hundred heretical inquiries that began in Cividale in the sixteenth century represented a confrontation between the codified ecclesiastical dogma of the church and the symbolic vitality of Friulian folk religion. In the uninhibited religiosity of the early benandanti, the plasticity of their beliefs, and the immediacy of their supernatural experiences, the clergy saw heretical motives. The mysterious behavior of the benandanti was translated through the legalistic work of the inquisitorial court into diabolical witchcraft. This simple maneuver permitted the activities of cult adherents to be scrutinized within the schema of demonological scholarship and canon law. The Inquisition achieved a cultural disenchantment, not by an extirpation of magical content, but through the imposition of an approved formula by which ritual and belief were incorporated into Catholic natural and supernatural domains.

The church had lost its rigid bureaucratic grip on evil by the twentieth century, while the Friulani narrowed and personified their view. The contemporary clerical role appropriated authority once exercised by the benandanti to protect the countryfolk from misfortune and malevolent spirits. This put the church in a parasitic relationship to traditional views of the supernatural world. The ongoing interplay between orthodox Catholicism and Friulian folk beliefs was not merely a matter of ideological deviance; on the contrary, it had real and very disturbing consequences for the daily lives of the countryfolk, inciting, in some cases, obsessive fears.

These people identified the sources of malevolence that touched their lives as the menacing wishes, desires, and jealousies of "witches," who were in reality the weak and socially estranged among themselves. Mired in their theological equivocations, the clergy were unable to thwart the morose obsessions of their parishioners and the antisocial consequences of their parishioners' anxieties. The apprehensions of the countryfolk revolved around imminent ruin and destitution, reflecting the vulnerabilities and insecurities implicit in the institutional relations that regulated their labor. The powerlessness of the Friulani was culturally transmuted and expressed in the idiom of witchery. These grim preoccupations were superimposed on the intimacies of rural life, and contributed to the fragility of community relations. As the belief in witches lost indigenous meaning, it gained a sterile psychological utility. The abstract formulas that ruled the social life of the countryfolk and determined their fate were projected on the play of supernatural forces. This mode of experiencing the world reflected impulses at the core of Friulian ethnic identity; these predispositions tenaciously gripped peasant-worker awareness and subverted the formation of an independent political outlook and identity.

Culture and Political Identity

The tasks of the White Alliance and its successor, the Partito popolare, were daunting. To transform the countryfolk with their traditional sensibilities into an active citizenry in a modern state required that a new cultural identity be crafted. The Catholic Movement had to instruct the rural populace to weigh their personal interests rationally and then bind them to a political agenda that represented those interests. What made this an unusual challenge was that the Catholic-backed movement attempted to fashion a modern political identity using the sacred authority of the church. The clergy fused their moral convictions with a detailed reform program. This ideological synthesis proved fragile and self-limiting. Political leaders achieved a mobilization of the countryfolk in the midst of a national crisis—they did not politicize them. While political elites focused on bureaucratic matters, the Friulani continued to adhere to their largely unquestioning identification with the church. For the majority of the rural populace, political participation was framed not in the idiom of rational interest, but in the idiom of their Catholic faith.

The frustrations and outright failures met by the White Alliance reflected deeper contradictions embedded in the theology and practice of the parish priest. As clerical elites struggled to redefine and politicize social conditions in the region, their coworkers in rural hamlets continued to frame their practices along ancient theological principles. The posture of the clergy on the parochial level was to demand from parishioners unwavering respect for both sacred and secular authority while holding out the promise of Christian salvation. The legitimacy of the church rested on the highly paternalistic and largely benevolent exercise of its social and ideological power. The formation of a fully politicized populace capable of an independent distillation of rights and interests, the framing of social and moral agendas and the delineation of systematic programs of agrarian reform, ran against the central clerical role, that of being unchallenged interpreters and mediators of earthly and supernatural power. The political agitation, much of which was orchestrated by the clergy, revealed precisely the abiding dependence of the church on the status quo. The full politicization of social conditions threatened to strip the clergy of their most prominent roles, spheres of responsibility, and sources of power. The rational discourse that dominated the public domain in the early decades of the twentieth century could not penetrate the traditional sensibilities that animated rural consciousness. Many aspects of this folk awareness were, ironically, ecclesiastical creations nurtured by clerical practice.

The interplay of family, patronage, bureaucracy, and political identity were expressed in the life of Domenico F., the Catholic activist described in chapter 5. Domenico was an arch rationalist in economic and political matters. His youth on the latifondo under the tutelage of his count shaped his relatively progressive social awareness. Like the clergy with whom he aligned himself, he was snared in traditional ties that frustrated the achievement of the political ideals that he publicly articulated. His patronal bonds with count and clergy could not be reconciled with his political convictions, family relations, or personal identity. The contradictions in Domenico's life forced him to abandon his public political role and retire to the life of a Friulian tenant farmer. The fate of Domenico contrasts with that of the cossans of le baracche who divorced themselves from the core of rural social and cultural life. The special circumstances afforded by the rural ghetto permitted the cossans to derive viable political identities, and the social relations necessary to sustain them.

THIS CHAPTER ENDS with a brief depiction of contemporary life in hamlet, comune, and region in terms of the two major themes of this study: peasant-worker society and cultural disenchantment. The fate of the clergy, the dismantling of the latifondo, the burgeoning of industry, and the current political situation are also briefly examined. These concluding remarks are intended not merely as a review of the issues that have dominated this study, but also as an effort to orient future research in this area.

The adoption of the Italian constitution of 1948—*Il secondo risorgimento*—redefined in a new, democratic idiom the principles governing institutional relations throughout Italy. Latifondi were prominent targets of legislative scrutiny. A series of legal restrictions, sponsored by the Left, made tenancy financially ruinous for the padroni, while the economic position and legal status of the fittavoli became increasingly secure. Many large estates in Friuli were slipping irretrievably into decay by the late 1950s. Simultaneously, state subsidies were enacted to

enable tenants to purchase their farmsteads and mechanize their operations (Douglass 1983: 191). By far the most important change came
with the extension of pension benefits and health and disability coverage
to the rural populace (Clark 1977; Holmes 1983). In the area around
Cividale and the Natisone valley, the Dc aggressively—some say reck-
lessly—secured these subventions for their rural constituency. These
subsidies, which were experienced by the countryfolk as entirely unanticipated windfalls, secured the autarchy that peasant-workers have
struggled to achieve for centuries.

The recent creation of an industrial zone in Cividale, also heavily
subsidized by government programs, dramatically expanded the opportunities for industrial employment in the vicinity of the comune
(Holmes and Quataert 1986). By 1985, 993 employees were working
for the various companies located in the zone. A service sector has blos-
somed in the shadow of this development, adding new employment alternatives. Controls on working conditions fought for by labor unions
and the political forces of the Left have eliminated the most egregious
forms of abuse and debasement in the workplace, while wages and benefits have steadily increased. The central socioeconomic uncertainties
of peasant-worker life have been, with remarkable speed, tempered, if
not resolved. In just over a generation the countryfolk have been pro-
pelled from a bare subsistence existence to an undreamed-of level of
material security underwritten by the welfare state. With the dramatic
rise in household income, many have even become beneficiaries of the
fanciful pleasures of the wider consumer-driven society of northern
Italy.

The emergence of the welfare state, or, more accurately, the mixed
economy, seems to punctuate an unexpected denouement in a long
cycle of cultural disenchantment in Friuli.[1] However, perturbations of
an equivocal character have accompanied these changes. As suggested
in chapter 5, the vigorous historical roles of the Friulian clergy as moral
arbiters, social activists and defenders of ethnic integrity were dissipated. The Rubignacchesi have experienced this change in a direct way.
In the late 1970s, the parish lost its full-time priest. The visiting cleric
who currently celebrates mass and ministers to the spiritual needs of the
parishioners is not fluent in Friulian. Elderly Rubignacchesi have found
this particularly upsetting. Far more important has been the incursion of
new forms of rationalization and disenchantment into the public life of
the Friulani. This cultural siege is intriguing because it does not operate
in the legal-bureaucratic idiom.

Messages, seductively conveyed by television, radio, film, and magazines, are the formulas that impel an unbound consumerism. There is a menacing genius to these new cultural codes. Like the contracts, they have a *translational* quality. They take human propensities for gregariousness and sociability and transpose those endowments onto relations that bind humans to objects. In the care lavished on a new Alfa Romeo, the fascination created by the latest Milanese style of clothing, and the frenzy incited by American rock music, passions are extended to things in ways that mimic intimacies between humans. Reciprocally, individual identity and self-worth become alloyed with these externalities. Human wants and needs are indulged vicariously with fetishized surrogates. This is hardly an unprecedented circumstance. Italian elites have been committed to conspicuous consumption for centuries. The relentless spread of these class prerogatives to a wider population and the investiture of consumerism as a dominant cultural preoccupation distinguish the post-1960 period.

A provocative Friulian response has been spawned to withstand these cultural incursions and to reassert an "indigenous" cultural integrity. It has taken the form of the Movimento Friuli, which is superficially a "political" organization, though it eschews the gloss of "party." Like the numerous subnational ethnic and religious groups that struggle for autonomy from Northern Ireland to the Ukraine, the Mf's tactics appear inscrutable. The movement was founded in the mid-1960s out of student demands for a university in Udine. It drew support from clergy who insisted on preaching in Friulian, in defiance of Rome. Intellectuals committed to linguistic and cultural preservation were also prominent in the founding of the movement. The current General Secretary describes the Mf as "avant-garde," a "party of ideas" rather than a potential powerholder. The leaders of the movement flirt with a breathtaking ambition—the reintegration of European society along regional and ethnic lines. Their hope is that the European Parliament will serve as a forum to achieve this new continental framework. Their achievements, however, have been far more modest. The most visible success to date has been the appending of Friulian place names to the road signs that line the region's highways.

The Movimento Friuli seems politically marginal to the outsider, who is tempted to dismiss it as a nostalgic and ephemeral phenomenon. Only on the cultural level does the movement have a nascent coherence. The impulses that draw together young urban residents in the Mf appear much like those that have impelled peasant-workers in the countryside for generations. The aspirations of the movement, however, may be

more formidable. The peasant-worker was content to maintain an en-
clave of enchantment in his domestic life and private broodings. The
Mf strives not only to stem new onslaughts of disenchantment, but to
retrieve remnants of ancient cultural ideals and ethnic practices, and
thus reenchant public life in the patria. How this cultural struggle will
unfold, we do not know.

Notes

1. The "disenchantment of the world" (die Entzauberung der Welt), a revision of Friedrich Schiller's phrase, the "disgodding of nature," is the central theme in Max Weber's analysis of Western cultural development (Bendix 1965; Tenbruck 1980). It refers to the progressive purging of the authority of magical ideas by modern secular societies. It is thus bound up with Weber's notion of "rationalization," which traces the processes by which "scientific" thinking displaces magical content in Occidental cultures (Weber 1946: 129–56; 267–359; 1951; 1952; 1958a; 1958b). "The great historical process of disenchantment of the world, which began with the ancient Jewish prophets and, in conjunction with Hellenic scientific thinking, condemned all magical means of salvation as superstition and blasphemy, was here [in the Protestant Reformation] completed" (Weber 1958a: 105). For an excellent discussion of these issues, see Wilhelm Hennis, "Personality and Life Orders: Max Weber's Theme" (1987); Stephen Kalberg, "Max Weber's Types of Rationality: Cornerstones for the Analysis of Rationalization Processes in History" (1980); Wolfgang Mommsen, "Personal Conduct and Societal Change" (1987); Guenther Roth, "Rationalization in Max Weber's Developmental History" (1987); Wolfgang Schluchter, "The Paradox of Rationalization: On the Relation of Ethics and World" (1979); Friedrich Tenbruck, "The Problem of Thematic Unity in the Works of Max Weber" (1980); and Jürgen Habermas's brief comments linking Weber's methodology with his prognosis for the bureaucratic dynamic of a capitalist economic order (1971: 63–66). For a thoughtful critique of Weberian "rationality" from a Marxist perspective, see Herbert Marcuse, "Industrialization and Capitalism" (1971). The most thorough effort to apply the notion of disenchantment and rationalization ethnographically is found in Pierre Bourdieu, "The Disenchantment of the World," in *Algeria 1960* (1979). David Landes makes use of the Weberian concept of rationalization in his famous study of European industrialization, *The Unbound Prometheus* (1969).

2. The distinction between "enchanted" and "disenchanted" orientations to the world is easily misconstrued. It is commonly reduced to a "primitive-modern" dichotomy. This equates enchantment and disenchantment with contrastive schemes such as mechanical and organic solidarity (Durkheim 1933), *Gemeinschaft* and *Gesellschaft* (Tönnies 1957), or the folk-urban continuum (Redfield 1941), thereby framing Weber's distinction in terms of evolutionary dynamics. Weber was concerned with the development of the modern world, but not in terms of a simple evolutionist scheme, as the following interpretation by Wolfgang Mommsen makes clear.

> [Weber] construed history as open-ended in principle and regarded development as not unidirectional. The triumphal march of rationalization in the West, which Weber described and analysed as a secular phenomenon, was

not the last word. For in as much as formal rationality was embodied in modern capitalism and bureaucracy, it was irrational when looked at from different perspectives or alternative models of rationalization. To this extent Max Weber could write as early as 1917 that despite the "magnificent rationalism of an ethically methodical conduct of life," which had originated from Jewish prophecy and had been victorious in its development, the problems of a rational orientation to the world had still not been solved: "The old, numerous gods deprived of their magic and so in the form of impersonal powers risen again from their graves strive for power over our lives and recommence their eternal battle with each other." . . . In light of this perception Weber undertook to formulate his programme of an ideal-typical reconstruction of Occidental history in a new way. The dialogue between rationalization that originally had been charismatically induced and its embodiment in the form of impersonal institutions and economic structures, which constitute the reality of history, is one that is fundamentally infinite and can never be concluded. (Mommsen 1987: 50–51)

The analysis presented in this study is consistent with Mommsen's interpretation. It treats the clash between enchantments and disenchantments as a dialectical process.

3. An important example of a Marxist orientation to rationalization and reification is presented in Michael Taussig, *The Devil and Commodity Fetishism in South America* (1980). Peter Berger and Stanley Pullberg (1965) have written an intriguing essay on reification that positions the concept within a sociology of knowledge. Karl Polanyi's (1957) discussion of "fictitious commodities," particularly in regard to labor, can also be equated with reification.

4. "Peasant-worker" is an awkward term. It is understood in northern Italy and widely used in the sociohistorical literature, and is hence employed herein.

5. S. H. Franklin's *The European Peasantry: The Final Phase* is one of the earliest and clearest efforts to treat seriously the empirical problems posed by the peasant-worker phenomenon. He notes that few scholars "have dealt with the worker-peasant as a feature of the evolution and the increasingly complex nature of the rural community. . . . Consequently the worker-peasant family, as a socio-economic type, remains largely uninvestigated. Never to my knowledge has an attempt been made to analyse the phenomenon of the worker-peasant family within the context of the theory of the peasant economy" (1969: 55). A growing international literature on the peasant-worker phenomenon has emerged since the publication of Franklin's book (Beck 1976; Bisselle 1973; Comaroff and Comaroff 1987; Johnson 1979; Laite 1981; Leys 1971; Lockwood 1973; Minge-Kalman 1978; Pitkin 1985; Prindle 1984; Sabel 1982; Stoler 1985; Weingrod and Morin 1971).

CHAPTER 2

1. For an excellent introduction to Friulian regional history see P. S. Leicht, *Breve storia del Friuli* (1951); Gian Carlo Menis, *Storia del Friuli: Dalle origini alla*

caduta dello stato patriarcale (1976); and Pio Paschini, *Storia del Friuli* (1953–1954).

CHAPTER 3

1. William Roseberry clearly defines the empirical problem posed by peasant-workers: "Particular peasants may spend a significant portion of the year engaged in both agricultural and nonagricultural sectors, perhaps travelling great distances to do so. Even so, a portion of the peasant family, and the entire family for part of the year, may be engaged in susbsistence agriculture. Are such persons to be defined as a 'rural proletariat' or as 'peasants'?" (1976: 46). This challenge is reflected in the Italian literature in reference to two related ethnographic issues, *combinazione* and the *figura mista*. Combinazione, in Silverman's (1971) words, refers to the practice by which a rural "cultivator typically combines a variety of different means of sustenance—from different pieces of land owned, rented and share-cropped, from wage labor, sporadic non-agricultural pursuits and anything else he can improvise" (see Davis 1973: 91; White 1980: 31–39). Figura mista refers to the individual who enacts the combinazione either in agricultural or nonagricultural settings (Rossi-Doria 1958). By far the finest analysis of the creation and recreation of combinazioni within an Italian family is presented in Donald Pitkin, *The House that Giacomo Built* (1985). Evidence of the persistence of peasant-workers in highly industrialized settings is presented by Donald Bell (1986: 96–97). Peasant-worker dynamics have been widely recognized; they have not, however, been seen as theoretically significant. One important exception is Charles Sabel's book, *Work and Politics: The Division of Labor in Industry* (1982), which examines the peasant-worker as an expression of a "new" European division of labor.

2. Though data regarding the braccianti are misleading in the case of eastern Friuli, this is not necessarily the case elsewhere. For example, David Kertzer's (1981, 1984) ambitious analysis of livelihood and coresidence in rural Bologna depicts the braccianti as a "real" (as opposed to phantom) group with distinctive social characteristics. Indeed, even in lower Friuli, *la bassa*, it is likely that agricultural wage earning was more important in defining a discrete social group than it was in the areas around Cividale.

3. The complexities of Italian migratory strategies have recently been analyzed by William Douglass (1983). Douglass also provides an excellent review of the relevant literature on the subject. Table 3.3 exploits a peculiar characteristic of Italian census data, the differentiation between *popolazione presente* and *popolazione residente*. This distinction between legal residents and those present at the time of the census permits inferences about whether a region is sending or receiving migrants (Douglass 1983: 195). In the Friulian case, the data are used to measure the scale of what I have referred to elsewhere as the "discontinuous peasant-worker strategy," by which I mean sojourners employed outside the region who continue to support their rural households in the patria (Holmes 1983; see also Schreiber 1973). The vast majority of sojourners appear to have been young males. However, one interesting example of an exclusively

221

female variant was found in Moimacco. It involved young mothers, who were recruited shortly after the birth of a child, to travel to Egypt and serve as wet nurses to English families. Unfortunately, I have scant data on these arrangements. They seem to have been part of a well-organized local business that thrived in Moimacco during the interwar period. For a discussion of the circumstances of Friulian settlers in Argentina, see Eduardo Archetti, "Rural Families and Demographic Behaviour: Some Latin American Analogies" (1984).

4. The notion of a society in constant flux with poorly developed boundaries parallels some of the ideas recently put forward by Eric Wolf (1982, 1984), and earlier by Sidney Mintz (1959).

5. There is good reason to believe that peasant-worker politics tend to be conservative. This has generally been the case in Friuli. However, there is also evidence that peasant-workers can display more radical political proclivities under special circumstances. For example, peasant-workers in historic Saxony were able to sustain long strikes against employers because they could return to their agrarian pursuits during walkouts (Jean Quataert, personal communication). Pitkin (1985) has also described the appeal of a leftist party to a young member of an Italian peasant-worker family in the 1970s.

<h2 style="text-align:center">CHAPTER 4</h2>

1. David Kertzer (1984) presents a thorough analysis of the social dynamics and historical development of Italian tenancy systems from the perspective of rural Bologna. Kertzer also provides an excellent bibliographic summary of the relevant literature on tenancy in Italy. Donald Pitkin (1959) laid the groundwork for this type of analysis with his article "Land Tenure and Family Organization in an Italian Village." Sydel Silverman (1975) added a historical perspective to the analysis in her study of classical mezzadria in Tuscany (see Gill 1983; Innocenti 1978). The aim of this chapter is to explore the social dynamics of the affitto misto tenancy system of eastern Friuli, much as Kertzer, Pitkin, and Silverman have done. However, I have also tried to raise an entirely new series of questions. These questions, as suggested in chapter 2, relate to the peculiar *cultural* formulas embodied by the affitto misto arrangements, which expressed the principles of a local bureaucratic capitalism.

2. The ideological component of patronage is set in a wider social context. Silverman puts it in the following terms: "Yet, the full significance of the ideology of patronage, and particularly the myth of public patronage, can be understood only by going beyond relationships between individuals to the structure of the community, and beyond the locality itself to its economic and political context" (1977: 14; see also Gilmore 1977, 1982). Caroline White suggests that patronage can influence the nature of community and political relations. "For what the 'patron' distributes (or withholds) are the means of subsistence and an acceptable standard of living, what the 'client' exchanges is not just his vote but his freedom to associate with others of his class in order to pursue their common interests. In short, he forgoes the right to engage in class struggle" (1980: 5).

3. James Scott stresses the underlying material reciprocities sustaining the patronal

bond. "Classically, the marginal tenant, sharecropper, or tied labourer has looked to his landlord for social insurance against periodic subsistence crises. For him the basic purpose of the patron-client contract, and therefore the cornerstone of its legitimacy, is the provision of basic social guarantees of subsistence and security. If and when the terms of trade deteriorate sufficiently to threaten these social rights which were the original basis for attachment and deference, one can anticipate that the bond will quickly lose its legitimacy" (1977: 30).

4. Ernest Gellner comes close to anticipating this type of relationship in his definition of patronage. "Patronage is unsymmetrical, involving inequality of power; it tends to form an extended system; to be long-term, or at least not restricted to a single isolated transaction; to possess a distinctive ethos; and whilst not always illegal or immoral, to stand outside the officially proclaimed formal morality of the society in question" (1977: 4).

CHAPTER 5

1. Six clerics were interviewed for this and the following chapter. Four were over sixty years old. Two of these older priests were particularly helpful in depicting the activities of the clergy in rural settlements, their political involvements, and their attitudes toward Friulian folk beliefs. The perspectives of these informants were often self-interested, expressing fierce loyalty to the Friulian church. Nonetheless, these priests were also capable of skepticism, even outright criticism of the role, activity, and outlook of the rural clergy.

2. The Socialists aggressively recruited members in the factories and workshops as well as in rural districts of the region through the *Leghe rosse*. The focus of the Red Leagues was on unionization and the improvement of wages and working conditions in industry and agriculture (Stella 1966: 81–83).

3. A full ethnographic depiction of Friulian fascism is beyond the scope of this study. It is, however, an issue that deserves immediate attention. Donald Bell provides references to the vast Italian sociohistorical literature on fascism (1984, 1986: 273–81).

4. A progression of relationships binding the rural poor to outside institutions and, particularly, the state, can be drawn from broker to patron to bureaucrat. Each represents a different type of mediating bond (see Blok 1969, 1974; Davis 1973; Eisenstadt and Roniger 1980; Gilmore 1980, 1982; Pitkin 1959; Schneider and Schneider 1976; Silverman 1965; White 1980).

CHAPTER 6

1. Carlo Ginzburg's (1966) data introduce this chapter and inspired the analysis that follows. The theoretical approach taken was also influenced by Pedro Carrasco, "Tarascan Folk Religion" (1957), and Michael Taussig, *The Devil and Commodity Fetishism in South America* (1980). There is a vast literature on Friulian folklore. The classic work of regional folklore is Valentino Ostermann,

La vita in Friuli (1940). A fine recent study is Andreina Nicoloso Ciceri, *Tradizioni popolari in Friuli* (1983).

CHAPTER 7

1. Eric Wolf has summarized the analytical challenge involved in probing the development of ideologies. "If ideology-making is social in nature, it follows that the processes through which ideologies are constructed take place in historic time and under definable circumstances" (1982: 388). This chapter is devoted to demonstrating the enormous complexity of the process by which ideologies are formulated, modified, and interchanged. The chapter has been influenced by Jean Quataert's (1985) superb article exploring how sexual ideologies coalesced in early industrial settings.
2. The work among the cossans was intended to further the analysis of peasant-worker society. The transformation of the cossans is a critical issue in its own right. More data is needed on the formation of working-class consciousness in the ghetto and the plight of the cossans after they left the barracks (Bell 1986; Levine 1984; Tilly 1981).
3. For a rich depiction of urban working class life and politics see David Kertzer's (1980) study of urban quartiere of Bologna, *Comrades and Christians: Religion and Political Struggle in Communist Italy*. Donald Bell's *Sesto San Giovanni* (1986) presents an excellent portrayal of the formation of working-class society and culture in an industrial suburb of Milan.

CHAPTER 8

1. This example of the instruments of the welfare state resolving the "iron cage" of capitalism sustains Herbert Marcuse's brilliant critique of Weber's concept of destiny: "For as an 'atrophied spirit' the machine *is not neutral*: technical reason is the comtemporarily dominant social reason: it can undergo changes in its own structure. As technical reason it can be transformed into the technology of liberation" (1971: 151). Thus, the Marxist rejoinder to Weber is that the "technical" reason that creates the "house of bondage" can also be used against the "iron cage" to free humanity. Reinhard Bendix (1971) responded to Marcuse's essay in an equally brilliant manner. Bendix's argument centers on what he believes is a misunderstanding by Marcuse of the highly ironic meaning of "rationality" in Weber's sociology.

References

Anderson, Perry. 1976. "The Antinomies of Antonio Gramsci." *New Left Review* 100: 5–78.

Arato, Andrew. 1972. "Lukács' Theory of Reification." *Telos* 11: 25–66.

Archetti, Eduardo. 1984. "Rural Families and Demographic Behaviour: Some Latin American Analogies." *Comparative Studies in Society and History* 26: 251–79.

Barbina, Guido, and Franca Battigelli. 1980. "Il paesaggio agrario friulano dalla fine dell'amminstrazione veneta all'annessione al Regno d'Italia." In *Contributi per la storia del paesaggio rurale nel Friuli-Venezia Giulia*, 339–401. Pordenone: Grafiche Editoriali Artistiche Pordenonesi.

Beck, Sam. 1976. "The Emergence of the Peasant-Worker in a Transylvanian Mountain Community." *Dialectical Anthropology* 4: 365–75.

Bell, Donald. 1984. "Working-Class Culture and Fascism in an Italian Industrial Town, 1918–1922." *Social History* 9: 1–4.

———. 1986. *Sesto San Giovanni: Workers, Culture, and Politics in an Italian Town, 1880–1922*. New Brunswick: Rutgers University Press.

Bell, Rudolf. 1979. *Fate and Honor, Family and Village: Demographic and Cultural Change in Rural Italy Since 1800*. Chicago: University of Chicago Press.

Beltrami, Daniele. 1955. *Saggio di storia dell'agricoltura nella Repubblica di Venezia durante l'età moderna*. Venice: Instituto per la collaborazione culturale.

———. 1961. *Forze di lavoro e proprietà fondiaria nelle campagne venete dei secoli XVII e XVIII*. Rome: Fondazione.

Bender, Byron, Giuseppe Francescato, and Zdeněk Saltzmann. 1952. "Friulian Phonology." *Word* 8: 216–23.

Bendix, Reinhard. 1965. *Max Weber: An Intellectual Portrait*. New York: Doubleday.

———. 1971. "Discussion on Industrialization and Capitalism." In *Max Weber and Sociology Today*, edited by O. Stammer. New York: Harper and Row.

Berger, Peter, and Stanley Pullberg. 1965. "Reification and the Sociological Critique of Consciousness." *History and Theory* 4: 196–211.

Bisselle, Walter. 1973. "Peasant-Workers in Poland." *Studies in European Society* 1: 79–90.

Bloch, Marc. 1962. *Feudal Society*. Chicago: University of Chicago Press.

Blok, Anton. 1969. "Peasant, Patron, and Broker in Western Sicily." *Anthropological Quarterly* 42: 155–70.

———. 1974. *The Mafia in a Sicilian Village 1860–1960*. New York: Harper and Row.

Bourdieu, Pierre. 1977. *Outline of a Theory of Practice*. Cambridge: Cambridge University Press.

———. 1979. *Algeria 1960: Essays by Pierre Bourdieu*. Cambridge: Cambridge University Press.

REFERENCES

Braudel, Fernand. 1972. *The Mediterranean and the Mediterranean World in the Age of Philip II*. New York: Harper and Row.

Bretell, Caroline. 1986. *Men Who Migrate, Women Who Wait: Population and History in a Portuguese Parish*. Princeton: Princeton University Press.

Brozzi, Mario. 1980. "L'alto medioevo (anni 568–1001)." In *Contributi per la storia del paesaggio rurale nel Friuli–Venezia Giulia*, 111–23. Pordenone: Grafiche Editoriali Artistiche Pordenonesi.

Cammarosano, Paolo. 1980. "Il paesaggio agrario del tardo medioevo." In *Contributi per la storia del paesaggio rurale nel Friuli-Venezia Giulia*, 125–35. Pordenone: Grafiche Editoriali Artistiche Pordenonesi.

Carrasco, Pedro. 1957. "Tarascan Folk Religion." In *Synoptic Studies of Mexican Culture*. Middle American Research Institute, Publication no. 17, 1–63. New Orleans: Tulane University Press.

———. 1959. "Comments [on Sidney W. Mintz's paper]. 'The Plantation as a Socio-Cultural Type.' " In *Plantation Systems of the New World*, edited by V. Rubin. Washington: Pan American Union.

Ciceri, Andreina Nicoloso. 1983. *Tradizioni popolari in Friuli*. Udine: Chiandetti Editore.

Clanchy, M. T. 1979. *From Memory to Written Word: England 1066–1307*. London: Edward Arnold, Ltd.

Clark, Gardner. 1977. *Agricultural Social Security and Rural Exodus in Italy*. Western Societies Program, Occasional Paper no. 7. Ithaca: Cornell University.

Clifford, James. 1981. "On Ethnographic Surrealism." *Comparative Studies in Society and History* 23: 539–64.

Comaroff, John and Jean Comaroff. 1987. "The Madman and the Migrant: Work and Labor in the Historical Consciousness of a South African People." *American Ethnologist* 14: 191–209.

Crew, David. 1978. *Town in the Ruhr: A Social History of Bochum, 1860–1914*. New York: Columbia University Press.

Davidson, Alastair. 1984. "Gramsci, the Peasantry and Popular Culture." *Journal of Peasant Studies* 11: 139–54.

Davis, J. 1973. *Land and Family in Pisticci*. New York: Humanities Press.

———. 1977. *People of the Mediterranean*. London: Routledge and Kegan Paul.

Denison, Norman. 1968. "Sauris: A Trilingual Community in Diatypic Perspective." *Man* 3: 578–92.

De Rosa, Gabriel. 1970. *Il movimento cattolico in Italia, dalla restaurazione all'età giolittiana*. Bari: Laterza.

Dionisopoulos-Mass, R. 1976. "The Evil Eye and Bewitchment in a Peasant Village." In *The Evil Eye*, edited by C. Maloney. New York: Columbia University Press.

Douglass, William. 1983. "Migration in Italy." In *Urban Life in Mediterranean Europe*, edited by M. Kenny and D. Kertzer. Urbana: University of Illinois Press.

Dublin, Thomas. 1979. *Women at Work: The Transformation of Work and Com-*

munity in Lowell, Massachusetts, 1826–1860. New York: Columbia University Press.

Duby, George. 1968. *Rural Economy and Country Life in the Medieval West*. Columbia: University of South Carolina Press.

———. 1974. *The Early Growth of the European Economy: Warriors and Peasants from the Seventh to the Twelfth Century*. Ithaca: Cornell University Press.

Dumont, Louis. 1980. *Homo hierarchicus*. Chicago: University of Chicago Press.

Durkheim, Émile. 1933. *The Division of Labor in Society*. New York: Macmillan.

Eisenstadt, S. N., and Louis Roniger. 1980. "Patron-Client Relations as a Model of Structuring Social Exchange." *Comparative Studies in Society and History* 22: 42–77.

Eley, Geoff. 1981. "Re-Thinking the Political: Social History and Political Culture in Eighteenth and Nineteenth Century Britain." *Archiv für Sozialgeschichte* 21: 427–57.

Eliade, Mircea. 1976. *Occultism, Witchcraft, and Cultural Fashions: Esssays in Comparative Religions*. Chicago: University of Chicago Press.

Evans, Robert. 1976. *Life and Politics in a Venetian Community*. South Bend: Notre Dame University Press.

Evans-Pritchard, E. E. 1976. *Witchcraft, Oracles, and Magic Among the Azande*. Oxford: Clarendon Press.

Facchin, Vanni. 1985. "Le streghe nella Bassa friulana di qua e di là del Tagliamento." *Ce fastu?* 61: 93–109.

Favret-Saada, Jeanne. 1980. *Deadly Words: Witchcraft in the Bocage*. Cambridge: Cambridge University Press.

Franklin, S. H. 1969. *The European Peasantry: The Final Phase*. London: Methuen.

Friedl, Ernestine. 1964. "Lagging Emulation in Post-Peasant Society: A Greek Case." *American Anthropologist* 66: 69–86.

———. 1976. "Kinship, Class and Selective Migration." In *Mediterranean Family Structures*. Cambridge: Cambridge University Press.

Garrison, Vivian, and Conrad Arensberg. 1976. "The Evil Eye: Envy or Risk of Seizure? Paranoia or Patronal Dependency?" In *The Evil Eye*, edited by C. Maloney. New York: Columbia University Press.

Gaspari, Paolo. 1976. *Storia popolare della società contadina Friuli*. Monza: Stampato nelle Officine Grafiche Piffarerio.

Gellner, Ernest. 1977. "Patrons and Clients." In *Patrons and Clients in Mediterranean Societies*, edited by E. Gellner and J. Waterbury. London: Duckworth.

Gill, Desmond. 1983. "Tuscan Sharecropping in United Italy: The Myth of Class Collaboration Destroyed." *Journal of Peasant Studies* 10: 146–69.

Gilmore, David. 1977. "Patronage and Class Conflict in Southern Spain." *Man* 12: 446–58.

———. 1980. *People of the Plain: Class and Community in Lower Andalusia*. New York: Columbia University Press.

———. 1982. "Anthropology of the Mediterranean Area." *Annual Review of Anthropology* 11: 175–205.

REFERENCES

Gilmore, David. 1987. *Aggression and Community: Paradoxes of Andalusian Culture*. New Haven: Yale University Press.

Ginzburg, Carlo. 1966. *I Benandanti: Stregoneria e culti agrari tra Cinquecento e Seicento*. Turin: Einaudi.

―――. 1980. *The Cheese and the Worms: The Cosmos of a Sixteenth-Century Miller*. Baltimore: Johns Hopkins University Press.

―――. 1983. *The Night Battles: Witchcraft and Agrarian Cults in the Sixteenth and Seventeenth Centuries*. Baltimore: Johns Hopkins University Press.

Gramsci, Antonio. 1978. *Selections from the Prison Notebooks*. New York: International.

Gregor, D. B. 1965. *Friulan: The Language of Friuli*. Northhampton, England: Letchworth.

Grinovero, Cesare. 1967. *L'Evoluzione dell'agricoltura friulana*. Udine: Del Bianco.

Guiotto, Luigi. 1979. *La fabbrica totale: paternalismo industriale e città sociale in Italia*. Milan: Giangiacomo Feltrinelli Editore.

Habermas, Jürgen. 1971. "Comment [on the article by Talcott Parsons], 'Value-Freedom and Objectivity.' " In *Max Weber and Sociology Today*, edited by O. Stammer. New York: Harper and Row.

―――. 1974. "The Public Sphere: An Encyclopedia Article (1964)." *New German Critique* 1: 50–55.

Hansen, Edward. 1977. *Rural Catalonia Under the Franco Regime: The Fate of Regional Culture Since the Spanish Civil War*. Cambridge: Cambridge University Press.

Harding, Susan. 1984. *Remaking Ibieca: Rural Life in Aragon under Franco*. Chapel Hill: University of North Carolina Press.

Hareven, Tamara. 1982. *Family Time and Industrial Time: The Relationship Between Family and Work in a New England Industrial Community*. Cambridge: Cambridge University Press.

Hennis, Wilhelm. 1987. "Personality and Life Orders: Max Weber's Theme." In *Max Weber, Rationality and Modernity*, edited by S. Whimster and S. Lash. London: Allen and Unwin.

Herzfeld, Michael. 1981. "Meaning and Morality: A Semiotic Approach to Evil Eye Accusations in a Greek Village." *American Ethnologist* 8: 560–74.

Holmes, Douglas. 1983. "A Peasant-Worker Model in a Northern Italian Context." *American Ethnologist* 10: 734–48.

Holmes, Douglas, and Jean Quataert. 1986. "An Approach to Modern Labor: Worker Peasantries in Historic Saxony and the Friuli Region over Three Centuries." *Comparative Studies in Society and History* 28: 191–216.

Innocenti, Gerard. 1978. "San Quirico: A Case Study of the Crisis of Mezzadria in Rural Pistoia, 1900–1960." Ph.D. dissertation, Bryn Mawr College.

Johnson, Robert. 1979. *Peasant and Proletarian: The Working Class of Moscow in the Late Nineteenth Century*. New Brunswick: Rutgers University Press.

Joyce, Patrick. 1980. *Work, Society and Politics: The Culture of the Factory in Later Victorian England*. New Brunswick: Rutgers University Press.

REFERENCES

Kalberg, Stephen. 1980. "Max Weber's Types of Rationality: Cornerstones for the Analysis of Rationalization Processes in History." *American Journal of Sociology* 85: 1145–79.

Kertzer, David. 1979. "Ideological and Social Bases of Italian Church-Communist Struggle: A Critique of Gramsci's Concept of Hegemony." *Dialectical Anthropology* 4: 321–28.

————. 1980. *Comrades and Christians: Religion and Political Struggle in Communist Italy*. Cambridge: Cambridge University Press.

————. 1981. *Famiglia contadina e urbanizzazione*. Bologna: Il Mulino.

————. 1982. "The Liberation of Evelina Zahi: The Life of an Italian Communist." *Signs* 8: 45–67.

————. 1984. *Family Life in Central Italy, 1880–1910*. New Brunswick: Rutgers University Press.

Kertzer, David, and Andrea Schiaffino. 1983. "Industrialization and Coresidence: A Life-Course Approach." In *Life-Span Development and Behavior*, edited by P. Baltes and O. Brim, Jr. New York: Academic Press.

Laite, Julian. 1981. *Industrial Development and Migrant Labor*. Austin: University of Texas Press.

Landes, David. 1969. *The Unbound Prometheus: Technological Change and Industrial Development in Western Europe from 1750 to the Present*. Cambridge: Cambridge University Press.

Lane, Frederic. 1973. *Venice: A Maritime Republic*. Baltimore: Johns Hopkins University Press.

Leicht, Pier Silverio. 1951. *Breve storia del Friuli*. Udine: Libreria Editrice Aquileia.

Le Play, Frédéric. 1982. *Frédéric Le Play: On Family, Work, and Social Change*, edited by C. Silver. Chicago: University of Chicago Press.

Le Roy Ladurie, Emmanuel. 1979. *Montaillou: The Promised Land of Error*. New York: Random House.

Levine, David, editor. 1984. *Proletarianization and Family History*. Orlando: Academic Press.

Leys, Colin. 1971. "Politics in Kenya: The Development of Peasant Society." *British Journal of Political Science* 1: 307–37.

Lockwood, William. 1973. "The Peasant-Worker in Yugoslavia." *Studies in European Society* 1: 91–110.

Löwith, Karl. 1982. *Max Weber and Karl Marx*. London: Allen and Unwin.

Lukács, Georg. 1971. *History and Class Consciousness: Studies in Marxist Dialects*. Cambridge: MIT Press.

McDonogh, Gary. 1986. *Good Families of Barcelona: A Social History of Power in the Industrial Era*. Princeton: Princeton University Press.

Maloney, Clarence, editor. 1976. *The Evil Eye*. New York: Columbia University Press.

Marcuse, Herbert. 1971. "Industrialization and Capitalism." In *Max Weber and Sociology Today*, edited by O. Stammer. New York: Harper and Row.

229

Menis, Gian Carlo. 1976. *Storia del Friuli: Dalle origini alla caduta dello stato patriarcale*. Udine: Società filological friulana.

Merli, Stefano. 1972. *Proletariato di fabbrica e capitalismo industriale: Il caso italiano: 1880–1900*. Florence: La Nuova Italia.

Messenger, Betty. 1975. *Picking Up the Linen Threads: A Study in Industrial Folklore*. Austin: University of Texas Press.

Minge-Kalman, Wanda. 1978. "Household Economy During the Peasant-to-Worker Transition in the Swiss Alps." *Ethnology* 17: 183–97.

Mintz, Sidney. 1959. "The Plantation as Socio-Cultural Type." In *Plantation Systems of the New World*, edited by Vera Rubin. Washington: Pan American Union.

———. 1974. *Caribbean Transformations*. Chicago: Aldine.

Mintz, Sidney, and Richard Price. 1976. *An Anthropological Approach to the Afro-American Past: A Caribbean Perspective*. Philadelphia: Institute for the Study of Human Issues.

Mommsen, Wolfgang. 1974. *The Age of Bureaucracy: Perspectives on the Political Sociology of Max Weber*. New York: Harper and Row.

———. 1987. "Personal Conduct and Societal Change." In *Max Weber, Rationality and Modernity*, edited by S. Whimster and S. Lash. London: Allen and Unwin.

Moretti, Aldo. 1986. "Scrivere in friulano." *Ce fastu?* 62: 207–26.

Moss, Leonard, and S. Cappannari. 1976. "Mal'occhio, Ayin ha ra, oculuc facinus, Judenblick: The Evil Eye Hovers Above." In *The Evil Eye*, edited by C. Maloney. New York: Columbia University Press.

Ostermann, Valentino. 1940. *La vita in Friuli*. Udine: Instituto delle edizioni accademiche.

Panizzon, Gaetano. 1967. *Aspetti demografici friulani del secolo: 1866–1966*. Udine: Del Bianco, reprinted 1986 in *Comparative Studies in Society and History* 25.

Parmeggiani, Nico. 1966. *Gli stadi dello sviluppo industriale nella provincia di Udine*. Udine: Del Bianco; reprinted 1986 in *Comparative Studies in Society and History* 25.

Paschini, Pio. 1953–1954. *Storia del Friuli*. Udine: Arte grafiche friulane.

Pellegrini, Giovanni Battista. 1972–1986. *L'Atlante storico linguistico etnografico friulano*. Padua: Instituto di glottologia e fonetica dell'università.

Pellizzoni, Elio. 1987. "Ancora sullo scrivere in friulano." *Ce fastu?* 63: 75–83.

Perrot, Michelle. 1979. "The Three Ages of Industrial Discipline." In *Consciousness and Class Experience in Nineteenth-Century Europe*, edited by John Merriman. New York: Holmes and Meier.

Perusini, Gaetano. 1939. *I contratti agrari nel Friuli durante il dominio veneto*. Rome.

———. 1961. *Vita di popolo in Friuli: Patti agrari e consuetudini tradizionali*. Florence: Leo S. Olschki-Editore.

Pitkin, Donald. 1959. "Land Tenure and Family Organization in an Italian Village." *Human Organization* 18: 169–73.

————. 1985. *The House that Giacomo Built: History of Italian Family, 1898–1978*. Cambridge: Cambridge University Press.

Pitt-Rivers, Julian. 1954. *The People of the Sierra*. Chicago: University of Chicago Press.

Polanyi, Karl. 1957. *The Great Transformation*. Boston: Beacon Press.

Poni, Carlo. 1976. "All'origine del sistema di fabbrica: Tecnologia e organizzazione produttiva dei mulini da seta nell'Italia settentrionale (sec. XVII–XVIII)." *Rivista storica italiana* 88: 444–97.

Prindle, Peter. 1984. "Part-Time Farming: A Japanese Example." *Journal of Anthropological Research* 40: 293–305.

Prost, Brigitte. 1973. *Le Frioul: Region d'affrontements*. Paris: Editions Ophrys.

Quataert, Jean. 1985. "The Shaping of Women's Work in Manufacturing: Guilds, Households, and the State in Central Europe, 1648–1870." *The American Historical Review* 90: 1122–48.

Rebel, Herman. 1983. *Peasant Classes: The Bureaucratization of Property and Family Relations under Early Habsburg Absolutism 1511–1636*. Princeton: Princeton University Press.

Redfield, Robert. 1941. *The Folk Culture of Yucatan*. Chicago: University of Chicago Press.

Reid, Donald. 1985. "Industrial Paternalism: Discourse and Practice in Nineteenth-Century French Mining and Metallurgy." *Comparative Studies in Society and History* 27: 579–607.

Roseberry, William. 1976. "Rent, Differentiation and the Development of Capitalism Among Peasants." *American Anthropologist* 78: 45–58.

Rossi-Doria, Manlio. 1958. "Land Tenure System and Class in Southern Italy." *American Historical Review* 64: 46–53.

Roth, Guenther. 1987. "Rationalization in Max Weber's Developmental History." In *Max Weber, Rationality and Modernity*, edited by S. Whimster and S. Lash. London: Allen and Unwin.

Sabel, Charles. 1982. *Work and Politics: The Division of Labor in Industry*. Cambridge: Cambridge University Press.

Schluchter, Wolfgang. 1979. "The Paradox of Rationalization: On the Relation of Ethics and World." In *Max Weber's Vision of History: Ethics and Methods*, edited by G. Roth and W. Schluchter. Berkeley and Los Angeles: University of California Press.

————. 1987. "Weber's Sociology of Rationalism and Typology of Religious Rejections of the World." In *Max Weber, Rationality and Modernity*, edited by S. Whimster and S. Lash. London: Allen and Unwin.

Schmidt, Carl. 1938. *The Plough and the Sword*. New York: Columbia University Press.

Schneider, Jane, and Peter Schneider. 1976. *Culture and Political Economy in Western Sicily*. New York: Academic Press.

Schreiber, Janet. 1973. "To Eat the Bread of Others: The Decision to Migrate in a Province of Southern Italy." Ph.D. dissertation, University of California, Berkeley.

REFERENCES

Scott, James. 1976. *The Moral Economy of the Peasant: Rebellion and Subsistence in Southeast Asia*. New Haven: Yale University Press.

————. 1977. "Patronage of Exploitation." In *Patrons and Clients in Mediterranean Societies*, edited by E. Gellner and J. Waterbury. London: Duckworth.

Scott, Joan, and Louise Tilly. 1975. "Women's Work and the Family in Nineteenth-Century Europe." *Comparative Studies in Society and History* 17: 36–64.

Silverman, Sydel. 1965. "Patronage and Community-Nation Relationships in Central Italy." *Ethnology* 4: 172–89.

————. 1970. "Exploitation in Rural Central Italy: Structure and Ideology in Stratification Study." *Comparative Studies in Society and History* 12: 327–39.

————. 1971. "The Italian Land Reform: Some Problems in the Development of a Cultural Tradition." *Anthropological Quarterly* 44: 66–77.

————. 1975. *The Three Bells of Civilization*. New York: Columbia University Press.

————. 1977. "Patronage as Myth." In *Patrons and Clients in Mediterranean Societies*, edited by E. Gellner and J. Waterbury. London: Duckworth.

Sozan, Michael. 1976. "Sociocultural Transformation in East Central Europe: The Case of the Hungarian Peasant-Worker in Burgenland." *East Central Europe* 3: 195–209.

Stella, Aldo. 1966. *Un secolo di storia friulana (1866–1966)*. Udine: Del Bianco Editore.

Stern, Alan. 1975. "Political Legitimacy in Local Politics: The Communist Party in Northeastern Italy." In *Communism in Italy and France*, edited by D. Blackner and S. Tarrow. Princeton: Princeton University Press.

Stoler, Ann. 1985. *Capitalism and Confrontation in Sumatra's Plantation Belt, 1870–1979*. New Haven: Yale University Press.

Strassoldo, Raimondo. 1987. "Il friulano in cifre—Una ricerca sociolinguistica in provincia di Udine." *Ce fastu?* 63: 111–20.

Tadic, Ljubomir. 1979. "Bureaucracy—Reified Organization." In *Praxis: Yugoslav Essays in the Philosophy of the Social Sciences*, edited by M. Marković and G. Petrović. Dordrecht, Holland: D. Reidel.

Tagliaferri, Amelio. 1966. "Aspetti dell'economia rurale Friulana tra il '600 e il '700." *Annali*, series 1, vol. 2. Verona: Palazzo Giuliari.

Taussig, Michael. 1980. *The Devil and Commodity Fetishism in South America*. Chapel Hill: University of North Carolina Press.

Tenbruck, Friedrich. 1980. "The Problem of Thematic Unity in the Works of Max Weber." *British Journal of Sociology* 31: 316–51.

Tessitori, Tiziano. 1972. *Storia del partito popolare in Friuli, 1919–1925*. Udine: Arti grafiche friulane.

Thompson, E. P. 1978. "Eighteenth-Century English Society: Class Struggle without Class?" *Social History* 3: 133–66.

Thorpe, Lewis. 1969. *Einhard and Nother the Stammerer: Two Lives of Charlemagne*. Harmondsworth: Penguin.

232

REFERENCES

Tilly, Louise. 1981. "Paths of Proletarianization: Organization of Production, Sexual Division of Labor, and Women's Collective Action." *Signs* 7: 400–17.

Tönnies, Ferdinand. 1957. *Community and Society*. East Lansing: Michigan State University Press.

Turner, Victor. 1967. *The Forest of Symbols: Aspects of Ndembu Ritual*. Ithaca: Cornell University Press.

Ventura, A. 1964. *Nobiltà e popolo nella società veneta del '400 e '500*. Bari: Laterza.

Visintini, Maria. 1980. "L'agro di Forum Iulii." In *Contributi per la storia del paesaggio rurale nel Friuli–Venezia Giulia*, 73–90. Pordenone: Grafiche Editoriali Artistiche Pordenonesi.

Weber, Max. 1946. *From Max Weber: Essays in Sociology*, edited by H. H. Gerth and C. Wright Mills. New York: Oxford University Press.

———. 1951. *The Religion of China: Confucianism and Taoism*. Glencoe, Illinois: The Free Press.

———. 1952. *Ancient Judaism*. Glencoe, Illinois: The Free Press.

———. 1958a. *The Protestant Ethic and the Spirit of Capitalism*. New York: Charles Scribner's Sons.

———. 1958b. *The Religion of India: The Sociology of Hinduism and Buddhism*. New York: The Free Press.

Weingrod, Alex, and Emma Morin. 1971. "Post-Peasants: The Character of Contemporary Sardinian Society." *Comparative Studies in Society and History* 13: 301–24.

Whimster, Sam, and Scott Lash. 1987. Introduction to *Max Weber, Rationality and Modernity*, edited by S. Whimster and S. Lash. London: Allen and Unwin.

White, Caroline. 1980. *Patrons and Partisans: A Study of Politics in Two Southern Italian Comuni*. Cambridge: Cambridge University Press.

Williams, Raymond. 1973. *The Country and the City*. New York: Oxford University Press.

Willis, Paul. 1981. *Learning to Labor: How Working Class Kids Get Working Class Jobs*. New York: Columbia University Press.

Wolf, Eric. 1959. "Specific Aspects of Plantation Systems in the New World: Community Sub-Culture and Social Classes." In *Plantation Systems of the New World*, edited by Vera Rubin. Washington: Pan American Union.

———. 1982. *Europe and the People Without History*. Berkeley and Los Angeles: University of California Press.

———. 1984. "Culture, Panacea or Problem." *American Antiquity* 49: 393–400.

Index